Public Administration and Public Governance in ASEAN Member Countries and Korea

Public Administration and Public Governance in ASEAN Member Countries and Korea

Pan Suk Kim
Editor

Daeyoung Moonhwasa Publishing Company
Seoul, Republic of Korea

Public Administration and Public Governance in ASEAN Member Countries and Korea

Edited by
Pan Suk Kim

ISBN 978-89-7644-326-7
Published by Choon Whan Lim
Daeyoung Moonhwasa Publishing Company
178-2 Chungpa-dong l-ga, Yongsan-gu, Seoul 140-869, Korea
TEL (02) 716-3883, (02) 714-3062
FAX (02) 703-3839
Published on October 15, 2009

Price KR₩ 17,000

Contents

Preface

The Association of Southeast Asian Nations (ASEAN) is a geo-political and economic organization of 10 countries located in Southeast Asia. ASEAN was established in 1967 in Bangkok by the five original member countries (namely, Indonesia, Malaysia, Philippines, Singapore, and Thailand). Later, five more countries joined it. Its aims include the acceleration of economic growth, social progress, cultural development among its members, and the promotion of regional peace. According to the ASEAN Secretariat, the ASEAN region has a population of about 583 million in 2009. Since ASEAN member countries as a whole perform well in general, many countries and international organizations recognize that ASEAN has become a very important organization in the world. However, general understanding of ASEAN member countries is generally not high enough. Although nowadays, many people are traveling to, and doing business with, these countries, they may not have an in-depth understanding of each individual ASEAN country. Accordingly, more substantial cooperative programs must be developed in order to promote awareness and understanding between ASEAN member countries and other parts of the world.

This book intends to be one of the mediums to promote understanding of ASEAN member countries in the areas of public administration and public governance.

Asia is diverse. Asia can be divided into sub-regions: Northern Asia, Central Asia, Western Asia, Southern Asia, Eastern Asia, and Southeastern Asia. ASEAN member countries and East Asian countries (China, Japan, Korea, etc.) are somewhat geographically distant. However, geographical distance should not be a serious barrier for promoting more cooperative relationships between ASEAN member countries and East Asian countries because we are living in an age of globalization and a boundaryless economy. Over time, more countries have wanted to develop a relationship with ASEAN, and this trend seems likely to continue into the future. Likewise, the relationship between ASEAN and East Asia will be expanded in the future. In order to expedite such a process, active scholarly dialogues and dissemination of comparative references would become a good vehicle for such transregional development.

In an era of globalization and information society, the Republic of Korea (ROK), as part of the Far Eastern group of countries, for example, needs to support a sustainable medium for ongoing professional dialogues in the region. Although ASEAN and ROK regularly emphasize to each other that they are close neighbors, there is still room for further development of more cooperative relationships in various sectors. Over the years, the economic and cultural relationships are growing rapidly between ASEAN member countries and ROK. Over the last 20 years, Korea-ASEAN relations have continued to develop in a wide range of areas, including the political, economic, social, and cultural fields. ASEAN has now emerged as Korea's third largest trading partner and second largest investment destination. Furthermore, about 3~4 million Koreans visit ASEAN member countries every year.

However, there is still a substantial need for a more broad range of cooperative projects between ASEAN and ROK, which could produce a great deal of mutual benefit in the future. In order to promote understanding and cooperation between and ASEAN and ROK, there might be a number of different approaches. Among several areas of interest, this book concentrates on public affairs because public affairs would be one of the common interests in ASEAN and the Republic of Korea. In Asia, public affairs, including public administration and public governance issues, are very important for the development of ASEAN member countries and ROK. Public administration can be broadly described as the study and implementation of public policy, and it is linked to pursuing the public good through various governmental apparatus in each country. Accordingly, this book aims to cover the following issues: overview of sociopolitical context (historical development, government, structure, and society), current status of public administration and public governance (the central government, local governments, civil service, public management, etc.), major issues or problems and public sector reforms in the recent years, public administration education and training (history of public administration education and programs, research, and professional associations in public administration), and challenges including newly demanding tasks and prospects in the future.

Up to now, few comparative studies have been done on the issue of public administration in Asia, and those studies which have been done are mostly focused on the regional economy or international relations. Accordingly, a comparative study of public administration systems in these countries could make a significant contribution to understanding the public sectors of the Southeast Asian region better and to promoting further mutual cooperation in the region. Understanding the public sector of these countries is one of the basic steps for further development of collaboration and progress in the regions. In that regard, this book could be timely and valuable in promoting an in-depth understanding of public affairs in ASEAN member countries and ROK. As many Koreans realize the significance and importance of ASEAN in an age of globalization more people want to get involved in various development and learning opportunities about ASEAN and ASEAN member countries. More substantial and advanced levels of dialogue should be developed. However, there have been limited opportunities of scholarly dialogue between ASEAN member countries and ROK. Even reference materials are rare in ROK. A number of regional studies programs have been developed recently in ROK, but most programs are targeted toward an American, Western, or East Asia-orientation. Comprehensive Southeast Asian programs have been weak in ROK. Therefore, it is time to promote more attention toward Southeast Asian countries because ROK-ASEAN cooperation will rapidly increase in the near future. This book could fill such a gap by promoting scholarly dialogues in the field of public administration and public governance.

In order to carry out a comparative study on public administration and public governance, selected experts from each ASEAN member country were involved in the process. This book is an outcome of the ROK-ASEAN Public Management Forum (hereafter, the forum). The forum was composed of a number of experts (academia and practitioners) in the areas of public administration, and the first forum was held in Seoul in late 2008. I hope that this kind of forum continues to take place with the support of the ROK-ASEAN cooperation project and hope that it becomes an effective vehicle to promote a shared awareness and understanding of ASEAN member countries and ROK. Through such meetings and cooperation, a series of publications and dialogues on public affairs can be sustainably developed between ASEAN member countries and ROK. Finally, but not least, my sincere thanks go to the ASEAN Secretariat in Jakarta and the Ministry of Foreign Affairs and Trade (MOFAT) of the Republic of Korea. I especially wish to thank Mr. Thongphane Savanphet, Ms. Dini Yunita, and Ms. Yeajin Yoon for supporting the related project and work. It is expected that a series of book volumes could be produced as an output of the project.

Pan Suk Kim

Chapter 1 Introduction

Pan Suk Kim

The Association of Southeast Asian Nations (ASEAN) was preceded by an organization called the Association of Southeast Asia, commonly known as ASA, which was an alliance consisting of Malaysia, the Philippines, and Thailand that was formed in 1961. As the Vietnam War reached its peak in the mid-1960s, interest in peace and security within the Southeast Asian region also escalated. In order to cope with the environmental changes and to achieve common prosperity through regional economic cooperation, the countries of Southeast Asia pursued the establishment of a regional alliance. ASEAN was founded on August 8, 1967 in Bangkok with the signing of the ASEAN Declaration by Indonesia, Malaysia, Philippines, Singapore and Thailand. Later, several other Southeast Asian countries joined ASEAN: Brunei Darussalam joined ASEAN on January 8, 1984, Viet Nam on July 28, 1995, Lao PDR and Myanmar on July 23, 1997, and Cambodia on April 20, 1999. Currently, ASEAN has 10 member countries. As of 2009, the ASEAN region has a population of about 583 million and a total area of 4.5 million square kilometers.[1)]

ASEAN establishes relations with countries outside the region

1) For more details, visit the ASEAN Secretariat's website at http://www.asean.org.

to cooperate on various matters of mutual interest. ASEAN currently has several dialogue partners. In recognition of security interdependence in the Asia-Pacific region, ASEAN established the ASEAN Regional Forum (ARF) in 1994. The ARF's agenda aims to evolve in three broad stages, namely the promotion of confidence building, development of preventive diplomacy, and elaboration of approaches to conflicts. The present participants in the ARF include: Australia, Brunei Darussalam, Cambodia, Canada, China, European Union, India, Indonesia, Japan, Democratic Republic of Korea (DRK), Republic of Korea (ROK), Lao PDR, Malaysia, Mongolia, Myanmar, New Zealand, Pakistan, Papua New Guinea, the Philippines, the Russian Federation, Singapore, Thailand, the United States, and Viet Nam.

The ASEAN Declaration states that the aims and purposes of the Association are, among others, to: (1) accelerate the economic growth, social progress, and cultural development in the region through joint endeavors in the spirit of equality and partnership in order to strengthen the foundation for a prosperous and peaceful community of Southeast Asian Nations; and (2) promote regional peace and stability through abiding respect for justice and the rule of law in the relationship among countries of the region and adherence to the principles of the United Nations Charter.[2] ASEAN becomes a rules-based intergovernmental organization with a legal personality with the entry into force of the ASEAN Charter on December 15, 2008. Some institutional changes include: (1) an improved structure to ensure greater efficiency and prompt implementation of ASEAN agreements and decisions; (2) convening of the ASEAN Summit twice a year; (3) creation of an ASEAN Coordinating Council; (4) single chairmanship for key high-level ASEAN bodies; (5)

2) Ibid.

creation of the Committee of Permanent Representatives in Jakarta; and (6) establishment of an ASEAN human rights body. The highest decision-making body of ASEAN is the meeting of the Heads of State or Government of the member countries. The Chairmanship of ASEAN is rotated annually, based on the alphabetical order of the English names of member states.3)

This book offers a collection of 11 formal essays submitted for the ROK-ASEAN Public Management Forum held in Seoul on December 5~7, 2008. This book aims to provide an insightful introduction of public administration and public governance in ASEAN member countries and ROK: an overview of socio-political the context (historical development, government, structure, and society), current status of public administration and public governance (the central government, local governments, civil service, public management, etc.), major issues or problems and public sector reforms in the recent years, public administration education and training (history of public administration education and programs, research, and professional associations in public administration), and challenges including newly demanding tasks and prospects in the future. Fortunately, highly distinguished experts from ASEAN member countries have participated in the process (For more details, please read the list of authors). Diverse experts from ASEAN member countries and ROK provide a unique mix of theoretical and empirical insight along with factual, informative information that will appeal to international readers in the academic, economic, and administrative spheres.

First, David S. Jones has written the chapter on public administration and public governance in Brunei Darussalam. This paper is comprised of two parts. In the first part, it examines the system of government and administration in Brunei, focusing

---

3) Ibid.

upon the structure and role of the civil service, its career schemes and personnel classification, and the nature of budgetary policy and management. In the second part, this paper considers the role of the government and the public sector in the social and economic development of Brunei. It highlights the extensive system of state social provision to underpin the living standards of the population. Also considered is the leading and interventionist role of the government in the economy of the country through public enterprises, public private partnerships, and through the regulation of business. This paper identifies the governance issues in Brunei that require the fine tuning of the existing framework of government administration and state interventionism. These include a need to both trim the size and enhance the efficiency of the civil service bureaucracy. Of particular importance is the streamlining of administrative processes, and the adoption of New Public Management practices, to make the civil service less centrally managed and more results-based. A further challenge is the need for the public sector to make the necessary adjustments to its central role in promoting economic development. These include determining new types of public private partnership that will attract investors and serve the national interest, corporatizing the remaining commercial functions of the civil service and trimming the more intrusive aspects of the system of business regulation.

Alain Benicy has written the chapter on public administration and public governance in Cambodia. In a mere few years, after decades of wars, Cambodia has achieved peace, stability, and security. Successive Royal Government rebuilt and strengthened the institutions of the State. The Civil Service is now unified, fairly stable, and functioning. The Prime Minister leads the reforms and is their primary advocate. The Deputy Prime Minister, Chairman of the Council for Administrative Reform directs implementation. The two Governance Action Plans (GAP) since 2001 attest to the sheer magnitude of the task at hand. The approach has been anchored in reality and in the maintenance of coherence among institutions. Cambodia has made substantial gains on a large front. Yet, Cambodia is at the beginning of a long and arduous journey. With the necessary in place, attention has turned to improving the quality and delivery of public services, particularly those that matter most to people. The third GAP now under preparation will directly target the development of institutional and human capacity to serve the people better. This paper provides an overall outline of the systematic progress made since the formation of the first Royal Government in 1993. In subsequent sections, it identifies sets of measures undertaken using the Administrative Reform as an example. It continues by providing insights into the upcoming National Program for Administrative Reform: the challenges, the strategy and the way forward. This paper finally concludes with lessons learned. The next phase of the reform will be more demanding than the two previous ones. The reform will confront well-embedded practices that have served the nation well.

Ismail Mohamad has written the chapter on public administration and public governance in Indonesia. One of the invaluable lessons from the extended economic and political crisis in East Asia is the fact that Indonesia has not finished developing its public administration system and good public governance suitable to the current progress. The understanding and implementation of the system has not run as smoothly as expected by the constitution, and has not consistently referred to the paradigm of new public management and governance models. This is due to, among others, the political dynamics in state administration, as well as institutional, human resource, and government management problems. Nevertheless, the Indonesian Government still believes that a good public administration system and good public governance which are suitable to the dynamical changes and people's demands can be implemented soon through various policy movements, significant changes of behaviors and attitudes of the public, and changes of governance paradigms. One important policy that should be made by the government is public bureaucracy reform. Successful implementation of bureaucracy reform will support the efforts of reforming other areas of politics, economy, and law enforcement in the country, as well as boosting readiness in anticipating tougher global competition in various areas.

Khammoune Viphongxay and Suresh Balakrishnan have written the chapter on public administration and public governance in Lao People's Democratic Republic. In four parts, this paper presents the evolution of public administration in Lao People's Democratic Republic and way forward. The first part provides an overview of the country, a historical perspective on the evolution of the Lao political system and the various social and political influences that have impacted this process. This overview underscores the challenges that the nation has taken on in the context of widespread poverty and underdevelopment. The second section describes the structure of public administration and related institutions and provides insights into how institutions are evolving. It describes, in brief, the different components of the political and administrative machinery and nuances related to the interplay of political and administrative systems. The third part highlights the array of governance reforms that are taking place in Lao People's Democratic Republic. It draws attention to the wide range of initiatives on decentralization, capacity development, and civil service strengthening, which the country has embarked on with the support of development partners. The concluding part provides some insights into the challenges that confront the nation as it modernizes its public administration. Oversight, coordination, and leadership are prominent issues discussed here.

Hong-Hai Lim has written the chapter on public administration and public governance in Malaysia. This essay examines public administration and its ability to serve society in multiracial Malaysia by looking at reforms for improving its performance. After describing the sociopolitical context and public administration in Malaysia, it presents the basic concepts and ideas that guide the subsequent examination of past reforms, outstanding needs for improvement, and needed future reforms. Past reforms have focused on strengthening the capacity of the bureaucracy and more reforms are needed for this purpose. However, the country's experience has underlined the need to strengthen public control for ensuring performance. Satisfactorily serving the country's multiracial society also requires a more racially representative bureaucracy. While these new directions in administrative reform are needed for meeting domestic and global pressures, they are also more politically challenging in the Malaysian context.

Tin Hla Kyi has written the chapter on public administration and public governance in Myanmar. This paper is presented in seven sections. First, background information on Myanmar's socio-economic situation and political economy is given. The second section then presents a brief overview of the development of government structure and administration since Myanmar gained independence from British rule. The current status of public administration is then described in the third section. The role of the State Peace and Development Council, the Ministry of Home Affairs, and the General Administration Department under it, the Civil Service Selection and Training Board as a central organ of civil service, the importance of the Ministry of Progress of Border Areas and National Races and Development Affairs in undertaking tasks for regional prosperity and development are highlighted in this section. This section also describes the civil service structure of departments and enterprises. The fourth section presents a list of economic reforms carried out by the State Law and Order Restoration Council and the State Peace and Development Council since 1988. Section five then describes the institutions that are intensively involved in providing education and training of public administrators. This paper then concludes after giving information on future prospects of public administration after the promulgation of the new State Constitution of May 29, 2008.

Alex B. Brillantes, Jr. and Maricel T. Fernandez have written the chapter on public administration and public governance in the Philippines. With the onset of globalization and its multi-fold challenges, countries in Asia Pacific are confronted with numerous challenges posed by poverty, corruption, environmental degradation, global warming, overpopulation, financial crises, adapting to information technology, etc. Reforms at various levels and in various sectors—including public administration and governance—have therefore become imperative. In the Philippines, public administration and public governance is a paradox. It is both dynamic and static but continues to evolve. One observes the conventional structures, institutions, and processes expected of any public administrative system (a bureaucracy in place, a governmental structure with executive, legislative and judicial branches; local government organized as sub-national institutions; accountability mechanisms, such as elections conducted regularly, etc.), and also the attendant challenges confronting public administrative systems in most developing countries (such as graft and corruption, weak implementation, lack of capacities, etc.). This chapter provides an overview of public administration in the Philippines. The various institutions, structures, and processes are discussed, together with the accompanying challenges, problems, and prospects.

M. Shamsul Haque has written the chapter on public

administration and public governance in Singapore. In this chapter, it is argued that for studying contemporary changes in the nature of public administration, Singapore represents a useful and interesting country, especially because there is limited research and education on this case. It begins with a macro-level analysis of Singapore's state-centric governance including the state formation, political system, politics-administration relation, and administrative scope. This is followed by a more micro-level analysis of recent reforms, such as pro-market policy shifts, structural and functional changes, normative reorientations, and so on. The chapter also examines the implications of such reforms for state capacity, state-society relations, and the people. Although there are diverse outcomes and new challenges created by these reforms in administration and governance in Singapore, there are reasons for taking this country's experience seriously in the current context of severe economic crisis worldwide.

Trinh Tien Dung has written the chapter on public administration and public governance in Viet Nam. This paper attempts to examine the question of how the open door and renovation process in Viet Nam has happened over the last 20 years. Can the relatively impressive and successful post-war economic growth and poverty reduction be attributed to a sound public governance and public administration? The paper explains that during the last two decades, while public governance and public administration reform has gained important accomplishments as documented below, they also faced major difficulties and still require fundamental solutions. For the next period of 10~15 years to come, when Viet Nam strives to become one of the middle income countries under the rapidly changing external and internal environment, public governance and public administration, Viet Nam should and could play a crucial role to successfully facilitate a much higher quality development process.

Sang-Il Han and Pan Suk Kim have written the chapter on public administration and public governance in the Republic of Korea. Korean public administration has been pivotal in both the country's economic and political success over the most recent six decades. The Korean government has been proactive and responsive to deal with the complicated challenges stemming from drastic developments, including industrialization, democratization, globalization, and the advent of an age of knowledge and information. It has implemented many structural reforms at the central level, transplanting business-oriented concepts to public organizations and encouraging public managers to become more attentive to their performance, more result-oriented, and more familiar with cost-effectiveness. In spite of all these reforms, the Korean government is criticized for neoliberalism, domination of administrative restructuring, and lack of consistency. Therefore, now is the time to clarify the goals and strategies of government reform to meet challenges in the future. This chapter first will review the historical development of Korean politics and public administration in four phases, followed by discussion of the current status of Korean public administration and governance, including the central and local governments, civil service, and public governance. After that, major issues in public sector reform and public administration education and research will be discussed, along with challenges and prospects for the future.

In sum, it is quite clear that public administration and public governance in ASEAN member countries and ROK are rapidly developing and moving forward. In modern history, public administration and social sciences in advanced countries significantly affected the development of public administration in Asia. Western influence is particularly salient in the developmental process of economy, politics, and academic fields including public administration. However, it is about time to promote indigenization and localization of its own ways in each Asian country. In terms of public sector reform, as well as the development of public administration in each country, indigenization becomes an important task for further development. For example, a reasonable way to decide what, and how, to reform is to first analyze various public affairs independently, and then carefully select reform goals and methods based on sound theory established in home-grown public administration research.

However, one of the common problems in developing countries is, without fully independent assessment of the reality, there is a tendency to mechanically imitate foreign experiences which have lots of differences with developing countries. If a country simply follows the experiences of the advanced countries and mechanically imitates their systems without indigenizing efforts, it is likely to make a mistake or fail. Some of the main reasons for such problems might be lack of understanding on socio-political dynamics between developing countries and advanced countries and every country has a different background (tradition, history, culture, religion, etc.) and a different path (nation building, industrialization, democratization, modernization, and institutionalization). Benchmarking is one of the developmental approaches and best practice might be transferable to another society, but not always.

Those who lead public sector reform should not neglect differences between developing and developed worlds and should not ignore the unique characteristics of a home country. Historically, there has been a long debate on the role of those who have flunkeyism or toadyism in many developing countries. When developing countries select reform measures, it is necessary to realistically review or analyze the nature of the issue and best possible solutions in the home country. In other words, it would be better to consider differences of the environmental factors and carry out pragmatic reforms based on an indigenized study of the reality. In that regard, it seems that public administration in ASEAN member countries and ROK need to promote theoretical and practical discourse in their own local context in addition to knowledge transfer from one country to another. I sincerely hope that this book could provide a basic comparative setting of public administration and public governance in ASEAN member countries and ROK as well as much closer collaboration between ASEAN Member Countries and other countries including ROK.

Chapter 2 Brunei Darussalam

David S. Jones

Introduction

Brunei Darussalam is a small sultanate situated on the north coast of Borneo, surrounded on its landward side by the East Malaysian state of Sarawak. Its population of 380,000 is mainly composed of Malays (about 66%), with Chinese, indigenous groups, and a large expatriate population (in both professional and low skilled occupations) comprising the rest. The small population of Brunei enjoys a high standard of living, with a GDP per head of US$28,700 (purchasing power parity), the fourth highest in Asia and slightly below that of Singapore. This affluence is largely due to Brunei's large reserves of oil and gas relative to its population size. Brunei has a mixed economy, with the state actively promoting economic development through state-owned enterprises and public-private partnerships. In addition, the high standard of living of the population is buttressed through an extensive system of state social provision. Due to the revenues from oil and gas, taxation remains low, the most notable feature of which is the exemption of income earners from personal income tax.

Although its population is affluent, Brunei has maintained a traditional ascriptive culture rooted in the predominant Malay society. Central to this are fine gradations of status based on customary titles and positions at the apex of which is the institution of the monarchy. Brunei has also retained a strong village culture based on close kinship ties, personal bonds and customary deference. At the heart of such traditions is a strong attachment to Islamic values and practices, with widespread observance amongst the Malay community of attendant obligations of worship, fasting, and pilgrimage.

System of Government

The system of government in Brunei is monarchal, as indicated above. Executive power resides in the Sultan who is supported by a Council of Ministers or cabinet. To reinforce his executive authority, the Sultan is Prime Minister (as well as Minister for Finance and Minister for Defense) and so has overall responsibility for the affairs of state. Day to day executive power and policy making are exercised by ministers in their different portfolios (Othman, 2002).

The Sultan and the cabinet are advised by a series of special councils: some are permanent while others are temporary and ad hoc. One of them is the Privy Council which advises the Sultan on any amendment or revocation of the Constitution and on the appointment of persons to Malay customary ranks, titles, honors, and dignities. Another is the Council of Succession which gives advice on matters related to the succession to the throne. The Council of Islamic Religion gives advice on matters of Islamic religious practice and observance. At a lower tier, there are several other councils including the Education Council, Economic Council, Defense Executive Committee, and various National Committees that deal with a range of social issues (Brunei Government [BG], 2008a).

While an elected parliament or national assembly does not

exist, a legislative council (LegCo) was re-introduced in 2004, having been prorogued in 1984. Presently it comprises 29 members, who are either ex-officio members or directly appointed by the Sultan. Fourteen of the 29 are government members and another 14 non-government members, with the remaining member serving as the speaker of the council. Ten of the government members are cabinet ministers, including the Sultan himself, and serve in an ex-officio capacity. The remaining 4 members on the government benches are appointed by the Sultan, presently consisting of three senior civil servants and the attorney-general. The 14 non-government members are also appointed by the Sultan, and are divided into three groups: those who possess customary titles and honors, those who have served the Brunei economy and society with distinction, and those representing each of the four districts of the country (Rosli, 2008; Brunei Resources [BR], 2005a).

The legislative council is essentially a consultative body which cannot override the executive in relation to policy and law making. It has, up to now, in its deliberations focused mainly on issues of local and specific importance such as payment of electricity bills, land leasing, and budget allocations. In doing so, it has been useful in raising such matters in the public domain which may then receive attention from ministers and civil servants. The reintroduction of the legislative council thus represents a cautious and pragmatic measure to widen the representative element in the policy and administrative process. It remains to be seen how the legislative council evolves, although it is envisaged, as announced by the Sultan at the opening of the council, that elections would be held for 15 of the 29 seats at some point in the future (Rosli, 2008; Mahmud, 2008).

The central tenet of the governing philosophy is Melayis-Islama-Berjaya (Malay Islamic Monarchy), which blends the monarchal principle of rulership with the upholding of Islamic values and laws and the preservation of Malay culture and traditions. It is the amalgam of these three elements, that shapes both the system of government and the wider political culture (BG, 2008b; Sainah, 2001; Othman, 2002).

In Brunei, the judicial system is based on three bodies of law. One is statute law, which is supplemented by and interpreted through English common law. Both statute and common law are enforced through a conventional four tier system of courts: magistrate courts, intermediate or district courts, the high court, and the court of appeal. Most statutes are supplemented by a considerable body of subsidiary legislation that comprises regulations, rules, orders, and notifications (BG, 2008c).

The other body of law in Brunei is the Islamic law (Shariah), which is applicable to cases involving family matters affecting the Muslim population, such as divorce and adoption. The Syariah law is also invoked in cases where prescribed forms of behavior under Islamic teaching have been contravened. The Syariah court structure is similar to the common law court structure except that it has no intermediate court. Magistrates and judges in both types of court are appointed by the government. To date, all have been appointed from the civil service with none thus far being appointed from private practice (BG, 2008c).

Government Administration

The Civil Service

The main institution of government administration is the civil service which consists of 13 ministries, employing just over 43,800 people (an increase of just under 10% since 2000) (IMF, 2008a:18). Annual recruitment increased from 1,332 persons in 2002 to 3,865 in 2005, falling back slightly to 3,137 in 2007

(Syohreni, 2008). Ministries are sub-divided into departments and directorates, which number more than 90. In a few cases, ministries are first sub-divided into divisions which are then sub-divided into departments (BR, 2008). The status of departments varies. For historical reasons, some departments have their own budgets separate from that of the parent ministry and, in many respects, may operate independently of that ministry. These are known as full-pledged departments, examples being the Lands Department and the Public Works Department in the Ministry of Development. Other departments do not enjoy separate budgetary status, and are more closely linked to the parent ministry (BR, 2008).

Executive responsibility for each ministry is exercised by a cabinet minister, who may be responsible for more than one ministry, with the administrative head as the permanent secretary. There are 21 permanent secretaries and it is not unusual for a ministry to have two or more (in the case of the Prime Minister's Office there are five, each responsible for a particular policy sector). Permanent secretaries are in turn assisted by deputy permanent secretaries. The main sub-divisions of a ministry are headed by director-generals, directors, heads of department, or commissioners, with the name varying from one ministry to another (BR, 2005c; BR, 2008; Sainah, 2001).

Policy making is undertaken at two levels. The Prime Minister's Office provides overall policy direction in key areas such as public finance, economic planning, energy, social welfare, crime and justice, and security, undertaken by specialist policy sections designated for each of these areas (Prime Minister's Office [PMO], 2008). This dovetails with specific policy making and rule drafting that is carried out within the ministries themselves, involving permanent secretaries, their deputies, and major divisional heads and their senior staff. Day to day management of operations and programs is handled by the middle managers in the departments etc., although many operational decisions emanate from or are checked by senior administrators, as mentioned below (BR, 2005b; BR, 2008).

The central responsibilities concerning the financial and human resource management of the civil service are performed by the Treasury in the Ministry of Finance and the Public Service Department within the Prime Minister's Office (in conjunction with Public Service Commission) respectively. There exists, in Brunei government administration, a balance between, on the one hand, the independent responsibilities undertaken by line ministries and departments, and, on the other hand, strategic and operational control exercised by the key central authorities, as mentioned above. It should be noted that many recruitment functions were delegated to the line ministries and departments in 2003, but were then reassigned to the Public Service Department and the Public Service Commission in 2007 (Syohreni, 2008).

There are three main organs of public accountability, which are located in the Prime Minister's Office (viz. the Public Service Commission), which are responsible for senior appointments, promotion, and discipline in the civil service, the Audit Department, which performs both compliance and value for money audits on ministries and departments, and the Anti-Corruption Bureau (Public Service Commission, 2008; International Organization of Supreme Audit Institutions, 2001; Anti-Corruption Bureau, 2008). The last mentioned has given high priority to the prevention of corruption through raising awareness and educational outreach, being one of the pioneers of this approach in South East Asia.

The fulcrum of government administration is the Prime Minister's Office. Apart from being the central policy making agency, it provides coordination for multi-sector programs and directs the human resource management of the civil service through the Public Service Department. In addition, it monitors the performance and enforces the accountability of ministries and departments (through the organs mentioned above) and initiates reforms of public management practices (PMO, 2008).

Within ministries and departments the decision making process is often multi-layered with decisions, sometimes in the form of recommendations, made at one level of management that are then referred for vetting and confirmation in one or more of the higher levels. An example is the granting of land titles or changing the terms of land titles. Recommendations relating to such matters are sent by the Commissioner of Lands, of the Lands Department, to the Permanent Secretary of the Ministry of Development, which are then submitted to the Prime Minister's office to be presented to the Cabinet for approval by the Sultan in Council. A related feature is that key operational decisions often require multi-agency approvals, an example being approvals for land development which involve both the Lands Department, Town and Country Planning Department, and Municipal Boards (Azaraimy, 2008).

Career Schemes and Personnel Classifications

Brunei civil service is divided hierarchically into various schemes of service. These divisions consist of the administrative and diplomatic services, special duties officers, the executive service, various professional and specialist services (such as engineering, accounting, medicine, and education), and a number of support services.

Cross-cutting these services are vertical rankings, called divisions, ranging from Division 1, the most senior division, to the lowest, Division 5. Division 1 is a small elite of officers at the senior management and policy making levels. Only 1.8% of the government workforce is designated as Division 1 officers.

They include permanent secretaries, deputy permanent secretaries, director-generals (with their deputies and senior staff), directors (with their deputies and senior staff), as well as some of the most senior officers in the professional and specialist services (BR, 2005b; BR, 2008; IMF 2008a: 18). Division 2 comprises officers at middle management levels, which include senior grades of the executive service and middle levels of the professional and specialist services. The 2nd Division comprises 17.5% of government employees. Division 3, totaling 23.4% of government employees, includes the bulk of supervisory staff, as well as a range of junior executive officers, qualified technical officers, assistant administrators, and inspectors. Division 4, numbering nearly 27% of government employees, is comprised of mainly those involved in clerical work. The lowest stratum, Division 5, consists of routine officers, junior clerks, and those in support services. This is the most numerous division, with over 30% of the government workforce (BR, 2005b; BR, 2008; IMF, 2008a: 19).

Appointments and promotions in the Brunei civil service are in part determined by merit, as measured by formal educational qualifications and the extent and type of training undergone. These indicators of merit prescribe the entry position of an officer and also how far he/she may be promoted. However, the recognition of merit criteria is balanced in promotional decisions by consideration for seniority in terms of years of service. Officers tend to move up the career ladder by age cohort with the most senior positions occupied by those in their mid or late career. Given the respect for seniority, no formal scheme of fast-track promotion for so-called "high flyers" exists. In addition, ethnic influences also affect appointments and promotions, with the preponderance of officers, including those in the senior ranks, drawn from the predominant Muslim-Malay population.

At the heart of Brunei's civil service is the administrative service, which is a distinct and elite scheme of service at the upper level of Division 1. Administrative service officers are generalists who exercise senior management and policy making responsibilities. Unlike their equivalent in Japan, they are appointed to the administrative service, instead of being appointed or attached to a particular ministry. In fact, during the course of their career, as discussed below, they move from one ministry to another on a frequent basis. Combining such mobility with similar educational backgrounds, tenured employment, and engagement in similar types and levels of responsibility, reinforced by a separate and clearly demarcated status, has instilled in the administrative service a shared set of values and a common professional identity (BR, 2005c).

The administrative service is stratified into four grade categories, with each category or grade within the category linked to a particular designation or level responsibility. The lowest category consists of the introductory grades (Administrative Officer Grade 1 and Administrative Officer Special Grade) to which new entrants into the Service are appointed. Above them is the Superscale category, consisting of four grades from Superscale C to Superscale Special. Above the Superscale category is the Group category, comprising three grades. The most senior category is the Permanent Secretary or Grade category, consisting of four grades from Deputy Permanent Secretary to Permanent Secretary (Grade A) (BR, 2005c).

Although there is no formal fast-track promotion as mentioned above, as a matter of practice, most administrative service officers are able to ascend the promotional ladder from the entry grade to the most senior grade in the Group category over a period of 25 years. Many of them will reach this grade before the age of 50. The interval between promotions ranges from five years at the lower level to three years for the higher posts. Although regular upward movement between and within the

Basic, Superscale, and Group categories can be expected, thereafter the process becomes more selective. Only the most able are chosen to enter the so-called Grade category, comprised of Deputy Secretary and various levels of Permanent Secretary (BR, 2005c).

In addition to satisfactory job performance, the key determinants of promotion of an administrative service officer are the years of service at a particular grade, the number of postings in different departments, and the successful attendance of two executive training courses (the last mentioned provide key milestones in an officer's career path). Promotion is also facilitated by the fact that grades are not necessarily linked to posts, with the result that any post can encompass more than one grade. Thus, an officer's promotion does not always depend upon a vacancy arising in a particular post (BR, 2005c). While most administrative service officers began their career in the service upon leaving a university, a number of promising officers have also been appointed from other schemes of service, such as the engineering and educational services. Although lessening the exclusive nature of the administrative service, mid-career entry has widened the pool of talented and suitable manpower that may be assigned to policy making and senior management roles.

Another feature of the career of an administrative service officer is the frequency with which he/she is moved from one ministry or department to another. In the first five years officers may be expected to occupy twelve different posts in different sections and departments, thus acquiring a wide ambit of experience (BR, 2005c).

The administrative service exerts crucial influence upon the formulation and administration of policy throughout the different ministries, especially by those officers who are permanent secretaries and deputy secretaries. Administrative service officers below this level (such as the directors mentioned above) are also engaged in policy work, but are also responsible for senior level operational matters. Administrative service officers are found in all ministries, working alongside officers of the professional and departmental services, and are normally concentrated in the headquarters and in the policy planning units of the ministries (BR, 2005c).

In light of the nature and diversity of their work, and the frequency with which they are moved from one post to another, administrative service officers can be regarded as generalists, often dealing with matters in which they do not have a trained specialization. In doing so, they may exercise the intellectual abilities of the good, all-round generalist, quickly understanding the essential issues, exercising analytical and problem solving skills, and adopting a comprehensive overview of a complex problem. In addition, from working in different postings, they often come to possess a breadth of understanding concerning the policy issues and administrative procedures in government administration.

The generalist character of senior administration in Brunei is reinforced by the wide spectrum of academic disciplines in which administrative service officers are educated, which includes humanities, social sciences, business studies, law, engineering, and science. The Brunei government has avoided the tendency evident in some countries, such as Singapore and Japan, to favor certain disciplines, such as engineering and law, in making senior appointments.

It should also be noted that the administrative service does not monopolize the senior management and policy making positions in the civil service. Occasionally, officers outside the administrative service are appointed to such positions, being designated as special duties officers. The grade structure for these officers is similar to that of the administrative service, although they are not guaranteed the same career advancement as their counterparts in the administrative service. The appointment of special duty officers to the positions mentioned above further adds to the diversity of backgrounds and specializations at the senior echelons of the Brunei civil service (BR, 2005c).

[Table 1-1] Designations and Grade Structure of the Administrative Service

Grade category
Permanent Secretary (Grade A)
Permanent Secretary (Grade B)
Permanent Secretary (Grade C)
Deputy Permanent Secretary (Grade D)
Group category
Senior Administrative Officer (Group 1)
Senior Administrative Officer (Group 2)
Senior Administrative Officer (Group 3)
Superscale category
Senior Administrative Officer (Superscale Special)
Senior Administrative Officer (Superscale A)
Senior Administrative Officer (Superscale B)
Senior Administrative Officer (Superscale C)
Basic category
Administrative Officer Special Grade
Administrative Officer Grade I

Source: Brunei Resources (2005c).

Training and Capacity Building

Civil servants in Brunei are required to undergo regular training throughout their career. For most civil servants 100 hours of training per year is mandated. Much of the training, but not all, is provided by the Civil Service Institute, or Institut Perkhidmatan Awam (IPA), which offers a range of courses to enhance management and administrative competencies of different grades of civil servant including senior officers. Typically, the courses cover such areas as total quality management, quality control circles, six sigma practices, project management, information systems, and office automation. Each course is targeted to a cohort of civil servants from a particular staff division (IPA, 2009). The Civil Service Institute is in the Prime Minister's Office, as is the Management Services Department, which undertakes research on how administrative reforms can be implemented to improve service delivery (Management Services Department, 2009).

In addition, senior and middle managers, mainly administrative service and special duties officers, are required to separately take an executive training course at the Institute of Policy Studies (IPS) of the University of Brunei Darussalam. The course exposes the participants to the most recent practices and reforms in policy making and public management and entails the completion of research projects and individual case studies relating to issues affecting the Brunei civil service. The course is a required stepping stone to further promotion. Upon completing the course, the middle managers can move up into the Superscale category and the senior managers into the Group category (Brunei Resources, 2005c; IPS, 2008; IPS, 2009).

Budgetary Administration and Government Finance

Government spending fell from a high of 46% of nominal GDP in FY 2002 to 32% in FY 2005/06, before rising again in FY 2006/07 to 43%. Overall, government spending as a share of GDP is much higher than in other states in the region. In FY 2006/07, 72% of total spending consisted of current expenditures, the most important item, comprised of wages and salaries (31% of total spending). The remaining 28% of total spending was devoted to capital projects, which was broadly in line with previous years, although 21% of the capital budget was underutilized in FY 2006/07 (Asian Development Bank [ADB], 2008: 224; Ministry of Finance[MOF] 2007: 5-6; IMF, 2008a: 24).

The sector breakdown of government spending is indicated in the five year spending projections enunciated in the current National Development Plan 2007~2012. The largest category of expenditure is that required for infrastructure development, which accounts for just under 40% of proposed expenditure over the five year period. This includes 11.2% of proposed expenditure for transport and communications, 15.7% for public utilities and drainage, and 12% for ICT services and hardware. Another important category of expenditure is social services, which comprises nearly one third of projected spending over the five years. This includes education, health care, and public housing, which is allocated the most funding. Just under 11% of the proposed expenditure has been allocated to industrial and commercial development and 6% to security (Council for the Long-Term Development Plan [CLDP], 2007: 213).

Government revenue at the outturn of FY 2006/07 totaled B$9.2 billion, which was 60% of GDP, attesting to the prominence of the state in the economy. Taxes comprise 60% of total revenue, mainly derived from the profits made in the oil and gas sector. A special corporate tax rate of 55% applies to this sector; the tax rate on other corporate businesses is 30%. Only a fraction of tax revenue is drawn from other taxes, such as customs and excise duties, vehicle taxes, levies on goods and services, and stamp duty, with no tax levied on personal incomes. The significant section of the revenue base comprising non-tax revenue consists of dividends earned by the government from its ownership stake in the oil and gas sector, and by royalties levied on oil and gas exploitation. Overall, the oil and gas sector accounts for 93.5% of government revenue (ADB, 2008: 223; MOF, 2007: 4; IMF, 2008a: 22, 24).

The flow of revenue from the oil and gas sector has enabled

the government of Brunei to earn large budget surpluses. A primary budget deficit of -5% of GDP was incurred in 2002, but in the subsequent years, sizable budget surpluses were achieved, which reached $4 billion, or 22% of GDP, at the outturn of FY2006/07 (MOF, 2007: 5-6; ADB, 2008: 221; IMF 2008a: 24, 25). Through substantial budget surpluses, largely derived from the oil and gas revenues, the Brunei government has little or no external borrowings and has instead accumulated significant foreign reserves and assets over the last 10 years, estimated to be B$45 billion in 2008. The ratio of overseas assets to GDP is high, at 2.5: 1, which is marginally higher than the ratio in Singapore (2.45: 1), reflecting the commitment of the Brunei government to building up foreign reserves and maintaining sound public finances (IMF, 2008b; Sovereign Wealth Fund Institute, 2008).

Conventional methods of public financial management and accounting are generally followed. These include the continued practice of cash accounting. Budget spending throughout the year continues to be "lumpy" and uneven. In FY 2005/06 and FY 2006/07 quarterly spending ranged from a low of 16% of yearly total in the first quarter to a high of 34% in the fourth quarter. In the two intermediary quarters, spending ranged between 24% and 26% (IMF, 2008: 25). A key reason for the biggest share of spending to be undertaken in the fourth quarter is the requirement for ministries and departments, as in many other states, to return unspent allocations to the consolidated fund at the end of the financial year.

The Public Sector's Role in Social and Economic Development

State Social Provision

An important aspect of public policy and government administration in Brunei is a comprehensive program of social protection, as reflected in the priority given to it in the current five year budget projections mentioned above. Although individual responsibility and entrepreneurship is encouraged, the government has over the years implemented a state model of welfare support and social provision, using the revenues from the oil and gas sector. This buttresses the living standards of the population, ensuring that its basic social needs are catered for, thus preventing any serious degree of poverty and privation amongst low income households. The commitment to comprehensive welfare provision was underlined in the current National Development Plan, which affirms the government's aim "to ensure that, as Brunei Darussalam prospers, its people are properly catered for through the provision of social safety nets." Key to this is the commitment to continue providing "an economically sustainable social security system for those of our people least able to cater for themselves" (CLDP, 2007: 21).

One of the cornerstones of state social provision in Brunei is the National Housing Development Scheme, whereby the government builds and makes available houses for families of all income levels, ranging from high class detached houses to semi-detached and terraced dwellings (CLDP, 2007: 147). The price of such houses is subsidized by the state and financed through a low interest advance from the Housing Development Department and repaid over 20 to 30 years. In addition to the National Housing Development Scheme is a special housing scheme for indigenous landless people known as the Landless Indigenous Citizens Housing Scheme. Another way of meeting the housing needs of the population is through the Temporary Occupation License Scheme, by which land lots are made available to householders to enable them to build their own residences. If they do this, they may then be given title to the ownership of the land (CLDP, 2007: 147).

Another important feature of state social provision in Brunei is the availability of a comprehensive system of health care. Many of the hospitals and clinics form part of a national health system and levy either no charges or charges which are heavily subsidized. This has made even expensive medical treatment available to low income groups (MOH, 1998). Alongside the national health system is a small private sector in health care whose charges approximate to market rates.

In keeping with the social welfare model, education is provided freely for all children at the primary level, and provided under a subsidized fee arrangement at the pre-school, secondary, and tertiary levels. Children of Brunei citizens who attend the small number of private schools at the primary and secondary levels may also be given an education allowance (Ministry of Education [MOE], 2008a). In addition, there are special scholarship schemes that enable some of the most able students to study overseas (mainly in UK colleges and universities) for both "A" levels and university qualifications, including post-graduate degrees (MOE, 2008b).

A further means of providing social protection is through price control and subsidization. Under the Price Control Act, the Price Controller may fix the price of certain goods by "declaring the maximum sale price or by prescribing that the sale price of the goods shall not exceed the price which they cost the seller plus a stated sum or a stated percentage of that cost price, or by prescribing the manner in which the maximum sale price of the goods shall be ascertained" (BG, 2002). Among the goods subject to price control and subsidization are staple foods, electricity, and petrol. Despite the rise in oil prices, the price of electricity and petrol at the filling station has remained unchanged. In January 2008, when the oil price was over US$100 per barrel, the price subsidy was 72% for diesel fuel, and 53% for high grade petrol (Too, 2008). Such controls have ensured price stability and helped to maintain living standards especially among low income groups (CLDP, 2007: 32).

Participation of the Public Sector in the Economy

Over the years, the state has played a leading role in the economic development of Brunei through direct investment and enterprise ownership. As a result, the reach of the public sector into the economy is significant. This has been achieved through exclusive public ownership in certain sectors such as tele-communication, postal services, electricity supply, civil aviation, and port services. In fact, postal services and electricity supply are still managed by departments in the civil service. Tele-communications was similarly managed until it was corporatized in 2005, but it is still wholly owned by the government.

Another way in which the Brunei government has played a leading role in the economic development of the country is through various partnership agreements with the private sector. This is no better illustrated than in the oil and gas sector. The main company producing oil and gas is Brunei Shell Petroleum (BSP) under a concession granted by the Brunei government and extending to 2022. The company is a joint-venture with 50% owned by Royal Dutch Shell and 50% owned by the Brunei government, which thus entitles each to 50% of the dividend profit. The Brunei government further augments its income from royalties and a special corporate tax levied on the portion of the profit earned by Royal Dutch Shell at a rate of 55%. Since the exploitation rights are based on a concession, title to the oil is transferred from the Brunei government to the BSP once the oil reaches the well-head, enabling the government to levy a royalty charge on the oil as it is extracted (Brunei Shell Petroleum, 2008).

Under a similar concession based on a public-private incorporated joint venture known as Brunei LNG, the natural gas that has been extracted by BSP is liquefied, with transport of the gas undertaken mainly by Brunei Shell Tankers (BST). The ownership stake in each of the companies is shared between the Brunei government, with 50% equity, and Mitsubishi and Shell, which each hold a 25% stake (Brunei LNG, 2008). Another company, Brunei Gas Carriers, which both services BST and also transports liquefied gas, is a joint venture partnership between the government of Brunei with an 80% holding and Shell and Mitsubishi, each with a 10% holding (Brunei Gas Carriers, 2007).

In recent years, the Brunei government has favored a different type of partnership arrangement in the exploration and exploitation of new oil and gas fields, known as a production sharing agreement (PSA), as distinct from a concession (CLDP, 2007: 80). The PSA has been a long-standing form of public private partnership in many oil producing countries. Under the PSA arrangements in Brunei, exploration and extraction of oil in four new or prospective oil and gas fields is managed by a wholly government-owned company, Brunei National Petroleum Company, formed in 2002. To do this, the company has sub-contracted or out-sourced the capital investment and operational work to an overseas consortium of companies in each field, forming a non-incorporated partnership with each of the consortia. In return, as part of the PSA, each consortium will recover its exploration and capital costs from income generated when the oil and gas begins to flow, with the net profits divided equally with the Brunei National Petroleum Company. The PSA gives the government of Brunei, through the Brunei National Petroleum Company, certain advantages in relation to control and risk. It retains title to the oil until it is exported, and continues to exercise ultimate executive control over the management of the oil field. Further, the PSA shifts the risk of capital losses to the consortia in the event of a failure to discover a commercially viable oil or gas field. However, in retaining ownership of the oil and gas, the Brunei government foregoes rights to gather royalties levied on the extraction of the oil (PetroleumBRUNEI, 2008: 9-10).

The most recent initiatives to diversify the Brunei economy have also involved public-private partnerships. One of the most important is the setting up of a methanol plant (due to come into operation in 2010) as part of a wider plan to establish a petrochemical sector, which has hitherto not existed. The plant will be owned and operated by an incorporated joint venture Brunei Methanol Company comprising the National Petroleum Company, and thus the Brunei government, with a 25% equity stake, and the Itochu Corporation and Mitsubishi Gas Chemical Company (Thambipillai, 2008: 156; PetroleumBRUNEI, 2008: 5-8).

Public-private partnerships have been established in a number of other sectors including agri-business, aquaculture, food processing, glassware, and production of timber products. As in the methanol project, the preferred partnership model is the incorporated joint venture, in which in the sectors mentioned above hold part of the equity stake, in this case the state-owned Semaun Holdings. The enterprises that have been set up based on this model have been small and medium scale (Semaun Holdings, 2008). Furthermore, in some of these sectors government has provided industrial sites and buildings, other infrastructure facilities, and technical services, as well as tax exemption for a period of 3 to 6 years for pioneer enterprises, post-pioneer companies which are expanding, or export-based industries (Brunei Industrial Investment Agency, 2004: 6-11). All this attests to the fact that much of the investment in Brunei is essentially state driven.

Government Regulation of Business

An important aspect of public governance is the regulation of businesses by government agencies. Under the auspices of the World Bank, two sets of surveys are regularly conducted to assess the regulation of businesses. One of the assessments is provided under the umbrella of its governance indicator measures, while the other is available under its Doing Business portal. The first assessment focuses on regulatory quality and is more general, measuring "the ability of the government to formulate and implement sound policies and regulations that permit and promote private sector development." This includes the whole range of substantive restrictions and requirements imposed on businesses. The second assessment is more concerned with the bureaucratic procedures that businesses are subject to (what may be termed as administrative as opposed to substantive regulations). It focuses upon the list of bureaucratic procedures, requirements, and formalities a business must follow in the different functions it discharges and the number of days it takes for these to be undertaken or completed, as well as the fees and charges levied in the process (Jones, 2008: 97-99). As such, it clearly displays the amount of red tape business are subject to.

Under the first assessment measuring regulatory quality, Brunei was ranked globally at the 82nd percentile in 2007 and given a point score of +1.00 in a range of -2.5 - +2.5. In East Asia, it was ranked third behind Singapore and Hong Kong, with the median percentile in the region being 51 and the median point score being − 0.13. Such ratings indicate that regulatory quality is high in Brunei, suggesting that policies are designed to promote business investment with few substantive impediments to conducting business imposed by government agencies (World Bank, 2008a). This is in accordance with the commitment of the government of Brunei to promote investment through equity partnerships, infrastructure, technical services, and the fiscal incentives mentioned above.

Under the second assessment, which considers the bureaucratic procedures that businesses have to follow in dealing with government agencies, Brunei has a lower ranking than under the first assessment. Globally, it is ranked 88th out of 181 countries surveyed in 2008, and in East Asia 15th out of 25 countries. Such rankings suggest that businesses encounter a significant amount of red tape and delay when dealing with government agencies (World Bank, 2008b). For example, in starting a business, it is estimated that 18 administrative formalities and bureaucratic procedures must be followed. These entail the need to obtain four approvals, two registrations and one license, and to involve four public agencies, with the entire process taking up to four months. In constructing a warehouse, a construction company or developer is required to follow 32 procedures in dealing with government agencies. These include six approvals and clearances before the project can begin, ten inspections, eight approvals, and one permit (occupancy permit) at the end of the project. The processing time involved both at both the beginning and the end of the project, before the building can even be used, is about 5.5 months (World Bank, 2008b).

Conclusion: Reforms and Challenges

While the government of Brunei has delivered stability and prosperity, challenges exist which necessitate adjustment in the role of the public sector and reform of the structure and processes of government administration. Some of these challenges have been highlighted in the current National Development Plan.

Although the public sector will continue to play a leading role in economic and social development of Brunei, there is a need to both trim the size and enhance the efficiency of the central bureaucracy (APEC, 2007: 4). Of particular importance is the streamlining of administrative processes and the consolidation of bureaucratic procedures, thus avoiding overlap, duplication, red tape, and wasted resources. Given that some services depend upon multi-agency processes, such as land administration, more efficient delivery will necessitate better coordination between various departments and ministries. The current National Development Plan has referred to the necessity for the "simplification of procedures" and improved coordination in the bureaucracy (CLDP, 2007: 5). Reflecting this necessity, presently a feasibility analysis is being undertaken to explore transferring control of land and infrastructure development, hitherto overseen by several agencies as mentioned above, into "a unified development and building control authority" (Azaraimy, 2008).

Another challenge is to pursue New Public Management reforms to create a system of government administration incorporating business management practices, and which is less centrally managed and more results-based. To this end, adjustments to financial practices may be required. These may include the introduction of bloc vote budgeting, which enables spending ministries and departments to control their own budget allocations (including virement), and the adoption of accrual accounting, which allows ministries or departments to levy charges on each other when providing services to each other and permits them to retain unspent allocations to avoid spending sprees at the end of the financial year.

An additional step to reform the system of administration to make it more results-based would be to establish a framework of performance indicators, target setting, and performance measurement. In addition, a further shift to a less centralized system of government administration would be achieved if those departments in the civil service that deliver specialist services to the public could be converted into more independent statutory authorities, and those undertaking trading functions ultimately into government owned companies outside the civil service.

Possible examples of such are the Lands Department, the Housing Department, the Electrical Department, the Registry of Companies, and the Post Office. The greater autonomy would give such entities greater flexibility to manage their operations, adopt business models, achieve efficiency savings, and reduce the red tape mentioned above.

A further challenge is to expedite diversification by striking a balance between state control of the economy and market freedom. The necessity for the government and the public sector to continue a leading role in the economy must be balanced against the desirability to avoid excessive dependence on that role, which could prevent the burgeoning of an independent private sector. Of particular importance is the future direction of public-private partnership which will continue to be a vital mechanism of investment. On the one hand, the shift from concession to production sharing agreements in the oil and gas sector suggests the necessity for greater state control. On the other hand, an argument can be made for lower state involvement in the other sectors through reduced equity stakes in joint ventures, while maintaining public provision of infrastructure and technical services, as well as fiscal incentives (IMF, 2008).

In keeping with the lower state involvement is the related concern to simplify the regulatory system under which business must be conducted, especially by minimizing bureaucratic procedures that can so often act as bindweed on business operations. The Crown Prince and Deputy Prime Minister, with reference to the World Bank Doing Business rankings for Brunei, has recently adverted to the intention of government to facilitate the various administrative processes with regard to key aspects of doing business, including the establishment of an online business license system (Othman, 2008).

References

Anti-Corruption Bureau (2008). *Background*, Brunei; Brunei Government: Available at HYPERLINK "http://www.anti-corruption.gov.bn" http://www.anti-corruption.gov.bn

APEC (2007). *Brunei Darussalam: Developments in Public Sector Governance*, in APEC, 2007 APEC Economic Policy Report, Singapore: APEC Secretariat: 45-49.

Asian Development Bank (2008). *Key Indicators for Asia and the Pacific 2008*, Manila: Asian Development Bank.

Audit Department (2008). *Types and Nature of Audit*, Brunei: Brunei Government: Available at HYPERLINK "http://www.audit.gov.bn" http://www.audit.gov.bn

Azaraimy, H. H. (2008). '"One Authority" for Land Development,' *Borneo Bulletin* (Brunei), 12 November.

Brunei Government (2002). *Price Control Act (Chapter 142)*, S 50/74, Brunei: Brunei Government.

Brunei Government (2008a). *System of Government*, Brunei: Government of Brunei: Available at http://brunei.gov.bn/government/

Brunei Government (2008b). *National Philosophy*, Brunei: Government of Brunei: Available at HYPERLINK "http://brunei.gov.bn" http://brunei. gov.bn/government/

Brunei Government (2008c). *Constitution of Brunei*, Brunei: Government of Brunei: Available at http://brunei.gov.bn/government/

Brunei LNG (BLNG) Sdn Bhd (2008). *About BNLG: The Shareholders*, Brunei: Brunei LNG: Available at http://www.blng.com.bn

Brunei Industrial Investment Authority (2008). *Investment Opportunities in Manufacturing Sector*, Brunei: Ministry of Industry and Primary Resources.

Brunei Resources (2005a). *The Legislative Council: Majlis Mesyuarat Negara*, Brunei: Brunei Resources.com: Available at http://www.bruneiresources.com

Brunei Resources (2005b). *The Brunei Civil Service: An Introduction*, Brunei: Brunei Resources.com: Available at http://www.bruneiresources.com

Brunei Resources (2005c). *The Brunei Civil Service; Explanatory Notes on Senior Administrative Officer and Special Duties Officer*, Brunei: Brunei Resources.com: Available at HYPERLINK "http://www.bruneiresources.com" http://www.bruneiresources.com

Brunei Resources (2008). *The Brunei Civil Service: Heads of Government Ministries and Departments*, Brunei: Brunei Resources.com: Available at http://www.bruneiresources.com

Brunei Shell Petroleum Company Sdn Bhd (2008). *About Us: Overview of Our Business*, Brunei: BSP: Available at http://www.bsp.com.bn

Council for the Long-Term Development Plan (2007). *Brunei Darussalam Long Term Development Plan: Wawasan Brunei 2035; Outline of Strategies and Policies for Development 2007~2017; National Development Plan 2007~2012*, Brunei: Government of Brunei.

IMF (2008a). *Brunei Darussalam: Statistical Appendix*, IMF Country Report no. 8/165, Washington: IMF.

IMF (2008b). *IMF Executive Board Concludes 2007 Article IV Consultation with Brunei Darussalam*, Public Information Notice no. 08/57, Washington: IMF.

Institut Perkhidmatan Awam (2009). *Training Programme* Brunei: Prime Minister's Office: Available at http://www.ipa.gov.bn

Institute of Policy Studies, Universiti Brunei Darussalam (2008). *Handbook: 6th Development Programme for Government Middle Management Officers*, Brunei: Public Service Department and Institute of Policy Studies, Universiti Brunei Darussalam.

Institute of Policy Studies, Universiti Brunei Darussalam (2009). *Handbook: 13th Executive Development Programme for Senior Government Officers*, Brunei: Public Service Department and Institute of Policy Studies, Universiti Brunei Darussalam.

International Organization of Supreme Audit Institutions (2001). *Mandates of Supreme Audit Institutions: Brunei Darussalam*, Vienna: International Organization of Supreme Audit Institutions: Available at HYPERLINK "http://www" http://www. intosaiitaudit.org/ mandates.

Jones, D. S. (2007). 'Regulatory Reform and Bureaucracy in Southeast Asia: Variations and Consequences,' *International Public Management Review*, vol. 8, no. 2 (December): 97-116.

Mahmud, Hadi (2008). "LegCo Session Begins Today," *Brunei Times*,

4 March.

Management Services Department (2009). *Tasks and Responsibilities*, Brunei: Prime Minister's Office: Available at http://www.msd.gov.bn/task.htm

Ministry of Education (2008a). *Education System*, Brunei: Ministry of Education: Available at http://www.moe.edu.bn/web/moe/edusys/

Ministry of Education (2008b). *Scholarship Schemes to Study Overseas for Year 2008*, Brunei: Ministry of Education: Available at http://www. moe.edu.bn/web/moe/

Ministry of Finance (2007). *Fiscal and Monetary Review-Q1 2007*, Brunei: Ministry of Finance.

Ministry of Health (1998). *Scheme of Charges for the Ministry of Health*, Brunei: Ministry of Health.

Othman, Azlan (2008). 'Govt to Make It Easy to Do Business in Brunei,' *Borneo Bulletin*, 12 November.

Othman, D. M. (2002). *Learning and Analyzing the Leadership Style of "The Caring Monarch,"* Brunei: Nira Kenchana Marketing.

PetroleumBRUNEI (2008). *Fuelling the Growth for Future Generations*, Brunei: Brunei National Petroleum Company.

Prime Minister's Office (2008). *Prime Minister's Office: About PMO*, Brunei: Government of Brunei: Available at http://pmo.gov.bn/government/

Public Service Commission (2008). *Latar Belakang & Objektif*, Brunei: Brunei Government: Available at http://www.spa.gov.bn/latar.htm

Rosli, Sobrina (2008). "A Primer on the Legislative Council of Brunei,' *Brunei Times*, 4 March.

Sainah, Hajah Saim (2001). *The Administrative System of Brunei Darussalam: Management, Accountability and Reform*, Brunei: Universiti Brunei Darussalam.

Semaun Holdings (2008). Joint Ventures and Link Companies, Brunei: Semaun Holdings: Available at http://www.semaunholdings.com

Sovereign Wealth Fund Institute (2008). *Brunei Investment Agency*, Roseville, CA: Sovereign Wealth Fund Institute: Available at http://swfinstitute.org

Syohreni, Adi (2008). "Recruitment in the Public Sector of Brunei Darussalam: Policy Issues and the Socio-cultural Influences on

Employee Recruitment," Unpublished Master of Public Policy Case Study, Universiti Brunei Darussalam.

Thambipillai Pushpa (2008). 'Brunei: Making a Concerted Effort,' in Daljit Singh & Tin Maung Than, *Southeast Asian Affairs 2008*, Singapore: Institute of Southeast Asian Studies: 89-104.

Too, Debbie (2008). 'Petrol Price Hike Will Have Ripple Effect On Economy,' *Brunei Times*, 11 January.

World Bank (2008a). *Governance Indicators: 1996-2007*. Washington, DC: World Bank: Available at http://www.worldbank.org/wbi/ governance/govdata

World Bank (2008b). *Doing Business: Measuring Business Regulations: Brunei*, Washington, DC: World Bank: Available at HYPERLINK "http://www.doingbusiness.org" http://www.doingbusiness.org

* Information on the Brunei civil service and public sector is available from the following web-sites:

HYPERLINK "http://www.bruneiresources.com" http://www.bruneiresources.com

HYPERLINK "http://brunei.gov.bn/government" http://brunei.gov.bn/government

HYPERLINK "http://www.pmo.gov.bn" http://www.pmo.gov.bn

Chapter 3 Cambodia

Alain Benicy

Introduction

Reforming the State is a political venture made of a myriad of inter-dependent actions. It is more art than science. The art of the possible is sustainable. It is about what can be done as opposed to what should be done. It is the result of clear goals, determination and resilience. The Prime Minister gives clear directions about priorities to reform State institutions and particularly the Administration. Reforms such as those undertaken require time to mature and take hold. Because of commitment and determination from hundreds of men and women, the reform of the Civil Service is now at the point where it can confidently confront challenges and make rapid progress to meet the needs of the people. The reform is a testament to the will of the Royal Government, in general, and of the Council for Administrative Reform, in particular, to take charge of the reform.

Relationships with development partners have not always been easy. At times, they were confrontational. From the very beginning, the Royal Government has sought to fully assume the ownership and leadership of the reform. The journey has been difficult every step of the way. The reform has arrived at a crossroad to serve people better through enhanced performance and accountability.

Historical Perspective

Following years of war and devastation, the Paris Peace Accords were signed in 1991. Free and fair elections, a necessary first step, were held in May 1993. Following the departure of the UN Transitory Authority in Cambodia in August '93, the new Royal Government set out to secure peace, security, and political stability and to rehabilitate and develop the country. In September 1993, a new constitution reestablished the Monarchy, setting the basis for a pluralist democratic political system, a liberal market economy, individual freedoms, sustainable economic and human development, social justice, and poverty reduction. To fulfill these responsibilities, the Royal Government undertook reforming state institutions and, in particular, transforming the Administration into a potent tool of public policy. By March 1994, the Royal Government and its international development partners had approved the National Program to Rehabilitate and Develop Cambodia (NPRDC). Reforming state institutions and particularly the Administration were at the core of the program.

The Administrative Reform has been just one of many reforms at the heart of the strategies of successive Royal Governments ever since. Following the 1998 elections, the Administrative Reform promptly accelerated. Other critical reforms included the Legal & Judicial Reform, the Reform of Public Finance, Decentralization and Deconcentration, the fight against corruption, and sectoral reforms such as those in Human Development and, particularly, in education and health. The example of the Administrative Reform illustrates well the sheer magnitude of the Cambodian reform program.

The strategy to reform the Administration was designed to first establish the Civil Service as a homogeneous institution, secondly to implement core management tools, and then to deepen the reform to serve people better. By the end of the first mandate of the National Assembly in 1998, critical institutions were created or strengthened. The Civil Service was becoming a unified institution integrating the administrations of the various political factions' party to the Paris Accords and elements of the Khmer Rouge. The legal framework to organize work and to manage and control the Civil Service (the Common Statute, Particular Statutes, and attendant regulations) was in place.

In 1999, the Royal Government and development partners approved the first National Program for Administrative Reform. In October 2001, the Royal Government had approved the Strategy to Rationalize the Civil Service (SRCS). By the end of the mandate in 2003, the SRCS implementation had reached important milestones: an exhaustive census had been conducted to ascertain the composition and distribution of the Civil Service and a comprehensive database on civil servants had been developed; a computerized Human Resources Management Information System to control the size and deployment of the workforce was operational; Particular Statutes were in place to anchor the career system; new pay and employment regimes more conducive to productivity and career progression had been introduced; innovative tools, such as the Priority Mission Groups program to marshal resources and enhance performance had been introduced; and a project was in place to kick-start capacity development within the Civil Service.

At its first meeting, following the 2003 election, the Council of Ministers of the new Royal Government approved the Rectangular Strategy for Growth, Employment, Equity and Efficiency in Cambodia. Based on the political platform agreed to by the partners into the coalition government, the strategy framed the policy and operational priorities of the Royal Government to 2008. Ministries were asked to produce detailed action plans for implementation. The strategy singled out a few reforms essential to success. The Administrative Reform was one of them. It also provided clear parameters to guide the reform notably with regard to remuneration within the Civil Service: the need for fiscal prudence and coherence among State institutions.

Following a national conference on reforming the Civil Service, the Royal Government updated the National Program for Administrative Reform in 2004. The focus was on Serving People Better. The program was designed to significantly improve the quality and delivery of public services in support of development and poverty reduction objectives. The NPAR was articulated around four strategic thrusts: improving the delivery of public services, enhancing pay and employment, developing the capacity of people and institutions, and promoting information and communications technologies. At the core of NPAR

[Figure 3-1] The National Program for Administrative Reform (2004~2008)

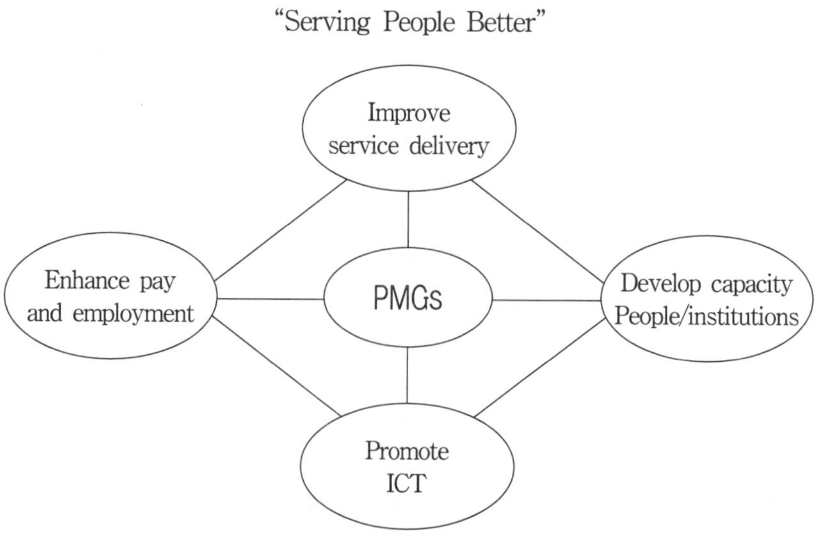

was the Priority Missions Group's scheme to enhance operational performance in priority areas and facilitate the implementation of reforms.

The Council for Administrative Reform set out to articulate a policy framework and implementation plan to guide the reform into the medium term to support the implementation of the National Strategic Development Plan 2006~2010. The policy framework to be developed included policies to: improve the delivery of public services, enhance the management and development of human resources, increase remuneration while maintaining fiscal stability and coherence among State institutions, redeploy civil servants towards priority needs particularly outside major centers, and make investments to develop the capacity of the Civil Service more effectively. Innovative instruments were designed and are still being deployed to increase performance and accountability within the Civil Service.

After the 2008 elections, with sound and sustainable foundations in place, the reform is currently at a crossroads to further deepen and widen its reach. The needs are clear: quality public services available when and where they are needed. The means are also clear: a transformed public administration, one closer to the people, more effective, accountable and transparent. In the next four years, the Administrative Reform will continue to focus on rapidly improving the quality and delivery of public services. The envisioned work can only proceed in full collaboration with other reforms and with development partners. Already, key ministries are well on their way to reforming both themselves and the delivery of their services with extensive assistance from development partners. Building on work in progress, capturing possible synergies, and sheer luck will all be critical to success.

[Table 3-1] Key Dates

- Signature of the Paris Accords-1991
- First general elections under UN supervision-May 1993
- New Constitution to reestablish the Monarchy and to support a pluralist democracy, market economy and individual freedoms-September 1993
- Establishment of the legal basis for a unified Civil service (Common Statute)-1994
- Integration of political factions into the Civil Service and Head Count-96, 98
- Second general elections-July 1998
- National Program for Administrative Reform (NPAR)-1999
- Integration of remaining Khmer Rouge officials into the Civil Service-1999
- Civil Service Census and establishment of comprehensive database-2000 the National Conference on "Democracy, Good Governance, and Transparency in Asian Context"-2001
- Approval of the Governance Action Plan-2001
- Approval of the Strategy to Rationalize the Civil Service-2001
- Introduction of new remuneration and classification regimes-2002
- Deployment of Priority Mission Groups to enhance performance-2003
- Completion of legal framework (Particular Statutes) - 2003
- Third general elections - July 2003
- National Conference on reforming the Civil Service-2004
- Approval of updated NPAR to Serve People Better-2004
- The National Conference on Strengthening Good Governance for Development and Poverty Reduction-2004
- Approval of the Second Governance Action Plan-2005
- Development of the policy framework to guide the reform in the medium term-2006
- Approval of the Policy on Public Service Delivery-May 2006
- Strengthening of management and control systems and development of innovative instruments to enhance performance and accountability-2007, 2008
- Fourth general elections - July 2008
- Deployment of innovative instruments to enhance performance and accountability in the Civil Service-2008
- Update of NPAR to target performance and accountability in support of service delivery-2008

Cambodia at a Glance

The Kingdom of Cambodia is a unitary state and a pluralist democracy. The National Assembly and the Senate anchor the Legislative Branch. Executive power resides with the Prime Minister and the Council of Ministers. Ministries and authorities have delegated executive power within their respective jurisdiction. It is the first time in some 500 years that the national government exerts sovereignty all over the country. The Royal Government undertook a vast reform to rebuild and develop institutions of the State, which had been totally destroyed during the Khmer Rouge regime.

Cambodia is a market-based economy. The private sector is the engine of growth while government is a strategist and facilitator. During the last 10 years, GDP grew by about 9.5% a year, on average. Growth peaked at 13.3% in 2005. Today, the garment and textile industry, tourism, construction, and agriculture lead the way. There are also promising new opportunities in oil and gas, bauxite, rubber, and agro-industries. As of 2008, Cambodia's population totaled about 14 million people with a GDP per capita of US$625. Future growth will hinge on continued political stability and prudent macro-economic policy, on the evolving world economic and trade environment, on the dynamism and competitiveness of the Cambodian private sector, and on continued improvements in governance.

Major central government organizations are: Office of the Council of Ministers, Ministry of Agriculture, Forestry and Fisheries, Ministry of Commerce, Ministry of Culture and Fine Arts, Ministry of Economy and Finance, Ministry of Education, Youth and Sports, Ministry of Environment, Ministry of Foreign Affairs and International Cooperation, Ministry of Health, Ministry of Industry, Mines and Energy, Ministry of Information, Ministry of Interior, Ministry of Justice, Ministry of Labor and

Vocational Training, Ministry of Land Management, Urban Planning & Construction, Ministry of National Defense, Ministry of Parliamentary Affairs and Inspection, Ministry of Planning, Ministry of Post and Telecommunication, Ministry of Public Works and Transport, Ministry of Religions and Cults, Ministry of Rural Development, Ministry of Social Affairs, Veteran and Youth Rehabilitation, Ministry of Tourism, Ministry of Water Resources and Meteorology, Ministry of Women Affairs, Municipality of Phnom Penh, Secretariat of Public Service, Secretariat of Civil Aviation, National Information Communications Technology Development, and others.[1] Capital and Provinces are Cambodia's First-level administrative divisions. Cambodian areas are divided into 23 provinces and the capital. Municipalities and Districts are the second-level administrative divisions of Cambodia.

The Context

The Royal Government enters its fourth mandate committed to the cause of peace, development, and prosperity for all. The Rectangular Strategy was updated to account for progress and evolving circumstances. Improving the quality and delivery of public services is one of four core strategic priorities. The Administrative Reform together with others such as deconcentration, decentralization, and sectoral reforms in every sector from health and education to land management is viewed as a key to unlocking capacity for poverty reduction and sustainable development for years to come.

The Royal Government is a government of reforms. As Prime Minister Samdech has said, reforms are a necessity; there is no choice. The Royal Government will reform the State in

1) For more details, visit the government website at http://www.cambodia.gov.kh/unisql1/egov/english/home.view.html.

fundamental ways for effective governance. Behavior will change, the capacity of people and institutions will be developed, and Cambodian resources will be mobilized towards priority needs and be duly accounted for.

The Royal Government approach to State reforms is based on three core principles: (1) securing peace, stability and security are necessary conditions to sustainable development, social justice and poverty reduction; (2) effective governance, performance and accountability are necessary conditions to a Civil Service that is loyal, motivated, professional and service oriented; and (3) making public services more transparent and more responsive to people's needs is essential to building trust for the well being of people and the prosperity of the Country. The following illustrates the extent of the Rectangular Strategy for Growth, Employment, Equity and Efficiency in Cambodia.

The Cambodian Civil Service

At the national level, the administration is subdivided into 27 ministries and some 34 authorities. At the sub-national level, there are 23 provinces, 26 cities, and 1,621 communes that interface directly with people. Vast programs are underway to bring government closer to the people and a new Organic Law specifying the responsibilities and authorities of the sub-national level was recently promulgated. The changes underway will have a determinant impact on the nature of the Cambodian Civil Service and the way it is managed.

The Cambodian Civil Service is a young institution. It was born in the footsteps of the Prime Minister win-win strategy for national reconciliation. It became a unified institution in 1999 with the integration of officials from the Khmer Rouge administration. Today's Civil Service is the result of national reconciliation and political stability imperatives. The Civil

Service is based on a career system whose main characteristics are stipulated in the Common Statute and in 21 Particular Statutes. The Common Statute is subdivided into five parts that define civil servant: regulate recruitment, provide for probation, permanent employment and removal, promotion, and discipline. The Particular Statutes classify civil servants into six cadres (e.g. administrators, foreign services, etc.) and provide for the specifics of the classification systems into grades and levels and for career progression. Progression is based on a mix of seniority and job performance. The following outlines key statistics concerning the Cambodian Civil Service, excluding the legislative and judiciary branches of the State, the armed forces and the police. They suggest that there may be room for deepening the reform (Numbers are rounded up).

[Table 3-2] Civil Service in Cambodia

Civil Service in Cambodia
Size of Civil Service in December 2008 (percentage at sub national level)
Total: 165,940 (80.3%)
Education: 96,294 (92.5%)
Health: 16,738 (88.4%)
As a percentage of population: 1.2%
Compensation in December 2008 (2001)
Average salary: US $ 68.6/month (US$ 19.5/month)
Average compensation (incl. benefits): US$ 78.9/month
Average compensation to GDP per capita: 1.50
Wage bill to GDP: 2.29%
Total wage bill to recurrent budget expenditures: 40.5%
Civil Service wage bill to recurrent budget expenditures: 27.5%

Current Public Administration Reform: The Situation

Management and control systems are operational and effective. However, they shall be made more supportive of performance, accountability, and merit. Innovative instruments to enhance performance and accountability are being deployed. However, they entail important risks that must be managed. There may be important exclusion issues. There is a broad base consensus on strategy and priorities to deepen the reform. The issue is one of capacity to implement and sustain. New partnership arrangements will need to be deployed rapidly based on principles of mutual trust and respect. Assistance by development partners will need to be harmonized and aligned with government needs.

Major complementary reform programs are underway. Ministries have taken the lead to reform their sectors with the assistance of development partners. Coordination and synergy among the reform will be essential to success.

The front is very wide. Urgent needs are many, and means are drastically limited. Thus, the need to prioritize critically and to sequence actions carefully is very important. Services provided must not only reduce poverty, delivery mechanisms themselves must promote the empowerment of collectivities, the development of the Civil Society, and the Private Sector. Not only should the administration be closer to the people, it should concentrate its efforts on what it can do best. Improving public services will bring about important changes in the attitude and behavior of both public servants and users of public services.

Public Administration Reform: The Vision and the Situation

To allow the values of loyalty, motivation, professionalism and service to characterize the attitudes and behavior, a Civil Service that is an effective provider of public services and a trusted development partner to better serve people must be created. The range of the Administrative Reform is far reaching. The next phase will be an extension of the previous ones. Upcoming initiatives will build on the significant successes achieved. The following is a list of the most significant ones. At the beginning of the Fourth Mandate, the Administrative Reform stands strong but challenges are daunting. The Civil Service is unified, stable and operational. However, capacity is lacking and means are scarce. To realize the vision of a loyal, motivated, professional and service-oriented Civil Service, systems and practices will need to be modernized, be made more performing and transparent, and behavior will need to change.

Secondly, the compensation regime (remuneration, social security, and pension) has been made more conducive to performance. Average compensation quadrupled since 2001. However, much more needs to be done for the Civil Service to be an effective provider of public services and a trusted development partner. Future improvements are a matter of affordability and thus of government revenues especially if coherence among state institutions is to be maintained.

Thirdly, management and control systems are operational and effective. However, they shall be made supportive of performance, accountability and merit. Innovative instruments to enhance performance and accountability are being deployed. However, they entail important risks that must be managed. There may be important exclusion issues.

Fourthly, there is a broad base consensus on strategy and priorities to deepen the reform. The issue is one of capacity to implement and sustain. New partnership arrangements will need to be deployed rapidly based on principles of mutual trust and respect. Assistance by development partners will need to be harmonized and aligned with government needs.

Lastly, major complementary reform programs are underway. Ministries have taken the lead to reform their sectors with the assistance of development partners. Coordination and synergy among the reform will be essential to success.

The front is very wide. Urgent needs are many, and means

are drastically limited. Thus, the need to prioritize critically and to sequence actions carefully is very important. Services provided must not only reduce poverty; delivery mechanisms themselves must promote the empowerment of collectivities, the development of the Civil Society, and the Private Sector. Not only should the administration be closer to the people, it should concentrate its efforts on what it can do best. Improving public services will bring about important changes in the attitude and behavior of both public servants and users of public services.

The Civil Service is an effective provider of public services and a trusted development partner to serve people better. Values of loyalty, motivation, professionalism, and service characterize attitude and behavior. During the current mandate, the reform will address five strategic objectives: (1) improving transparency and quality in the delivery of public services, (2) improving accountability and efficiency in public services, (3) developing human and institutional capacity, (4) enhancing human resources management and compensation, and (5) strengthening cadre management and deployment.

[Figure 3-2] The Scope of the Reform

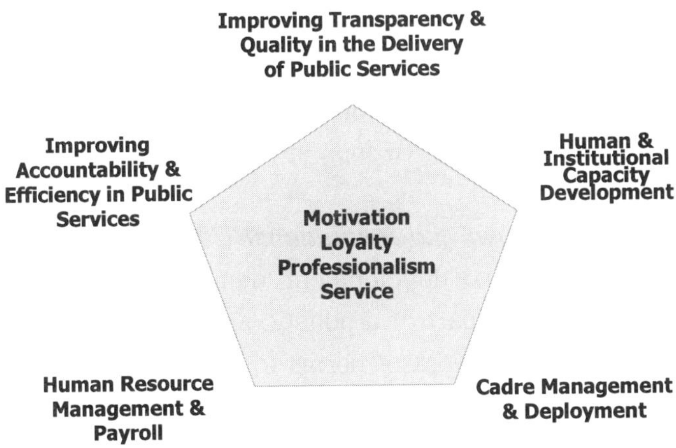

The approach will be prudent, step by step, and executed according to capacity and circumstances. The direction is clear and the action plan being prepared will specify initiatives, their timing, and sequencing. Much will depend on partnership arrangements between those concerned that have yet to be agreed upon. To illustrate the scope of the reform, the following are examples of initiatives to be undertaken:

Improving Transparency and Quality in the Delivery of Public Services: Making public services delivery processes more transparent, responsive, and easier to access are cornerstones of the administrative reform. Priorities include: the ongoing implementation of the Policy on Public Service Delivery, updating the Governance Action Plan to focus on improving public services by ministries, completing and widely disseminating the compendium on public services to enhance transparency and access, promoting the use of ICT in support of delivery processes.

Improving Accountability and Efficiency in Public Services: The objective is to focus on people. In support of priority activities of the Royal Government and to provide better public services to the people, the Administrative reform will focus on enhancing accountability and efficiency through: ongoing implementation of a yearly increase of 20% in basic salary, ongoing performance enhancement through targeted allowances, and the deployment of Performance and Accountability tools such as Priority Mission Groups and Merit Based Performance Incentives.

Developing Human and Institutional Capacity: The objective is to make capacity development demand more driven and "Cambodianized" as part of a holistic program where ministries lead within the framework of norms to enhance coordination and value. Priorities include: finalizing the policy and guidelines on Capacity Development, finalizing policy and guidelines on Human

Resource Development, deploying Performance Management and Accountability System, and completing the management frameworks and processes to support capacity development.

Human Resource Management and Payroll: The objective is to strengthen human resource processes and practices to enhance performance, accountability, and merit. Priorities include finalizing the policy on human resource management and its implementation plan and further development of the functionalities of ICT-based processes supporting personnel management and the payroll.

Cadre Management and Deployment: The objective is to deploy staff were most needed while ensuring effective control mechanisms and maintaining the number of civil servants to an acceptable level. Priorities include: the promulgation of a policy on the deployment of civil servants, effective control of the establishment, ongoing strengthening of the classification system, ongoing implementation the retirement policy through the use of ICT, the implementation of mechanisms to increase mobility and deploy civil servants where they are needed, mostly including local recruitment.

For a reform to succeed, the Royal Government believes that it must be owned and lead by Cambodia, and the initiative must be practical and sustainable. The strengthening of institutions, improving governance, and rapidly developing domestic capacity are keys of the Royal Government approach. The establishment of strong partnerships among ministries and between the government and its development partners is the way to empower Cambodia to meet its societal objectives. To be effective, partnerships must be based on principles of mutual respect, trust, and accountability. Dialogue, participation and transparency are essential attributes of any such arrangement at the program, activity, or project level.

Performance and Accountability

Performance and accountability instruments such as Special Operating Agencies, Priority Missions Groups, and Merit Based Performance Incentives will serve as wedges to introduce needed reforms. The CAR, ministries, and development partners developed four innovative and complementary instruments to enhance performance and accountability in the Civil Service. The Royal Government is deploying these instruments in coherence with reality, in ways that respect the fundamentals of the Cambodian Civil Service and that do not threaten its stability. They are innovative tools and they entail risks. The Council for Administrative Reform is monitoring their deployment closely to manage and mitigate risks.

Special Operating Agencies (SOAs): SOA type institutions are being used, with success, as part of reform programs that, much like the Royal Government's strategy, mainly aims to improve the quality and delivery of public services, to enhance performance, and develop human and institutional capacity. A Royal Decree provides the legal framework for ministries to design, establish, and manage SOAs within their jurisdiction.

Priority Mission Groups (PMGs): The Royal Government has been deploying PMGs since 2005 to enhance performance. Lessons were drawn and the PMG scheme has been strengthened for performance while incentives were also updated. PMGs, as SOAs and MBPIs, focus on achieving agreed results in return for better compensation. The new scheme facilitates the involvement and participation of development partners. PMG schemes target operational priorities while enhancing performance and capacity.

Merit-Based Performance Incentives (MBPIs): A Sub-Decree provides the legal framework for ministries to design, establish, manage, and monitor MBPI schemes within their jurisdiction.

Like the other two instruments, the MBPI instrument was designed to enhance performance and accountability in the Civil Service. Individual MBPI schemes in ministries or institutions will target core strategic priorities of ministries, participation will be strictly limited and implementation will be closely monitored.

Performance Management and Accountability Systems (PMAS): PMA Systems link ministries strategic and operational plans to work-units and staff. These systems will be deployed step by step first through SOAs, PMGs and MBPIs. It is through PMAS that staff are assigned responsibilities, monitored for results and held to account. These systems are a primary source to identify capacity development needs and to gradually change attitudes and behavior.

PMAS are an essential tool to the good functioning and success of SOAs, PMGs, and MBPIs. The PMAS guide is intended to assist ministries and the set of managers and staff, monitor and evaluate work priorities, targets and indicators, and to identify institutional and individual capacity development needs. The manual was developed to assist ministries and institutions establish, manage, and monitor performance and accountability in each of the three instruments.

SOAs, PMGs, and MBPIs complement one another and, when used together, they can significantly help achieve strategic, operational, or service delivery priorities. Together, these instruments will serve as wedges to transform the Civil Service into an effective provider of public services and a trusted development partner to serve people better, thereby enhancing the well-being of people and the prosperity of the nation. It is for ministries and institutions to use these instruments. Implementation guides were prepared to facilitate the work of ministries. An extensive program is underway to build the capacity of ministries in using them.

Lessons Learned

Reforming the public administration is a political venture made of inter-dependent actions. It is more art than science. The art of the possible is sustainable. It is about what can be done as opposed to what should be done. Reforming the State is a long arduous process that involves a complex array of activities that must mutually reinforce one another. In a context such as that of Cambodia, success depends on marshaling all available resources and being innovative. Success also knows what not to do. It is about doing better and accomplishing more with the available means. Many lessons can be drawn from the Cambodian experience. Following are ten of the major ones: (1) reforms should be anchored in one's reality (The issue is not determining what should be done, but what can be done. It is about focusing on the essential and high-return opportunities in ways that are practical and sustainable. Design and implementation must reflect the capacity to implement); (2) the importance of ownership and leadership (Reforms gradually transformed the Civil Service, but the behavior and attitudes of civil servants changed radically. Cambodian ownership and leadership of reforms are essential for the results to be sustainable, so ministries and civil servants must be actively involved); (3) the importance of a clear vision and political commitment (Reforms such as those undertaken are daunting and highly complex. To succeed they require well-understood and shared objectives, clearly articulated strategies, and unwavering political support); (4) reform activities shall be practical and realistic (The scope and pace of reforms shall be a function of available means and the capacity to sustain the course. Expectations shall be realistic and widely shared); and (5) reform activities and their sequencing shall be demand driven (A reform should support government wide and sectoral priorities. It shall address operational needs in a timely way. Ministries are ultimately responsible, reform councils are instigators, facilitators, and coordinators).

Moreover, additional lessons can be learned: (1) the importance of people (It is individuals that make the reforms succeed. Leadership, discipline, commitment, and participation are all necessary conditions of success. Political will and "savoir faire" are determinant factors); (2) the importance of effective governance (State building goes through the establishment of effective, transparent, and accountable institutions. Coherence among State institutions, Cambodian leadership, and ownership are determinant); (3) the importance of making optimal use of available means and thus of innovation (Without means, the best of plans remain mere dreams. The use of innovative approaches and mechanisms are often determinant to use available resources optimally); (4) the importance of inclusion, participation, and communications (Government, the private sector, civil society, and development partners shall work together, reinforcing one another in support of priorities. Inclusion, participation, and communications are determinant); and (5) coping with the dysfunctions of technical assistance (Technical assistance in general, but particularly TA of substitution, is often counter-productive when it comes to developing ongoing capacity within institutions of the State).

The Way Forward

The direction the Royal Government set for itself through its strategies and action plans is clear. Considering Cambodia's reality, the issue is how, together with its partners, the government can make this strategy succeed. More precisely what shall the reform do to further the cause of good governance in Cambodia? What should it do to promote capacity, performance, and accountability? The administrative reform is entering a particularly difficult phase: public service delivery processes will be soon be more streamlined, the workforce will be redeployed closer to the people and towards priority poverty reduction areas, entrenched attitudes and behavior will be changed, and new skills will be acquired. This will require long-term commitment and the deployment of important resources. New partnership arrangements will need to be put in place.

The challenges are formidable. The current administration is relatively young, a result of previously autonomous factions being integrated as recently as early 1998. The foreseeable MTEF and Fiscal Framework limit options that would allow sustainability without significant investments by development partners. Reforms such as those envisaged will require difficult policy and programming choices. The capacity of people and institutions must be developed urgently. Compensation shall motivate civil servants and attract the necessary talent, but competition is fierce. In addition, the programming and resourcing of initiatives is not any less challenging. Early next steps will include: (1) achieving a broad base consensus on the NPAR 2009~2013, (2) establishing partnership arrangements to meet priorities, (3) deploying innovative instruments to enhance performance and accountability, and (4) promulgating policies to make HRM, HRD, capacity development and deployment more effective.

Conclusion

The reform faces important challenges to modernize the Civil Service into an effective provider of public services and a trusted development partner. They include: (1) the need to increase the accessibility, transparency and responsiveness of public services particularly those that matter most to the people,

(2) the need to promote loyalty, motivation, professionalism and service culture within the Civil Service, (3) the need to develop programs to develop human and institutional capacity to implement and to sustain, (4) the need to improve performance and accountability in a controlled manner, and (5) the need to better use available resources. All are difficult and arduous tasks that will tax the best of determination and resources. As experience shows around the world, modernizing civil services can only be an ongoing work in progress.

Because of financial and human capacity constraints, Cambodian reform will continue to focus on the main priorities of government and on supporting the implementation of strategic sectoral reforms. The Administrative Reform shall better support reforms whose purposes are to improve the quality and delivery of public services. The approach will be prudent and fiscally responsible, particularly when it comes to the introduction of incentive instruments and to improving compensation in the Civil Service.

The Council for Administrative Reform will complete consultations with ministries, development partners, and other stakeholders in the coming months on a sequenced action plan. In early 2009, a national seminar will be held to offer advisement on the specifics of a multi-year action plan. Once the National Program for Administrative Reform is approved, partnerships involving ministries and development partners will be established to carry out the process of implementation.

References

Royal Government of Cambodia (2001a). *Good Governance Action Plan I.* Phnom Penh, Cambodia: Royal Government of Cambodia.

Royal Government of Cambodia (2001b). *Strategy for Rationalization of the Civil Service (2002~2006).* Phnom Penh, Cambodia: Royal Government of Cambodia.

Royal Government of Cambodia (2002). *National Poverty Reduction Strategy 2003~2005.* Phnom Penh, Cambodia: Royal Government of Cambodia.

Royal Government of Cambodia (2003). *Constitution of the Kingdom of Cambodia.* Phnom Penh, Cambodia: Royal Government of Cambodia.

Royal Government of Cambodia (2004a). *Rectangle Strategy for Growth, Employment, Equity and Efficiency in Cambodia.* Phnom Penh, Cambodia: Royal Government of Cambodia.

Royal Government of Cambodia (2004b). Speaking Notes by Samdech Akka Moha Sena Padei Techo Prime Minister Hun Sen, National Seminar on Administrative Reform, August 25. Phnom Penh, Cambodia: Royal Government of Cambodia.

Royal Government of Cambodia (2004c). Speaking Notes by H.E. Sok An Deputy Prime Minister, Minister in Charge of the Office of the Council of Ministers, Chairman of the Council for Administrative Reform, National Conference on Strengthening Good Governance for Poverty Reduction and Development, December. Phnom Penh, Cambodia: Royal Government of Cambodia.

Royal Government of Cambodia (2005). *National Strategic Development Plan 2006~2010.* Phnom Penh, Cambodia: Royal Government of Cambodia.

Royal Government of Cambodia (2006a). *Good Governance Action Plan II.* Phnom Penh, Cambodia: Royal Government of Cambodia.

Royal Government of Cambodia (2006b). *Policy of Public Service Delivery.* Phnom Penh, Cambodia: Royal Government of Cambodia.

Royal Government of Cambodia (2008). Speaking Notes by Samdech Akka Moha Sena Padei Techo Hun Sen, Prime Minister of the Kingdom of Cambodia, National Conference on the Prosperity of People Through

Achievements from the Implementation of the Rectangular Strategy by the Royal Government 2004~2007, June. Phnom Penh, Cambodia: Royal Government of Cambodia.

World Bank (2004). *Cambodia at the Crossroads, Strengthening Accountability to Reduce Poverty*. Washington, DC: World Bank.

World Bank (2007). *Sharing Growth: Equity and Development in Cambodia*. Washington, DC: World Bank.

Office of the Council of Ministers (www.ocm.gov.kh)
Ministry of Economy and Finance (www.mef.gov.kh)
Ministry of Foreign Affairs and International Cooperation (www.mfaic.gov.kh)
Ministry of Information (www.information.gov.kh)
Secretariat of Public Service (www.sspf.gov.kh)
Ministry of Planning (www.mop.gov.kh)
Secretariat of Public Service (www.sspf.gov.kh)
Permanent Mission of the Kingdom of Cambodia to the United Nations (www.un.int/cambodia)
National Institute of Statistic (www.nis.gov.kh)
The Council for the Development of Cambodia (www.cdc-crdb.gov.kh)

Chapter 4 Indonesia

Ismail Mohamad

Introduction

Indonesia is a *republic* with a *presidential system*. As a *unitary state*, power is concentrated in the national government. Following the *resignation of President Suharto* in 1998, Indonesian political and governmental structures have undergone major reforms. Four amendments to the *1945 Constitution of Indonesia* have revamped the *executive*, *judicial*, and *legislative* branches. The President of Indonesia is the Head of State, Commander-in-chief of the *Indonesian Armed Forces*, and the Director of Domestic Governance, Policy-making and Foreign affairs. The President appoints a Council of Ministers not required to be elected members of the legislature. The highest representative body at national level is the *People's Consultative Assembly* (MPR). Its main functions are supporting and amending the constitution, inaugurating the president, and formalizing broad outlines of state policy. It has the power to impeach the president. The MPR comprises two houses: the *House of Representative Council* (DPR), with 550 members, and the Board of Regional Representatives (DPD), with 128 members. The DPR passes legislation and monitors the executive branch. Party-aligned members are elected for five-year terms by proportional representation. Reforms since 1998 have markedly increased the DPR's role in national governance. The DPD is a new chamber for matters of regional management. Administratively, Indonesia consists of *thirty-three provinces*, five of which have special status. Each province has its own political legislature and governor. The provinces are subdivided into regencies (*kabupaten*) and cities (*kota*), which are further subdivided into subdistricts (*kecamatan*), and again into village groupings (either *desa* or *kelurahan*). Following the implementation of regional autonomy measures in 2001, the regencies and cities have become the key administrative units, responsible for providing most government services. The village administration level is the most influential on a citizen's daily life, and handles matters of a village or neighborhood through an elected lurah or kepala desa (village chief). Based on this socio-political condition, this paper attempts to describe the dynamics of public sector reform implementation in order to establish better public governance in Indonesia than its earlier periods.

Since the Asian financial crisis in 1997~1998, Indonesia has been faced with various challenges in many sectors. Since those days, several development indicators have shown Indonesia's catastrophies in the fields of economy, politics, law and justice, as well as in the fields of clean government, good public governance, and good corporate governance implementation. These conditions have triggered the demand for changes and reforms in the state administration. For fulfilling the demand, one fundamental step taken was the amendment of the 1945 State Constitution. Up until now, there have been amendments four times. The first one was taken in October 19, 1999, the second in August 18, 2000, the next on November 1, 2001, and the last one was conducted in August 10, 2002.

The 1945 State Constitution and its four amendments have adopted various new insights; among others they: (1) confirm the implementation of the thoughts of democracy and nomocracy at the same time for complementary fulfillment to each other's principles, (2) strengthen the separation of power as well as checks and balances mechanism, (3) purify the presidential government system, and rejuvenate the idea of unity in diversity under the scheme of the Unitary State of the Republic of Indonesia. The implementation of people's sovereignity is channeled through the constitutional procedures established in the laws and the constitution (constitutional democracy). The implementation of the principles of people's sovereignty (democratie) and law's sovereignity (nomocratie) at the same time is just like the two faces of a coin. The government system chosen is presidential because of previous failures of parliamentary government implementation in the past. For Indonesia, the presidential system guarantees more stability in government. This system can also be practiced by incorporating the multi-party system through a constitutional arrangement to reduce the negative impacts or hereditial weaknesses of this presidential system (Ashiddiqie, 2003). This amendment also confirms that the Republic of Indonesia is a democratic state of law as well as a lawful state of democracy (constitutional democracy) which cannot be separated from each other. This evidence is also strenghtened by the improving enforcement and protection of human hights.

The amendments of the 1945 State Constitution have formed a better constitution in developing a state governance system and have shown strong commitment to the values and principles of good governance. These efforts were done in order to provide strong fundamentals for the implementation of massive reform agendas in government administration as the key leverage of development dynamics towards advanced, prosperous, just, and self-sufficient people of Indonesia as stated in the opening remarks of 1945 state constitution. Realizing that the successful implementation of the principles of good governance in state government management would highly depend on the government bureaucracy, the bureaucracy mission, as an elaboration of the opening remarks of the 1945 state constitution, is then to uphold quality, efficiency, and effectiveness of service provisions to the people in a just and equal manner. Bureaucracy, according to its tasks, roles, and functions, will master the knowledge and information which are supported by great resources which other parties would not have. Thus, bureaucracy should have strong access to formulate technocratic-nuanced policy and gain political support as well as holding an important position in implementing various policy decisions. This implies the importance of having a competent, neutral bureaucracy which can take the roles of government engines to carry out their duties professionally and measurably.

However, history has also noted that ever since the Indonesian independence was proclaimed, government bureaucracy matters were always related to the adopted political systems. By the end of the new order regimes (1998), civil servants were often involved in various political activities and those made them distracted from their professional duties. The reform era (1998 up to now) has opened a large opportunity for the civil servants to develop their professional competence and to be released from practical political games. However, the extended crisis and political, as well as democratic, euphoria have caused various obstacles to the targeted improvements. The implementation of decentralization and local autonomy as assigned by the constitutions has not shown the expected impacts, and has even created and escalated more complex problems as various overlapping policies made by central and local governments, authority problems between central and local government, local proliferation problems, and sectoral egos in development (Effendi, 2008).

Although government bureaucracy in Indonesia before the era of reform was designed as a bureaucracy based on the principles of rationality, efficiency, certainty, and calculability (Weberian bureaucracy) which had strong roots to the intellectual cultures of developed countries, in daily practice it was still influenced by strong hierarchical patterns and feudalistic cultures. This created an inefficient and authoritarian bureaucracy, one conducive for corruption, collusion, and nepotism to take place. Therefore, as the time goes by, bureaucracy reforms have become a shared commitment, turning into a national movement in the reform era and also manifesting into a national policy agenda which, among others, was stipulated in the Law No. 17 of the year 2007 on The National Long Term Development Plan 2005~2025. This law states that "state apparatus development is carried out through bureaucracy reforms in order to improve their professionalism to realize good governance in central and local governments to support the successful development of other areas." Furthermore, the Presidential Regulation No. 7 of the year 2005 on the National Middle Term Development Plan 2004~2009 states the policy steps aiming at an institutional and mechanical system of state apparatus, quality of human resources, and over sighting systems, as well as effective auditing, in order to realize good governance.

Successful implementation of bureaucracy reform will support the efforts of reforming other areas of politics, economy, and law enforcement in the country, as well as boosting readiness in anticipating tougher global competition in various areas. This implies that bureaucracy reform is an important step in the efforts of improving public administration in realizing good public governance. However, the understanding and implementation of bureaucracy reform in Indonesia has not run as smoothly as expected by the constitution, and has not consistently referred to the paradigm of New Public Management and governance model. This is due to, among other things, the political dynamics in state administration, as well as institutional, human resource, and government management problems.

This paper will generally describe the public administration and public governance in Indonesia, with the focus on the dynamics of the implementation of government bureaucracy reforms. This focus is chosen because the government bureaucracy problem will not only obstruct the productivity and competitiveness of Indonesia, but may also interfere with its bilateral and multilateral relationships.

Current Status

Indonesia is a country with a population of 237.5 million and is ranked fourth in the world's most populated countries (as reported per July 2008). It is a very culturally diverse nation of about 350 recognized ethnolingusitic groups, with 1.9 million square kilometers of total land area and 7.9 million square kilometers of total sea area and thus named as the largest archipelagic nation in the world. It compasses more than 17,000 islands, about 5,100 kilometers at its greatest east west extent, and about 1,888 kilometers at its greatest expanse north to south. The vast complexity and diversity has influenced on the formulations and configurations of political powers in the society and has impacted to the development of multi-party components in democracy system, as well as to the development of public administration.

Politics and Democracy

Up to now (2008), the political development in Indonesia has not become as stable as expected by the people. This can be seen through the growing numbers of political parties, which is probably the largest number in the world. In terms of population and democracy practices, Indonesia is ranked third for democratic countries in the world, after India and the United States of America. There are 34 political parties that have been registered and factually verified to compete in the 2009 general election. For comprehensive descriptions of the complexity of the political parties and democracy practices in Indonesia, the following are short reviews on the general elections that have taken place in this country since 1955 up to the preparation stage of the next 2009 general election.

The First General Election

The first general election was conducted in 1955. This general election was acclaimed as the most democratic general election in Indonesia. The general election was carried out under an inconducive security condition where some areas of Indonesia were still threatened by fear and havoc. In this situation, both the armed forces and national police corps were also entitled the right to vote. However, the general election managed to be conducted peacefully. This general election was carried out to choose members of House of Representatives and constituantees. From 172 participating political parties, only 35 managed to obtain seats both in the house and in the constituantees, with five major political parties acclaimed to have majority votes.

A Period of Guided Democracy

The next general election was supposed to be conducted after the first election, that is, in 1960. However, due to the release of the Presidential Decree on July 5, 1959, the general election was cancelled. This decree dispersed the constituantees and stated the commitment to re-embrace the 1945 state constitution, as well as formed the "gotong royong" house of representatives and temporary people consultative assembly whose members were elected by the president and proclaimed the procurement of guided democracy. Furthermore, in September 1963, Sukarno, who was the President at that time, proclaimed himself as President for life. This tense and hostile atmosphere was broken on September 30, 1965 by a form of coup by the Indonesian Communist Party and ended the era of Sukarno regimes after 22 years of power (August 18, 1945~March 12, 1967).

The New Order Era

On March 11, 1966, the power was transferred from Sukarno to Suharto, and the Indonesian Communist Party was formally banned the following day. One year later, the new order regimes began when Suharto became the Acting President on March 12, 1967. The new order was more authoritarian but was more successful in bringing stability to the nation with its enormous economic achievements and undeniably improved well-being of Indonesians. In terms of general election participation, there was a significant reduction in its number. In 1971, only 10 political parties participated in the general election. While in the next general elections in 1977, 1982, 1987, 1992, and 1997, it was followed by only 3 contesting political parties, namely, the United Development Party (PPP), the Golongan Karya (Golkar), and the Indonesian Democratic Party (PDI). Throughout the era, the Golkar had always won the elections, becoming the single majority, and dominated the house and the even government. Government bureaucracy became partisan and took the side of the ruling Golkar. Bureaucracy became unneutral (Thoha, 2000: 64). That caused the alleged sustainability of the new order regime for more than 30 years. This was also related to the fact that Suharto was the Chairman of the Executive Board of Golkar.

Suharto provided strong leadership but did not provide for a wise transition, and in his last years clung to power and favored family and friends. There was corruption on a large scale. When the Asian crisis hit in 1997~1998, the New Order Regime lost the economic justification that had guaranteed much of its public support, and there was a widespread call for Suharto to step down. Suharto resigned on May 21, 1998. Suharto's administration (the new order) lasted for 32 years before it came to an end (March 12, 1967~May 21, 1998).

Reform Era

On May 21, 1998, Suharto was succeeded by B. J. Habibie (May 21, 1998~October 20, 1999) who began a new and more open electoral process. In this reform era, political opportunities were widely open, the constitution guaranteed freedom for unity, and everyone was entitled the right to establish political parties. This encouraged a multi-party political system to take place once again. In 1999, following Indonesia's first freely contested parliamentary election since 1995, Abdurrahman Wahid (Gus Dur) became the president. The 1999 general election was participated in by 43 political parties. Later, leadership styles and health reasons encouraged the oppositions to unite and build a strong movement for Gus Dur's impeachment. He was dismissed from the office in July 2001 in favor of Megawati Sukarnoputri, his vice president. Gus Dur was in power only from October 20, 1999~July 23, 2001 while Megawati ruled from July 23, 2001~October 20, 2004.

Then, as instructed by the constitution, in the year of 2004 another general election was conducted for electing the members of House of Representatives and of the Board Regions of Representatives, in which 24 political parties participated. There were also two rounds for the Presidential and Vice Presidential elections. The first round was administered on July 5, 2004 and was partcipated in by 5 paired-participants. Since there was no pair that won more than 50% of the votes, the second round was held on September 20, 2004 and was participated by two winning pairs from the first round, Susilo Bambang Yudhoyono–Jusuf Kalla and Megawati–Hasyim Muzadi. Based on the general election results announced on October 4, 2004 and from registered voters of 150,644,184, there were actually 116,662,705 (77.44%) voters that showed up on the election day. From the total votes, there were actually 114,257,054 (97.94%) were deemed as legal votes and the rest were considered impaired. Susilo Bambang Yudhoyono and Jusuf Kalla won this election by gaining more than 60% votes while Megawati-Hasyim Muzadi only took less than 40% votes.

[Table 4–1] The Result of the Presidential Election

NO.	Paired Candidates	Numbers of Votes	%
1.	Megawati - Hasyim Muzadi	44,990,704	39.38%
2.	Susilo Bambang Yudhoyono - Jusuf Kalla	69,266,350	60.62%

Susilo Bambang Yudhoyono and Jusuf Kalla were elected the President and Vice President from October 24, 2004 and still remain in power up until now.

2009 General Election

The 2009 general election was scheduled to take place in April 9, 2009 to simultaneously elect 560 members of the national House of Representatives, 132 members of Board of Regions of Representatives as well as members of local houses of representatives in all municipalities and regencies in Indonesia for service years of 2009~2014 on July 7, 2009. The General Election Commission has announced 34 names of political parties that are factually verified to participate in the 2009 general election. Among the 34 political parties, there are 18 newly contesting political parties who are participating for the first-time in the elections. Meanwhile, the direct election for the President and Vice President is scheduled for July 2009, after the legislative election finishes.

The elaboration of political and democracic development since the first general election in 1955 and the upcoming 2009 above describes the long journey of democracic development in Indonesia. It also shows the political and democracic euphoria which, among others, have impacted tough competition (and possible conflicts) among political parties and elites who are supposed to be "role models" in the society. This has caused more confusion and prolonged detoriation of trust to the people. They have witnessed "the polemics" become "daily bread" to the public countenance (Effendi, 2008: 8). This situation also impacts the "health" of government bureaucracy since the bureacracy itself cannot be separated from the government that is controlled by political power. This is also true because bureaucracy is directly influenced by how the power is exercised and operated. Bureaucracy reform is therefore strongly related to the process of democratization since it is also related to the escalating transparency of the fulfillment of people's basic rights, people empowerment, decentralization and public accountability.

Public Administration Development

Redeveloping government bureaucracy has become a continuous effort of public sector reform (Thoha, 2000). Bureaucracy reform is actually the effort of fundamentally renewing and changing the government administration system, especially related to the aspects of institutional (organization), administrative (systems and procedures), and human resource development (The Ministry for Empowerment of State Apparatus, 2008: 9). The current status of developing government bureaucracy in the reform era, as mentioned above, is as follows.

Institutional Aspects

For the interest of achieving the goals of the nation, various organizations/institutions have been established for running the state administration. Sovereignity of the people is manifested through "the three arms of power," which are horizontally divided by the seperation of power into the power of various state institutions that have controls over one another to establish "checks and balances."

Indonesia in a unitary state whose juridictions are divided into autonomous regions of provinces, municipalities, and regencies. The power whose limitations are prescribed by the state consitution are established in Central Government. The power relationships between the central, provincial, and municipal or regencial governments adopt the principles of decentralization (autonomy) and auxiliary tasks (medebewin). Based on this concept, People's Consultative Assembly's Decree No. XV/MPR/1998 was formulated. This decree arranges the administration of local autonomy, the just and wise usage of the national natural resources exploitation, and financial balances between the central, provincial, and local governments under the scheme of the unitary state of the Republic of Indonesia. Autonomy is aimed at providing more authority and responsibility to the autonomous regions in managing and administering local people's best interest through their own intents or people's aspirations.

State Institutions: State institutions that are established in the government system in Indonesia are as follows: (1) Legislative bodies, which are comprised of the House of Representatives (DPR) and the Board of Regional Representatives (DPD), together they form the People's Consultative Assembly (MPR) with all their members, (2) the Executive body is the President, and the (3) Judical body is represented by the Supreme Court (MA) and the Constitutional Court (MK). Besides these, there is also the Financial Audit Board (BPK), which is free and independent in performing auditing functions as an external oversighting body. Other institutions are in forms of commissions: the judicial commission (KY), general election commission (KPU), and corruption eradication commission (KPK). Besides that, there are also various state boards and institutions under the branch of the executive arm whose independence is also prescribed in the constitution with regard to their roles and duties. These executive institutions, among others, are the Bank of Indonesia as the central bank, The National Police Corps (POLRI) and General Attorney as law enforcement agencies, and the Indonesian National Armed Forces (TNI) as state defense organization.

Central Government Organizations: Central government organizations are unitary state apparatus in the central government which hold the responsibilities of executives agencies and whose duties are conducting various business in the government within the authorities of the central government. According to the Law No. 39/2008 on State Ministry, it is said that the central government format comprises presidential institutions, ministries, and non-ministry organizations. The current ministerial terms as Department, State Ministry, and others are acknowledged by this law until the establishment of new ministerial institutions prescribed by regulations in this law. The central government organizations play the roles of maintaining administrations in the fields of foreign affairs, defense, security, monetary and fiscal affairs, religious affairs, judicial affairs, as well as formulating policies, norms, standards, and criteria for other fields of development which are the authority of local governments.

Local Government Organizations: Provincial, municipal, and regency governments do not have hierarchical relationships to one another. This means that provincial governments are not heading municipal and regency governments. However, each province as a jurisdictional administrator holds the responsibity as coordinator of the municipalities and regencies in its territory. In establishing the municipality and regency as autonomous areas, a split model was used in order to create the pure autonomous areas and does not take the duties of administrative jurisdictions which can take the deconcentration missions.

The autonomous regional governments are comprised of a local government (representing the executive) and a local house of representatives (representing the legislative). The position of the local house is equal and becomes a partner of local government. The local apparatus is comprised of secretariat, local authority offices, and local technical institutions. In municipalities and regencies, there are districts which are also parts of municipalities and regencies' apparatus. Disctricts' apparatus are called "desa" (villages) (however, names vary due to local cultures). In the villages, there are village governments and villages representative boards.

One of the impacts in regional autonomy in Indonesia is the escalating proliferations from village levels to provincial levels. General descriptions of provincial proliferation is summarized in Table 4-2. Up to June 2008, there have been establishments of 191 and autonomous areas, comprised of 7 provinces, 153 regencies, 31 municipalities, making a total of 33 provinces, 386 regencies, and 91 municipalities if added to the previously established ones. Table 4-3 shows the growth of the new autonomous areas before 1999 and up to June 2008 above. Although proliferations can bring the government closer to its people in public service provision, but up to now what has really been observed is the ineffciency and ineffectiveness of

[Table 4-2] The Number of Regions in Indonesia 1945 until Now

1945~1950	1950~1966	1966~1998	1999~sekarang
Sumatera	Sumatera Utara Daerah Istimewa Aceh Jambi Riau Sumatera Barat Sumatera Selatan Lampung	Sumatera Utara Daerah Istimewa Aceh Jambi Riau Sumatera Barat Sumatera Selatan Lampung Bengkulu	Sumatera Utara Nangroe Aceh Darussalam Jambi Riau Kepulauan Riau Sumatera Barat Sumatera Selatan Lampung Bengkulu Kepulauan Bangka Belitung
Jawa Barat	Jawa Barat	Jawa Barat	Jawa Barat
			Banten
	Daerah Khusus Ibukota Jakarta	Daerah Khusus Ibukota Jakarta	Daerah Khusus Ibukota Jakarta
Jawa Tengah	Jawa Tengah	Jawa Tengah	Jawa Tengah
	Daerah Istimewa Yogyakarta	Daerah Istimewa Yogyakarta	Daerah Istimewa Yogyakarta
Jawa Timur	Jawa Timur	Jawa Timur	Jawa Timur
Sunda Kecil	Bali	Bali	Bali
	Nusa Tenggara Barat	Nusa Tenggara Barat	Nusa Tenggara Barat
	Nusa Tenggara Timur	Nusa Tenggara Timur	Nusa Tenggara Timur
Borneo	Kalimantan Barat	Kalimantan Barat	Kalimantan Barat
	Kalimantan Tengah	Kalimantan Tengah	Kalimantan Tengah
	Kalimantan Selatan	Kalimantan Selatan	Kalimantan Selatan
	Kalimantan Timur	Kalimantan Timur	Kalimantan Timur
Sulawesi	Sulawesi Utara	Sulawesi Utara	Sulawesi Utara
			Gorontalo
	Sulawesi Tengah	Sulawesi Tengah	Sulawesi Tengah
	Sulawesi Selatan	Sulawesi Selatan	Sulawesi Selatan
			Sulawesi Barat
	Sulawesi Tenggara	Sulawesi Tenggara	Sulawesi Tenggara
Maluku	Maluku	Maluku	Maluku
			Maluku Utara
	Irian Barat	Irian Jaya	Papua
			Papua Barat
		Timor Timur	
8 provinsi	25 provinsi	27 provinsi	33 provinsi

Sumber : www.depdagri.go.id

[Table 4-3] The Development of Region

Before and After 1999

Regions	Before 1999	Up to June 2008
Provinces	27	33
Regencies	233	386
Municipalities	60	91
Total	320	510

Source: www.depdagri.go.id

bureaucracy in terms of institutions, financial management, and development budgets.

Privatization: To meet the demands for efficiency, the government has also privatized several state-owned enterprises. This policy was made due to several considerations such as: (1) to improve the performance of state-owned enterprises as well as to create and increase companies' added values based on the principles of good corporate governance, (2) to enlarge public participation in the ownerships of the companies' shares, (3) to improve economic efficiency, to stimulate, and to become milestones for economic growth through investments and through more efficient technology transfers, (4) to develop stock markets in the country, and/or (5) to add resources of state incomes and revenues (LAN, 2008). The implementation of privatization policy until now is still encumbered with pros and cons due to both its political and economical advantages and disavantages.

Administrative Aspects (System and Procedures)

Tremendous political and institutional changes have marked Indonesia's transition to a much more open and competitive society. Constitutional reforms securing direct elections have created a new accountability framework at all levels of the political system. The decentralization process that started in 2001 is bringing control over resources closer to the clients/end-users, providing new opportunities for participation and monitoring of service delivery. Regions have become key players in service delivery. As a result, users say that the quality of services has improved sharply over the past two years. According to a survey, around 70% of users think that the quality of health and education service has improved. The quality of administrative matters and policing have likewise improved. Public demand for good governance has also been championed by a free media and more effective pressure from civil society organizations (APEC, 2007: 72).

Transparency and Accountability: The Indonesian public sector has published, or made available, its laws, regulations, procedural rules, and administrative rulings of general application through several media channels. Information on policies related to government agencies is published and available on the agencies' websites. In addition, the same things apply for the activities of state-owned companies, which can also be accessed via their websites. In this case, there has been an enactment of Law No. 14/2008 on Public Information Openness, which will be effective in April 2010. The establishment of this law will change public organization cultures, not only in the executives, but also in the legislatives and judiciary as well as in non government organizations that are partly or fully funded by public budgets or public contributions or foreign donors, to provide access on all public information that they have. When this law takes effect the government's role will be only as an information administrator. Failure to follow this law will result in the public organization paying the penalty of Rp. 5 millions or one year imprisonment. There is actually still permissible classified information which can only be accessed through a court order.

In terms of accountability, Indonesia has implemented a performance based budget system that makes the public sector more accountable. In addition, a performance accountability system called SAKIP (Performance Accountability System for Government Agencies) was also developed. SAKIP includes the development of strategic planning and performance management as parts of its mechanism. Based on this system, government agencies are required to submit their performance accountability reports (LAKIP) to the president every year, *via* The Ministry for Empowerment of State Apparatus (Menpan). This system is an effort to improve the managerial accountability of the government apparatus. In terms of financial accountability, government agencies are audited by the Financial Audit Board (BPK) and the Financial and Develoment Supervisory Board (BPKP). Furthermore, for improving financial management, auditing, and implementation of SAKIP, there are also development of government internal controlling systems in the efforts of efficiently and effectively achieving organizational goals, as well as improving performance, transparency, and accountability in state financial management and minimizing financial fraud and corruption in government institutions.

In relation to the improvement of public accountability, non-government organizations (NGOs) serve as partners in supervising the government's activities, including the preparation and the implementation of rules and regulations. Some of the NGOs are engaged in advocacy issues, while others work for promoting good governance and increasing public participation in public affairs. Many NGOs promote transparency and accountability, and some are directly concerned with issues of corruption.

To enhance transparency, accountability, and efficiency in the procurement system, the government has intoduced new procedures, including developing an electronic government procurement system (E-GP) to foster competition in bidding for government contracts. In early 2008, the government conducted E-GP pilot projects in several line ministries and selected provincial/local governments. In the future, the E-GP will be progressively implemented in Indonesia.

Control of Corruption: Furthermore, as an important aspect of implementing good governance, an extensive effort of controlling the corruption is deemed very important. The better the control, the more accountable public institutions are. To see the development and current progress of corruption control in Indonesia in more detail, the description below is presented, starting from the time the reform began.

The large scale of corruption that took place in many sectors in the era of the new order regimes, were mainly caused by limited access for the people, and for media to freely inform and communicate to the public the corruption cases conducted by the government officials. People were not able or were not encouraged to disclose various corruption scandals that took place but were difficult to prove. Therefore, it was understandable why various policies and strategies that had been meant to reduce the corruption did not seem to work effectively. The crisis of confidence in the government was worsened by the financial crisis that hit in 1997~1998 and ended the new order regimes. After the fall of the new order, people's critical awareness began to rise to directly criticize each policy that was not in the best interests of the people. The state administration was also required to change so that it was no longer state-oriented, but more people-oriented (Kleiden, 2003).

By the beginnging of the reform era, President B. J. Habibie conducted various efforts to make fundamental changes based on the people's needs, among others, through widening the opportunity for media to establish social control. The government efforts were also supported by the legislature who produced the Decree of People Consultative Assembly No.XI/MPR/1998 on Corruption, Collusion, and Nepotism-Free State Administration. Based on this decree, Law No. 28/1999 was released to facilitate the efforts. Further efforts were made through the enactment of Law No. 31/1999 on Corruption Eradication. This law brought the impetus for the formulation of Corruption Eradication Commissions for State Administrators.

In the time of President Abdurrahman Wahid, the National Ombudsmen Commission was also established through Presidential Decree No. 44/2000 (which was later replaced by Law No. 37/2008 on Ombudsmen) which emphasizes improvement of the oversighting quality to public service provision. Besides that, a team for corruption eradication directly chaired by the President was also assembled. After that, there were also establishments of such non-government institutions as Transparency People of Indonesia, Indonesian Corruption Watch, as well as Transparency International Indonesia and other organizations as watchdogs over corruption cases in Indonesia. All these organizations along with the donor organization/ countries as well as with the civil society and the government have encouraged public sector reforms in Indonesia.

In the time of President Megawati, Law No. 15/2002 on Anti-Money Laundering was enacted. This law brought the impetus to the establishment of Center for Financial Transactions Report and Analysis, which analysizes and reports various financial reports. The efforts of corruption eradication was further strenghtened by Law no. 30/2002 on Corruption Eradication Commission. Moreover, in 2004, the House of Representatives along with the government established Judicial Commissions whose responsibility, among others, is to monitor and evaluate the performance of state judges.

Government efforts to eradicate corruption was further significantly strenghtened. In the time of President Susilo Bambang Yudhoyono, people's optimism has improved. People's optimism was recorded under the survey of Transparency International in the year 2005 entitled Global Corruption Barometer, where more than 81% of Indonesian people were optimistic that corruption will significantly decrease. This percentage greatly surpassed the average of 19% and bettered other countries such as Uruguay (57%), Nigeria (51%), Kosovo (50%) as can be observed in Table 4-4.

[Table 4-4] The Biggest Optimists
(Countries Where the Public Thinks Corruption will Decrease)

Country	2003	2004	2005
Indonesia	55%	66%	81%
Uruguay	N/A*	28%	57%
Nigeria	39%	27%	51%
Kosovo	N/A*	52%	50%
Sample average	19%	17%	19%

* Country not included in Global Corruption Barometer 2003/2004.
Source: Transparency International Global Corruption Barometer 2005.

People's confidence on the reduction of corruption case in Indonesia is shown by the decrease of corruption perception index, that is, from 2 in the year 2004 to become 2.6 in the year 2008 (International Transparency, 2008) for the scale from 0 (very corrupt) to 10 (very clean). The increase of the Corruption Perceptions Index (CPI) has put Indonesia in a better place compared to the Philipines (2.3), Pakistan (2.5), and Bangladesh (2.1). Although the CPI position of Indonesia was not better than Thailand, Malaysia, and Singapore, the current progress shows

Indonesian's position is moving towards improvement, seeming very promising. Details of the recent progress of CPI can be seen in the following Table 4-5:

[Table 4-5] CPI Indonesia and Other Asian Countries (2001~2008)

	2001	2002	2003	2004	2005	2006	2007	2008
Singapore	9.2	9.3	9.4	9.3	9.4	9.4	9.3	9.2
Hong Kong	7.9	8.2	8	8.3	8.3	8.3	8.3	8.1
Japan	7.1	7.1	7	6.9	7.3	7.6	7.5	7.3
Taiwan	5.9	5.6	5.7	5.6	5.9	5.9	5.7	5.7
Malaysia	5.0	4.9	5.3	5	5.1	5	5.1	5.1
South Korea	4.2	4.5	4.3	4.5	5	5.1	5.1	5.6
China	3.5	3.5	3.4	3.4	3.2	3.3	3.5	3.6
Thailand	3.2	3.2	3.3	3.6	3.8	3.6	3.3	3.5
Philipines	2.9	2.6	2.5	2.6	2.5	2.5	2.5	2.3
India	2.7	2.7	2.8	2.8	2.9	3.3	3.5	3.4
Vietnam	2.6	2.4	2.4	2.6	2.6	2.6	2.6	2.7
Pakistan	2.3	2.6	2.5	2.1	2.1	2.2	2.4	2.5
Indonesia	1.9	1.9	1.9	2	2.2	2.4	2.3	2.6
Bangladesh	0.4	1.2	1.3	1.5	1.7	2	2	2.1

Source: International Transparency, 2001~2008.

Another positive issue that can be regarded as an improvement is the prosecution of corruptors, which have significantly increased in recent years. Before the reform, from 1994~1998, the number of corruption cases being put on trial was only 124 cases. After the reform the corruption cases being put on trial reached 513 cases, an improvement of more than 400% (Davidson et al., 2006).

Government efforts in eradicating corruption as described above at least managed to fulfill people's expectations. These efforts also influence the improvement of Indonesia's competitiveness in recent years. The survey conducted by the World Economic Forum (WEF) entitled Global Competitiveness Report 2006~2007 shows Indonesia's competitiveness sharply increased to number 50 out of 125 countries or increased by 19% if compared from the previous year's competitiveness, which put Indonesia on number 69 of 107 countries being surveyed (Seputar Indonesia, May 20, 2007).

Although the above information shows a positive image of government committment in handling corruption problems, other problems also emerged. Several surveys indicate "close relationships" between some local government officials and some members of the local house of representatives caused new forms of corruption, collusion, and nepotism. From the local houses of representatives corruption cases that were exposed, there were at least 1,437 members of the local houses of representatives all over the country that have been legally prosecuted and sentenced to imprisoment. Meanwhile, between years 2004 up to 2006, the number of local government officials that have conducted corruption reached 1,000 cases both in provincial and municipal/regencial levels. There were also corruption cases which involved Governors, Mayors, and Regents. Figure 4-1 shows corruption cases conducted by local officials (Kompas, April 6, 2006).

[Figure 4-1] Corruption Cases Conducted by Local Officials (2004~2006)

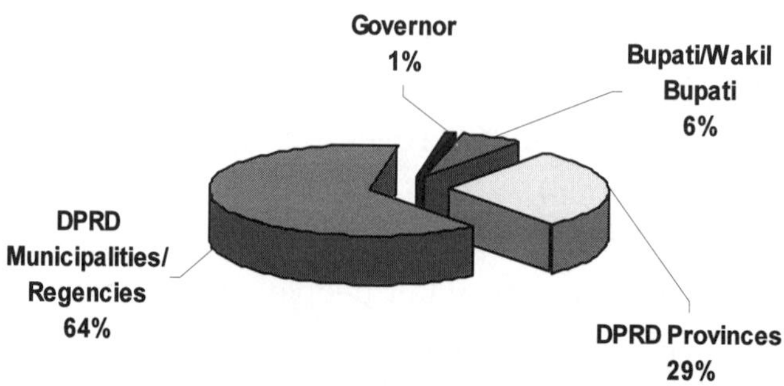

All these facts show that great challenges lie ahead of the government and all components of the nation to realize clean government and good governance.

Human Resorces Apparatus Aspects

The challenges of political and democratic dynamics, as well as of decentralization and regional autonomy, with proliferation problems and of public accountability as the heart of good governance, implementation becomes more complex when bureaucracy reform is challenged by objective conditions of the government's human resources in the bureaucracy.

Workforce: The current number of civil servants in Indonesia has reached 4,061,854 which are dispersed in central and local goverment. 55% of that number (2,254,382) are male and 44.50% (1,807,472) are female. These numbers increase from year to year to meet the needs of new recruits for replacing the retired ones or fulfilling any other necessity. When compared with the number in 2003, these figures show a big leap, especially the one that took place in 2007. Table 4-6 shows the increase of civil servant numbers from 2003~2008:

[Table 4-6] Total Number of Civil Servants (2003~2008)

Gender	Year					
	2003	2004	2005	2006	2007	2008
Male	2,172,285	2,130,299	2,131,674	2,144,320	2,292,555	2,254,382
	59.5 %	59.4%	58.2%	57.6%	56.4%	55.5%
Female	1,475,720	1,457,038	1,530,662	1,580,911	1,774,646	1,807,472
	40.5 %	40.6%	41.8%	42.4%	43.6%	44.5%
Total	3,648,005	3,587,337	3,662,336	3,752,231	4,067,201	4,061,854

Source: www.bkn.go.id, 2008.

The increasing number of civil servants above is mainly caused by the hiring of a temporary workforce who will become permanent civil servants. The number of temporary workers at the end of 2003 was about 900,000 (including village officers, part-time teachers, etc.), the result of previous years' tenders. These large numbers become problematic to the government in terms of personnel management. Since 2005, a political decision was made to gradually promote the temporary workforce to become permanent civil servants and finish by the end of year 2009. After that, there will be no more temporary workers. This policy was realized as contradictive to the political will of the government to reform the bureaucracy since this policy will later cause problems in terms of career paths, professionalism, composition, and competency of the civil servants (Effendi, 2008: 44-45).

Meanwhile, the quality of civil servants in Indonesia can be illustrated by the levels of educational background in the workforce. The current composition of Indonesian civil servants based on their educational background can be shown in Figure 4-2.

From this graphic, it is known that the majority of educational

[Figure 4-2] The Number of Civil Services based on Educational Background

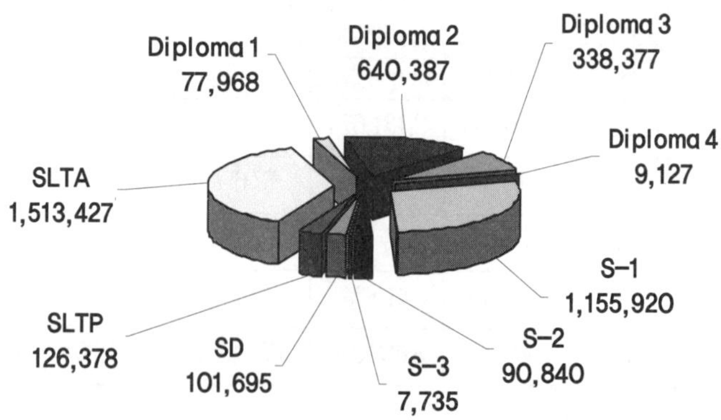

background of civil servants in Indonesia is Senior High School, which reaches the number of 1,513,427 persons. This number is 37.3% of the total population of civil servants in Indonesia. After that, diploma 1 and diploma 2 graduates compose the total 1,155,920 (28.5%) and 640,387 (15.8%) respectively, and the bachelor and post graduate backgrounds compose 1,254,495 persons or 30.9% of the total population (BKN, 2008).

In order to boost the competence of civil servants and to end the patronage system cultivated from the time of the new order regimes, the government has made efforts since 1999 to implement meritocracy principles through various policies, that put more emphasis on the significance of implementing performance oriented personnel management. These policies are aimed at putting competency as the benchmark for developing education and training for the civil servants. To do so, an education and training system for civil servants which adopts open competition and more flexibility is part of the progress of development and sooner implementation.

Remuneration Reform: In the unhealthy situation of civil servants, reflected by the composition based on educational background as mentioned above, bureaucracy reform is also challenged by the most fundamental problem: Civil Servant Prosperity. Civil servants in Indonesia are relatively badly compensated. This condition surely affects the condition of government service they can provide to the society while influencing their morality, behavior, and motivation. The government has always made efforts to improve the prosperity of the civil servants gradually, according to its ability. In the time of reform, the civil servants have experienced several salary raises. The first one was conducted in the time of President Abdurrahmman Wahid in 2001 for 10% increase. In the time of President Megawati, a policy to give a thirteenth salary on school intakes seasons was released. In the time of President Susilo Bambang Yudhoyono, since 2005 up to now there has been a 15% increase per year while the rise for professional bonuses for structural and functional officials ranges from 22~60% during the same period.

Up to now, four major weaknesses have emerged in the remuneration system of civil servants in Indonesia: (1) the scale of civil servant salaries has nothing to do with the workload of a position, and the dispersement is also irrational where unequality takes place vertically or horizontally; (2) the value of the salary is not competitive as a huge gap exists between the salary of civil servants and private sector employees, especially at the level of medium managers and above; (3) there are not incentives for well-performing civil servants; and (4) there are also too many supplements outside of official salaries, and this makes it difficult to control the budget for fair remuneration. Therefore, it is a must to make a policy that can regulate merit based remuneration system with the purpose of: (1) improving civil servants' motivation to competitively produce high or better performance; (2) maintaining the existing professionals within or attracting new professionals to join the civil service; and (3) controlling the budgets for personnel expenditures so that proper management can be implemented (Effendi, 2008: 72). The scale of salaries of each group of civil servants in

[Table 4-7] Civil Sevice Salaries

Scales (Golongan)	Salary (Rupiah)	
	Minimum	Maximum
Golongan I	910,000	1,410,000
Golongan II	1,151,700	1,913,300
Golongan III	1,440,600	2,365,500
Golongan IV	1,700,300	2,910,000

Sources: Government Regulation No. 10/2008.

Indonesia is shown in Table 4-7.

For the time being, a merit-based remuneration system is under pilot projects within three government institutions; the Department of Finance, the Supreme Court, and Financial Auditing Board. In this pilot project, the scale of incentives is renumerated on the basis of each civil servant's performance. The following table shows the implemenation made in the Department of Finance which is conducted under the Decrees of Finance Minister No. 289/KMK.01/2007 and No. 290/KMK. 01/2007 on the Scale of Special Incentives for State Financial Fosterment which range 27 grades as the basis of incentive payments, with the highest amount of Rp. 46,950,000 (US$ 4,500) per month and the lowest amount of Rp. 1,330,000 (US $100) per month as shown in Table 4-8.

[Table 4-8] Scale of Special Incentives for State Financial Fosterment

No.	Grade	Incentives	No.	Grade	Incentives
1	27	46,950,000	15	13	4,370,000
2	26	41,550,000	16	12	3,800,000
3	25	36,770,000	17	11	3,450,000
4	24	32,540,000	18	10	3,140,000
5	23	24,100,000	19	9	2,850,000
6	22	21,330,000	20	8	2,590,000
7	21	18,880,000	21	7	2,360,000
8	20	16,700,000	22	6	2,140,000
9	19	12,370,000	23	5	1,950,000
10	18	10,760,000	24	4	1,770,000
11	17	9,360,000	25	3	1,610,000
12	16	6,930,000	26	2	1,460,000
13	15	6,030,000	27	1	1,330,000
14	14	5,240,000			

Source: Decrees of Finance Minister No. 289/KMK.01/2007 and No. 290/KMK.01/2007.

Up until now, this new merit based renumeration system has not been applied in all government institutions due to predicted impacts of an exessive budget load to all the state budgets.

Civil Service Education and Training Reform: Government bureaucracy reform is a strategic movement in forming and developing government apparatus, profiles, and behaviors so that they have integrity and high productivity, as well as feeling the responsibility, and possessing the ability to provide a service of excellence to the public. They should also be clean, efficient, effective, transparent, and accountable, as well as equipped with a very reliable competency in order to be competitive, anticipative, and innovative in carrying out their duties.

In order to achieve those objectives, the Indonesian government has continuously made efforts to develop and improve the civil service education and training systems with various types and levels. The development of education and training systems is an inherent part of capacity building implementation as a government effort to improve the competencies, expertise, and skills which will be required by a person, an organization, and even a system to achieve their intended goals. Beside those, civil service education and training is also aimed at preparing the civil servants with competencies to deal with the dynamic changes of strategic environments like politics, economics, social, and technology, both locally and globally.

One of the approaches in Indonesia's future civil service education and training system considered most appropriate is Competency Based Training (CBT). The implementation of CBT requires a directory of competency which will be used in every government organization in performing Training Need Analysis (TNA). TNA is needed in order to identify, or find out, whether or not competency gaps exist in performing an organization's main duties and functions. If an individual or an organization possesses a competency gap in performing its duties, then a series of education and training programs can fill the gap.

The main approaches of the CBT in its delivery will be andragogy (adult learning) and learner-centered ones. To support this CBT, various facilities and infra-structures should be available in order to accommodate the various necessities resulted. Facilitating classrooms, learning utensils, learning media, as well as facilitators, and teaching and learning strategies should be prepared to support the implementation of CBT and its andragogy. The CBT model requires all participants to pass education and training programs which are related to "core competencies" which are parts of orientation programs for the Indonesian civil service and are also related to the national interest. While specific competencies are developed on the basis of each unit or organization's needs in performing their duties, an individual's competencies are assessed by considering his/her previous knowledge and skills. These specific competencies are called bureaucracy professions (task units related to state management and bureaucracy).

Challenges and Prospects in The Future

Although the government bureaucracy reform in Indonesia basically has been conducted since the time of the earliest government in Indonesia through various efforts in improving bureaucracy performance, until now it has not shown the expected results. This has happened because government bureaucracy reforms which are currently conducted are very partial and unrelated to one another. There have not been integrated efforts of reforms among government institutions and departments. Likewise, the case for the relationships among regions and between regions to the central governments is not integrated. The achievement made has normally been partial and has not made greater impacts to the country as a whole. These symptoms show unintegrated reforms (Thoha, 2008). Other presumed causes are the limitations of resources available compared to the size of the problem faced, as described in the earlier parts of this paper. Others are the uncomprehensive and unsystemic approaches employed and this makes an impression that reform is only a matter of rhetorics.

These conditions have forced Indonesia to face various challenges in its efforts to improve public administration and the quality of public sector governance. From the perspective of government management and bureaucracy performance, several challenges can be generally identified as follows: (1) developing, maintaining, and securing the public and political committment and supports to public sector reform, (2) improving law enforcement and corruption eradication, (3) developing and sustaining government management systems, (4) managing the organization and its business process and procedures, (5) improving the competency and prosperity of apparatus human resources, (6) developing public accountability, transparency, and participation, (7) debureaucratization in the management of public affairs, (8) improving and strengthening ICT, (9) improving the awareness of the necessity of public sector governance among civil society and other stakeholders, and (10) strengthening good leadership.

To answer those challenges and to implement public administration reforms, a grand design becomes a must (Thoha, 2008; Effendi, 2008). In this grand design, a systemic bur-eaucracy redesign should be employed by considering not only the internal conditions of bureaucracy but also the strategic challenges that surround them. Today, the Ministry for Empowerment of State Apparatus is the Initiative Ministry, along with other government institutions, in developing “the grand design of public bureaucracy reforms" comprehensively.

In this context, several successful and unsucessul implementations can be used as invaluable lessons learned. Among others are as captured in the "2007 APEC Economic Policy Report on Indonesia: Development in Public Sector Governance" as follows: (1) in some districts decentralization has led to innovations in public service provision, the result being a clear and positive improvement in both service provision and the number of people covered (important factors for the success of this innovation are decentralization and good leadership); (2) decentralization of functions and budget to regional governments, particularly at the distric level (kabupaten and kota) is bringing greater authority over local public services to regional officials; (3) the granting of greater authority to district levels has made local politicians and citizens more interested in good governance; (4) there has been increasing demand for public sector reform in the regions; (5) the fight against corruption has been progressing: the legal framework to fight corruption has been strengthened, new anti-corruption institutions have been created or are in the process of being created, and strong efforts are being made to pursue legal cases against corrupt individuals; (6) Indonesia's formal accountability framework is undergoing a remarkable transformation, but the impact on accountability remains weak; and (7) public awareness is increasing. An expanding civil society and a newly free media are helping citizens monitor the performance of implementing agencies and service delivery, and citizens themselves are learning to speak out.

Through these lessons learned, and other policy movements, as well as various efforts that are conducted recently, the future prospects of implementing public administration reforms become very promising and realistic to accomplish. This is strengthened by the existence of long term, middle term, and short terms of develoment plans which are comprehensively integrated into one another, as well, the policy of improving public administration and public governance will widen the opportunity of boosting shared committment to implement thorough, gradual, and sustainable reforms.

Conclusion

One of the most invaluable lessons from the extended economic and political crisis is the fact that Indonesia has not finished developing public administration systems and good public governance suitable to the current times. The Indonesian Government still believes that good public administration systems and good public governance that are suitable to the dynamic changes and demands of the people will be able to be implemented soon through various policy movements taken and through adjustment to significant changes of behaviors and attitudes of the public, and changes to the governance paradigm. One important policy which should be made by the government in order to realize a more responsive public administration system to the people's need is public bureaucracy reform. This effort should be supported by implementing various policies which have important characteristics of good governance as dispersal of power: checks and balances, transparency, public participation, accountability, decentralization, rule of law, and respecting human rights.

Several of these efforts have produced various improvements and fundamental changes such as changing the government system from very centralised to decentralised, improving public service provision, improving the efforts and results of corruption eradication, improving the ethos of public bodies to become more transparent and accountable, improving press freedom, power separation between the armed forces and police corps, improving respect for human rights, as well as improving mass media and non-government organization involvement in supervising the development. However, all those efforts have not reached their fundamentally expected goals. This is caused by the unfinished pre-conditional development for implementing good governance in Indonesia; for instance, democratic governance, which is aimed not only at the existence of the general elections and press freedom but also at a democractic system based on rational, honest, open, accountable cultures and guaranteeing egilitarianism as well as availabilty of incentives, corporate restructuring implementation, public participation behaviours and strong law enforcement. All these should be supported by a highly productive, clean, efficient, effective, transparent, and accountable state appararatus/bureaucracy displaying integrity and the ability to provide service of excellence.

References

Asshiddiqie, Jimly (2003). "Indonesia Governance Sructure After the 4th Amendment of the 1945 State Constitution," presented in National Symposium at the Ministry of Justice and Human Rights. Jakarta: Government of Indonesia.

APEC (2007). "*APEC Economic Policy Report: Indonesia: Development in Public Sector Governance*": 72-76, www.apec. org/apec/

Deloitte and Ash Institute (2004). "Government by Network: The New Public Management Imperative," A Joint Study by Deloitte Research and the Ash Institute for Democratic Governance and Innovation at the John F. Kennedy School of Government at Harvard University.

Effendi, Taufiq (2008). "Challenges and Improvement of State Apparatus Human Resources in Anticipating Global Competitions," presented in Seminar of Developing State Human Resource Apparatus in Diponegoro University, Semarang, May.

Government of Indonesia (2008). Government Regulation No.60 of the year 2008 on "Government Internal Controlling System." Jakarta: Government of Indonesia.

Government of Indonesia (2008). Law No.14 of the year 2008 on Public Information Openness. Jakarta: Government of Indonesia.

Government of Indonesia (2008). Law No.17 of the Year 2007 on "The National Long Term Development Plan 2005~2025." Jakarta: Government of Indonesia.

Government of Indonesia (2008). Law No. 39 of the Year 2008 on "State Ministry." Jakarta: Government of Indonesia.

Kleden, Ignas (2003). "Indonesia after 5 years reform (1998~2003)." Analisys CSIS, no.2: 164.

Larbi, George A. (1999). "The New Public Management Approach and Crisis States," in UNSRID Discussion Paper, no.1, 12, September.

[Indonesian] Ministry for Empowerment of State Apparatus (2008). "General Guideliness for Bureaucracy Reform." Jakarta: Government of Indonesia.

[Indonesian]. National Institute of Public Administration (LAN) (2003). "SANKRI." Jakarta: LAN.

[Indonesian]. National Institute of Public Administration (LAN) (2008). "White Book on Public Administration Reform." Jakarta: LAN.

Polidano, Charles (1999). "The new public management in developing countries," IDPM (Institute for Development Policy and Management) University of Manchester, UK, Public Policy and Management Working Paper no.13, November. (Source: http://idpm.man.ac.uk/11/1999)

Government of Indonesia (2005). "President Regulation No. 7 of the Year 2005 on the National Middle Term Development Plan 2004~2009." Jakarta: Government of Indonesia.

Sarker, Abu Elias (2006). "New Public Management in Developing Countries: An analysis of success and failure with particular reference to Singapore and Bangladesh," *International Journal of Public Sector Management* 19 (2): 180-203.

Soren Davidson, Visnu Juwono dan David G. Timberman (2006). "Curbing Corruption in Indonesia 2004~2006: A Survey of National Policies and Approaches." Washington, DC: The United States-Indonesia Society (USINDO) and Centre for Strategic and International

Studies (CSIS).

Thoha, Miftah (2008). "Government Bureaucracy Reform," presented at a focus group discussion in the National Institute of Public Administration (LAN-RI), Jakarta: LAN.

www.bkn.go.id.

www.depdagri.go.id

www.icgg.org

Chapter 5 Lao PDR

Khammoune Viphongxay and Suresh Balakrishnan

Introduction

The Lao People's Democratic Republic (PDR in short) is a landlocked country in South East Asia, surrounded by Thailand, Myanmar, China, Vietnam, and Cambodia. Divided into sixteen provinces with Vientiane, the Capital City, Lao PDR has a land area of 236,800 square kilometers. With a population of 5.62 million inhabitants, Lao PDR has one of the lowest population densities in the region (24 people per square kilometer). The population, consisting of 2.82 million females and 2.80 million males, grew at 2.1% per annum during the previous decade. The age-pyramid of Lao PDR reflects a young population as about 40% of the population was below the age of 14 in 2005. Urban areas take up less than one percent of the total land area. About 70% of the country is mountainous, while the rest of the country consists of the Mekong floodplains and other river valleys. Forest covers over a third of the country, making it one of the most heavily forested countries in the region. The population is predominantly located in rural areas (over 70%). The country has a multi-ethnic population; the census classifies them into 49 main ethnic groups.

Development Status

Lao PDR is also one of the least developed countries in South-East Asia. It is ranked 130 out of 177 countries in the global Human Development Index 2007~08; its rank is, however, higher than some of the other countries in the region, such as Timor Leste, Myanmar, and Cambodia. Estimates suggest that poverty has declined from 46% in 1992~93 to about 33% by 2002, and further to about 27% by 2008 (GoL and UN, 2009). However, malnutrition remains a significant concern with 37% of children below five years of age being underweight and chronic malnutrition affecting children in that age group (GoL and UN, 2008). Education achievement levels have seen significant improvement in recent years. About 16% of the population had completed primary school, 6% completed lower secondary, and 5% upper secondary schools, respectively. Among persons of age 6 years and above, 26% were found to have no education, which is a major improvement from 43% without education in 1995. Around 78% of the population derives their livelihood from agriculture, fishing, and related occupations. There has been a significant increase in population employed in the service sector, which now accounts for about 17%.

Social Systems

Lao society displays a strong Buddhist influence in all walks of life including its political culture. This influence has given rise to a widespread sense of morality, diligence, self-discipline, self-reliance, honesty and transparency (Keuleers, 2002). Strong kinship connections and extended family relationships play a role in both public affairs and business activities, and Lao people are found making great efforts to maintain them. From this perspective, giving presents, granting tax reductions or other advantages to members of the kinship has been widespread and socially accepted. As a result, there is evidence of soft social control systems, inspired by tolerance, compassion, respect for authority and seniority, loyalty to kinships and confrontation-avoidance.

Early Political Development: It is, however, important to keep in perspective the long and complex history of this country. While the rise of the Kingdom of Lan Xang Hom Khao in the 12th century around Luang Prabang is often attributed to its crucial role in the trade that passed through this region, recorded history suggests this strength continued until the 16th century. Thereafter, the development of maritime kingdoms and stable sea routes in the following period reduced its strategic significance, and came to consist of four kingdoms, Xieng Dong Xieng Thong (Luang Prabang), Xieng Khoang, Vientiane (Sikhottabong) and Champasak (Chamberlain, 2007). As the strength of the Lao kingdoms diminished, they came under the sphere of influence of the French from the 19th century who brought three Lao kingdoms under the royal house of Luang Prabang and managed it as part of French Indochina. This continued until the middle of the 20th century but for a small period when the Japanese took control of the country during the Second World War and the few months immediately after, when it was controlled by Lao Itsara nationalists, before the French resumed control. Laos' first French-written and monarchical constitution was promulgated on May 11, 1947 and declared it to be an independent state within the French Union. The military defeat of French at Dien Bien Phu in 1954 led to the withdrawal of the French from the region and was followed by elections under the Lao monarchy. The revised constitution of 1957 was much the same as the first constitution, but removed reference to the French Union, though the country continued its close educational, health, and technical ties with the former colonial power. Successive national and right wing governments controlled most of the country with US backing in the years that followed, while the revolutionary Pathet Lao gathered strength in the northeastern and eastern regions. The victory of communist forces in Viet Nam and Cambodia was followed by the victory of the Lao People's Revolutionary Party, who removed the Lao monarchy and allies from power and established the Lao People's Democratic Republic in 1975.

The National General People Meeting of the Lao People's Revolutionary Party in 1975, which unanimously proclaimed the establishment of the Lao PDR, appointed the Supreme People Assembly, President of the Republic, and its Council of Ministers. The 1957 Constitution was abrogated on December 3, 1975, after the People's Republic was proclaimed. For the next decade, the country was managed on the basis of revolutionary socialist principles–collectivization, nationalization, re-education, and the like. Chairmen of provincial administrative committees were appointed in 1975 to provide political and administrative leadership in a highly decentralized manner and reported to the Prime Minister. The Ministry of Interior ceased to control the provincial administration. People's Assemblies existed at provincial and district levels. The Lao state, at that stage, was an extension of the revolutionary movement of two decades and operated under the direct guidance of the Lao People's Revolutionary Party and leadership of its Political Bureau, supported by several levels of leadership extending to the village level.

More Recent Political Developments: The Supreme People's Assembly First Legislature adopted the First 5 Year Plan of Socioeconomic Development (1980~1985) and passed a number of new laws, such as the Law on the Council of Ministers, the Law on Local Administration Authority, and the Law on Foreign Investment. In the decade that followed, it became clear to the national leadership that such orthodox policies were not delivering required results. The high degree of decentralized administration meant that service delivery was part of the mandate of local government and led to wide divergence in procedures followed, standards adopted, and recruitment of large numbers of civil servants (Keuleers and Sibounheuang, 1999). In several instances, facilities like teacher training colleges were created without adequate equipment or with faculty possessing limited qualifications.

At the 4th Party Congress in 1986 the political leadership adopted the New Economic Mechanism, its prime feature being a pronounced shift from a command and centrally planned economy to a market economy. While economic transition was high on the reform agenda, the New Economic Mechanism also required supporting reforms in the public sector. An impressive set of fiscal reforms were introduced in the late 1980's alongside some major political initiatives that gained momentum in the 1990's.

The People's Supreme Assembly Second Legislature was elected in March 1989. The most important achievement of the People's Supreme Assembly Second Legislature was drafting the Constitution of the Lao Republic, adopted on August 14, 1991. The new Constitution of the Lao PDR was promulgated shortly after this and marked the transition from direct administration by the Party towards a modern state governed by the rule of law. The Constitution established the legislature, the judiciary, and the executive as the main institutions of the state, with guidance of the Party. According to the Constitution, Lao PDR is a people's democracy, with a single political Party, the Lao People's Revolutionary Party (LPRP). Party committees at each level support the local authorities in the implementation of the country's socio-economic development plan. After the Third Legislature was elected in 1992, the Supreme People's Assembly changed its name to the National Assembly. The National Assembly, as a legislative organ, implements its rights and duties defined in the Constitution and the Laws on the National Assembly. From the time of the Third Legislature, regional assemblies ceased to exist.

A major personnel downsizing policy was implemented in the early 1990's. The reassertion of central control was highlighted by the Central Bank of Lao PDR taking over the monetary management and the formulation of a national budget covering central and local expenditures that had to be approved by the National Assembly. All recruitments to the civil service had to be proposed to the Department of Public Administration in the Prime Minister's Office for scrutiny, modification and approval. The economy grew rapidly between 1992 and 1996 when the average annual rate of growth was 7%, which was followed by the Asian financial crisis and much slower rate of growth. However, since 1999, annual economic growth has resumed at a rate of around 6%.

Central and Local Administration in Lao PDR

The Constitution of 1991 and its subsequent amendments (GoL, 2003b) conceive of the Lao PDR as a political system composed of the National Assembly, the President of the Republic, the Government headed by the Prime Minister, the Local Administrations and the judiciary. The National Assembly is mandated to supervise and oversee the functioning of the executive and judicial organs and elects (and remove) the President of the Republic. The President of the Republic is the Head of State, with powers to promulgate laws approved by the National Assembly, to appoint or remove (with National Assembly approval) the Prime Minister and members of the Government, and to appoint provincial Governors and municipal

Mayors on the recommendation of the Prime Minister. The Government, headed by the Prime Minister, has broad executive responsibilities and includes ministers, deputy ministers and deputy chairmen of ministry-equivalent committees, as well as deputy Governors, deputy Mayors and district Chiefs. The Local Administrations–provinces, municipalities, districts and villages, are headed respectively by appointed Governors, Mayors, Chiefs, and Headmen. The judiciary, made up of the People's Courts, is present at national, provincial, municipal and district levels.

Government

The government currently has 16 ministries to administer the country, with the support of 17 agencies under the Prime Minister's Office. The Ministries of the Government are the Prime Minister's Office, Ministry of National Defense, Ministry of Public Security, Ministry of Foreign Affairs, Ministry of Justice, Ministry of Finance, Ministry of Agriculture and Forestry, Ministry of Industry and Commerce, Ministry of Energy and Mining, Ministry of Public Work and Transport, Ministry of Education, Ministry of Public Health, Ministry of Information and Culture, Ministry of Labor and Social Welfare, Ministry of Planning and Investment and the Bank of Lao PDR. The 17 agencies set up to address specific tasks under the guidance of the Prime Minister's Office are Public Administration and Civil Service Authority, State Inspection Agency, National Audit Office, National Science & Technology Authority, Water Resources and Environment Authority, National Tourism Authority, National Land Management Authority, National Post and Communication Authority, Lao National Sport Committee, Institute of Social Science, Department of National Geography, Department of National Document, National Business Promotion Office, National Committee for Inspection and Control of Drugs,

Committee for the Advancement of Women, National Leading Committee for Rural Development and Poverty Eradication, and National Science Assembly office.

While the overall leadership is provided by the Prime Minister and Deputy Prime Ministers, the work of Ministries is supervised by Ministers with the assistance of Deputy Ministers. Some of the agencies in the Prime Minister's Office are headed by Minister's who are also designated Chairpersons. The Government currently comprises of 240 departments and sub-departments across the ministries and agencies (excluding Ministry of National Defense).

Local Administration

The country is administratively divided into 16 provinces and one equivalent organization (Vientiane Prefecture), which are further divided into 141 districts. Provincial governors, who are representatives of the central government, are appointed to the position by the President of State after being recommended by the Prime Minister. Governors usually hold party positions, and are often elected as the secretary of the provincial party organization by the local party members.

Until 1991 the state administration was composed of 5 tiers: central government, provinces, districts, tassengs (sub-districts), and villages (Keuleers, 2001). However, the 1991 Constitution significantly changed the structure of the local administration. The Provincial People's Councils were dissolved, as were the local administrative committees. The tassengs, intermediate units between the district and village authorities, were abolished, thereby reducing the number of administrative levels in the country from five to four, leading to increased and direct responsibilities for districts over a larger number of villages without necessarily having additional resources or improved capacities. District Chiefs are appointed by the Prime Minister on the recommendation of the provincial Governor to administer the area, implement development plans, and coordinate activities of field offices of the line ministries in the district. Provincial governors and district chiefs are civil servants appointed by the state, whereas village chiefs are elected representatives.

Culture in Administration

As in the domestic culture, the approach to administration in the government is non-confrontational; civil servants in supervisory positions often pay more attention to the performance of their team of colleagues than on the performance of individual staff members. When it comes to decision-making, Lao political institutions and public organizations strongly comply with the principles of centralized democracy. In essence, all relevant stakeholders in the institution get the opportunity to present their opinions and suggestions, giving rise to a collective view or decision. Village chiefs or district chiefs often address minor disputes through local mediation. When mediation fails, matters come before the courts of law. This approach stems from the tradition to avoid confrontation, the need for individuals in conflict to save face, and limited awareness of the legal system.

The Lao Civil Service

While the major political reforms associated with the new Constitution commenced in 1991, public personnel management continued to be directly managed by the Party Committees. From 2001, the responsibility for personnel management in the civil service was transferred from the Central Committee of Organization and Personnel to the Department of Public Administration and Civil Service in the Prime Minister's Office, with the Central Committee of Organization and Personnel only retaining responsibility for the management of high leadership positions. The Department of Public Administration and Civil Service has subsequently become the Public Administration and Civil Service Authority, a sub-ministry in the Prime Minister's Office. At the provincial and district levels, the Party's Committees for Organization and Personnel provide guidance on management of the civil service and staff of mass organizations.

Size and Scope of Civil Service

The country is administered by the Civil Service, consisting of 104,726 civil servants, of which over a third is female (excluding soldiers and work force of the police). The size of civil service is less than 2% of the population and not considered excessive by international standards. Ministries at the national level account for over 13,000 personnel, while staff of these ministries, placed at sub-national offices (in provinces and districts), are about 80,000. The remaining personnel consist of about 6,000 and 5,000 staff in the provincial and district administrations, and over a thousand in mass organizations. The increase in size of the civil service during 2007~08 was 6,681, which is roughly 6%. The responsibility for hiring civil servants varies somewhat depending on the level and location of the job. Generally, hiring rests with the ministries. Wage levels for civil servants are low; re-indexing the wages during 2008 was estimated to increase the wage bill by about 14%.

Structure of Civil Service

The civil service in Lao PDR (GoL, 2003a) is classified into five grades, and each grade has 15 steps matching respective salary indexes. This classification excludes high-ranking officers (Vice-Minister and above), military, police, employees of State Owned Enterprises, and State employees working on a contractual basis. Civil servants at grades I and II are "Administrative Support Staff" and in grades III, IV and V are

"Professional Staff." Civil servants eligible for Grade V are required to have passed through Grade IV. Each grade is divided further into levels based on the level of education and seniority in the civil service. Application of grades and steps are based principally on the level of education or managerial position. For example, the appropriate step for civil servants in Grade IV with a Doctoral degree or equivalent are eligible for step 7, those with a High Graduate Diploma for step 6, and those with Bachelor's Degree or equivalent for step 2. Article 66 of the Civil service decree provides for grade promotion of civil servants based on certificates/qualifications obtained, level of seniority, and through examination. The Organization and Personnel Department of Ministries manage grade promotion and step advancement annually, with ratification by the Minister, Governor, or Mayor, before recommending the same to the central agency for civil service management.

The norms for administrative positions of Lao civil service (GoL, 2008) also cover civil servants in the organizational structure of the Party, the Government, Lao Front for National Construction, and Mass Organizations at central and local level. Administrative positions in the Lao Civil Service fall into eight classes. The first class positions are Vice Chairperson of designated agencies and Sub-Ministries, Committee members of the Central Committee for Inspection, President of the Regional People's Court and the Regional People's Prosecutor. The second class administrative position covers Department Director General and equivalent positions such as Head of Cabinet Office of Ministries and Sub-Ministries, Vice President of the Regional People's Court and the Regional People's Prosecutor, District Head and Dean of the National University.

Given the key role played by the civil service in delivering services and implementing development programmes, the Government of Lao is actively reviewing compensation and allowances for civil servants sent to work in remote areas. This has become a serious concern because of a significant shortage of staff willing to be placed in remote areas, therefore many civil servant positions remain unfilled. All civil servants must spend two of their first five years at a District or Village location (GoL, 2003a), but this is yet to be implemented in a comprehensive manner.

Capacity Building in Civil Service

The Government has encouraged civil servants to upgrade their educational qualifications. An incentive for pursuing higher qualifications is embedded in the civil service structure with higher steps offered in their grades on securing higher degrees. Recruitment by the ministries has also tried to focus on candidates with higher technical/specialized (rather than general) qualifications. The number of civil servants with postgraduate qualifications more than doubled since 1998.

The first institutional arrangements for training civil servants were established in 1991 in the form of the National School of Administration and Management. This school subsequently merged in 1995 with the National Political School of the LPRP to create the National Organization for Studies of Politics and Administration, renamed the National Academy of Politics and Public Administration in 2007. The National Academy organizes workshops as well as short and long-term (four to ten month) training courses to upgrade the qualifications of senior Government managers to prepare them to take on higher responsibilities. Since 1992, four-year Bachelor-level degree courses covering subjects such as public administration, management and political theory have been organized. Ministries also have their own technical level schools in order to teach public servants the technical skills required for their particular sector.

Governance Reforms and Challenges

The Government proposed framework for governance reform is reflected in the National Socio-Economic Development Plan for the period 2006 to 2010. The strategic plan on governance emphasizes the government's commitment to building "an effective, efficient, well-trained, honest and ethical public service that is able to meet the needs of the multi-ethnic Lao people" (GoL, 2006). It highlights the need for greater accountability, transparency and public participation in planning and decision-making as well as more accessible and efficient legal enforcement institutions. Given the projected increases in public revenues over the life of the current NSEDP period as a result of investments in the energy and mining sectors, there is an immediate requirement to strengthen governance for more accountable and transparent service delivery. The Government's framework identifies four major governance themes: "Public Service Improvement, People's Participation, Rule of Law, and Sound Financial Management." Each of these areas was seen as playing critical roles in ensuring the balanced and sustainable development of Lao society and administration.

Public Service Improvement

The Government has addressed the goal of Public Service Improvement through several activities related in four strategic areas-improving the state management regulations and administrative framework, reforming organizational machinery and administrative framework of state agencies, improving civil service management, and strengthening central-local relationships.

The government of Lao PDR has put in place several regulations and frameworks to support substantive and sustainable change, concentrating on improving the roles, functions, duties and organizational structure and appropriately modifying deployment and appointment of staff. At the central level, the focus has been on enabling Ministries to address their macro management roles, while enabling decentralization of work, authority and responsibilities to the local level and technical units. The Government has issued a significant number of Resolutions, Decrees, Decisions and Instructions for this purpose. It has also established and simplified the administrative regulations making them more precise in facilitating the delivery of public services. The Prime Minister's instructions regarding expansion of One-Door-Service to all provinces (Ordinance 86) provided an impetus for effective decentralization of services used by large numbers of people. Peer-to-peer learning on these simple innovations has followed with several provinces visiting the successful pilot at Xaysetha district in Vientiane Capital.

The process of reorganizing ministries and offices of the government is an ongoing activity. In keeping with the priority to support internal efforts for improvement, a manual and tools for analysis and restructuring are seen as key steps forward. The roles, functions, and rights of a number of Ministries have been reviewed. In recent years, the Prime Minister's Office provided several decrees on the role and structure of several ministries and offices. Some specific tasks were transferred to Ministries and equivalent agencies to ensure more efficient management. A number of new organizations have been established with the specific aim to respond to the actual work during the new period. In an effort to streamline this strategic effort, the Government reorganized and established the Ministry of Public Works and Transport to deal with the core functions of infrastructure development, and set up separate agencies to handle the other tasks. On a similar note, a Ministry of Planning & Investment was established to help the Government provide direction and technical support to all offices and agencies, and provide direction to align different tasks to be carried out under the 6th NSEDP.

Civil Service Management

The strong support of the Government for implementing the NSEDP has led to strengthening of Civil Service Management on a continuing basis. The policy framework is provided by the Civil Service Statute of the Lao PDR based on Decree No. 82/PM issued of May 19, 2003, an amendment of decree No. 171/PM of November 11, 1993. Several regulatory documents have been provided to help discharge key civil service management functions such as selection, recruitment and deployment, grade and step determination, training and development, award granting and disciplinary measures, resignation, and retirement.

Job descriptions have been implemented in organizations at the central and local levels throughout the country. Actions have been taken to make a separation between administrative personnel and technical personnel in the education and health sectors in order to facilitate the employment of new civil servants and the application of policies in an appropriate manner. The Government has also concentrated on the transfer of civil servants from the central level to the local level. Efforts have been made to increase the number of civil servants at the district level by increasing the recruitment quota of new personnel at the district level.

An assessment of the capacity-building initiatives for the civil service was completed (GoL, 2008) and the lessons provide important insights for detailing out the National Civil Service Training and Development Framework, which will include such elements as a National Training and Development Policy and Procedures and Training Curriculum. The government has also initiated steps to set up an Information and Training Centre at PACSA (on civil service management and public administration).

The Training Centre is expected to develop and deliver training programs for public servants in high priority areas of governance, such as human resource management and e-governance, provide a platform for leadership development including build up of result-oriented management, and establish core values for quality service delivery and citizen-oriented administration.

The Draft Code of Conduct for civil servants has been developed and is being circulated for feedback on implementation mechanisms. This Code will help civil servants have clear guidance on matters that have a significant bearing on performance and effectiveness *vis-a-vis* the civil service as well as the people they serve. The systematic management of civil servants can be well supported by leveraging information technology. An Information Technology-enabled Personnel Information Management System has been initiated and steps taken to provide an internet based platform to facilitate updates of the database. This system will be expanded to support payroll operations with close support of all ministries. The government has initiated systematic efforts to improve the salaries and remuneration of civil servants, which are currently at a very low level.

Sub-national Administration

The Government has also taken important steps towards creating stronger local administration in urban areas. The decisions regarding the scope of functions and the delegated authority for municipalities are being made and will be first implemented in the World Heritage City of Luang Prabang. The lessons from Luang Prabang will be reviewed and plans drawn up to establish the Municipality of Vientiane Capital. Local administrations in select districts are now provided with authority and financial resources to plan and implement small investments for strengthening local service delivery–these include renovation of rural schools, construction of small water supply systems and footbridges, etc. While the past transferred funds are not very large, the big achievement is capacity created at the district level to take on greater responsibilities in local development.

The Government is closely looking at the need for capacity development and improvement of machinery for district administration. The Prime Minister's Instruction in this regard has been followed with pilot efforts in some districts. Given the capacity constraints in the districts, frameworks are being developed to assist the district administrations. The Government has also initiated steps to strengthen the performance of the lowest levels of administration–at the village and village clusters. Mechanisms are being developed to oversee performance and support capacity building for the village and village clusters level.

These developments have been accompanied by significant steps taken to better manage revenue collection and fiscal transfers. The Ministry of Finance has reorganized the revenue collection process so that all revenue collection activities are directly managed by the Ministry through its offices at the sub-national level. Hence, the role of provincial Departments of Finance has greater focus on public expenditure administration.

Rule of Law

The institutions working on strengthening Rule of Law are the Ministry of Justice, the People's Supreme Court and Office of the Prosecutor General. Effective "Rule of Law" is a vital part of the development of governance systems in Lao PDR. The Legal Sector Master Plan has been drafted, and a major national programme will commence soon to implement the Plan in a systematic manner. While there is need for several laws and legal instruments, the government has systematically identified the priorities in lawmaking, keeping in view the social and economic development goals of the country. Laws related to several critical functions are being formulated so that social and economic activities can be effectively carried out. The development of about 20 laws has taken place recently, including the Law on Accounting, Law on Education, Law on Commercial Bank, Law on Value Added Tax, Law on the Protection of Rights of Children, Law on Audit, Law on Inspection, and the Law on Public Security.

The Government of Lao PDR attaches great importance to having an informed citizenry who can contribute to the development of the nation. Mass media plays a major role in this endeavor. The recently passed Law on Mass Media is an important step toward providing the media with a clear mandate to carry out its work. This law enables journalists and mass media to expand their activities. The Government continues to provide leadership for the industrial and economic development of the country. While there is increasing scale of private enterprise, State Enterprises and Joint Ventures continue to play a major role. The Law on Management of State Investment is an effort to ensure that state enterprises perform their mandated role and are managed effectively. In line with the strong role played by the Government in supporting the country's development, there was need to actively manage the country's financial resources. The Law on Treasury is being drafted to enable the Government to manage treasury operations, which leverages the availability and use of Information Technology in the government. A Department of Enforcement of Judgment of the Ministry of Justice has been established to deal with and improve the situation in relation to the low level of judgment enforcement.

The Government of Lao PDR is committed to its role in the

global community, and is signatory to several international treaties and covenants. The Government signed the International Covenant on Civil & Political Rights in 2003, which has yet to be ratified. If it is passed, a framework for several parts of the Government to respond to requirements on the international commitments, provided through the Presidential Ordinance on Conclusion and Implementation of Treaties, will be a major step to speedy implementation of several measures by the Government.

Providing access to relevant information is another key priority in the legal sector. Given the limited reach of mass media, radio has been the preferred medium for awareness-building efforts. Radio has the potential to reach all parts of the country and is widely used by rural communities for receiving information and entertainment. While the materials are developed in Lao language, used by the largest segment of the population, the needs of members of ethnic communities who are not fully conversant with Lao language have also been addressed. For example, radio programmes have been specially translated and broadcasted in local languages. Other mass media, such as newspaper and television, are also used to promote legal awareness. Information about several programmes and events are shared with the citizens through these media.

The People's Supreme Court, District Courts and Courts of Appeal are growing gradually. Capacity-building for judicial personnel is an important priority. The judicial system has also addressed the needs of specific segments of society. Emphasis has been placed on establishing women and juvenile units in courts. A Women Advancement Unit is being set up in the Supreme Court. The Prosecutor's Office too has been expanding and Appeal Prosecutor Offices have been established in the North, Central and South of the country.

Participation

People's participation is a cross-cutting priority addressed by different institutions ranging from representation in the National Assembly to participatory planning at the village. As it is an elected body with members chosen by the Lao people, the National Assembly plays a vital role in promoting people's participation in governance. As an institution, it enables people's participation through representation, oversight, and legislative appraisal.

Press coverage of the National Assembly's activities has also increased. Every day, during the National Assembly's sessions, the National Assembly's activities are published in newspapers and broadcast live on TV and radio. The National Assembly performs oversight through a variety of means: by scrutinizing the performance of line ministries, through question time, and through debates in plenary. In general, public participation in these processes is indirect. By contrast, the petitions system provides a more direct form of participation by giving the public a way to address grievances relating to judicial and administrative cases. To strengthen the petitions system further, several consultations have been held to clarify the respective responsibility of the judiciary, executive and legislature in handling petitions. Consultations have also been held on upgrading the existing Department for Public Petitions to a Committee, possibly with ombudsman-like functions. Internally, capacity has been built by training of provincial parliamentary staff on petitions processing.

The National Assembly hotline is another important channel for direct people's participation. Since 2006, the hotline works during each ordinary session of the National Assembly. It receives anonymous comments, suggestions, and concerns from the general public by telephone, fax, letter, and email. At the end of each day, a summary report together with full transcripts is sent to each member, as well as relevant line ministries. Many issues have fed into parliamentary debates, helping increase the quality of legislative scrutiny, oversight and debate. The hotline reports are also passed to the local media, thereby increasing the quality of press coverage and analysis of important social issues.

Parliamentary inquiries have also commenced in Lao PDR, with the first by the Committee for Social-Cultural Affairs focusing on the education sector. The inquiry collected inputs from the Ministry of Education at the central level and from education officials, teachers and parents in the north. Consultations are beginning on the feasibility of establishing an official gazette, which will be an important step in promoting awareness of new legislation.

A Citizen Report Card has been piloted as a baseline activity whereby communities have been asked to benchmark the quality of services, provide insights into key areas where improvements are of high priority, and provide assessments of how services have improved. The decree on Civil Society Organizations has been prepared after wide consultations and signed by the Prime Minister. This will provide strong support for expanding the scope of civil society support for development activities in the country. Discussions have also been initiated to explore the scope for Local Councils and to strengthen people's participation at the sub-national level. This is at an early stage, and the options are being put together for further discussion and review.

Conclusions and Policy Implications

The reforms and changes mentioned earlier signal major steps forward; however, there remain a number of significant challenges that need to be overcome if the reform agenda is to be addressed in a meaningful and lasting manner. This would be best addressed through a governance reform master action plan, which needs to be developed to detail the steps various agencies should take to realize the intention of the governance strategy. Governance issues cut across different sectors and agencies. It is also necessary to strengthen policy linkages between improved public administration and service delivery which will include addressing specific planning and finance policy initiatives along with civil service management policy. The oversight, steering, and monitoring of reforms needs to be positioned at a high level involving all relevant institutions.

The plans and agendas in this sector are implemented through the Government of Lao PDR. The effectiveness of implementation depends on investment, development assistance and better technology. It is also about the larger policy framework, organizational mechanisms, as well as staff capacities to translate these plans into results. While these can be addressed to some extent within sectors or ministries in the short run, the challenge is to work together to set in place government-wide improvements on an incremental, and most importantly, sustainable basis.

Downward accountability mechanisms remain weakly defined and poorly operationalized. The Law on Local Administration allows for consultative process at local levels but is vague as to how this is to be institutionalized. Recent guidelines on the establishment of community structures at sub-district levels refer to village development groups with political and functional responsibilities. The decentralization policy and related regulations lack clarity on fiscal assignments and functional responsibilities. Planning continues to be centralized, budgets highly constrained, and capacities weak. There is need for more effective local level planning and service delivery as intrinsic parts of a more decentralized approach to service delivery, especially in key sectors such as agriculture, health, and education.

Fiscal decentralization remains a critical issue clouded by notions of fiscal self-reliance at provincial level that have resulted in the absence of any transparent process for the collection and distribution of revenues linked to a systematic and equitable process of inter-governmental fiscal transfers. Important steps are now underway as a result of mounting pressure for public expenditure management improvements. The new Budget Law of 2006 has initiated this process with the centralization of treasury, customs, and tax functions, and offers room to develop new proposals for inter-governmental fiscal transfers.

Whilst there has been some restructuring of ministries and agencies to date, there is a major challenge to develop a more systematic approach to organizational change. This will need to include a linked process of functional review, job analysis, workforce planning and systems development with a focus on improved access to services, especially for the poor and vulnerable. There is also an important need to devise systems improvement initiatives that will impact provincial and district planning, finance, and management systems as a priority. At present, there is no coherent linkage between planning systems and budgets. This is largely due to weak expenditure management systems and inadequate revenues to ensure budgetary certainty and predictability. This will need to be addressed through further support of policy development.

While there has been good progress in conducting a civil service staff census, which will be linked to the new personnel management information system. A key challenge will be to establish a fully functioning civil service staff planning and management capability and to translate human resource management policy into practices that will improve work performance. At the same time there is a need for greater buy-in of key stakeholders to change management processes. The preparation of job descriptions is only a first step towards this objective.

There has been a substantial effort to date in the provision of *ad hoc* training programs and workshops in support of specific project initiatives. However, there is now an urgent requirement to build a sustainable HRD and training structure with sufficient outreach to provinces and districts. This can best be achieved by leveraging established training institutions and resources to increase the capacity to train civil servants. It will also be important to ensure training more closely matches the work and office environment and provides opportunities for trainees to put into use knowledge and skills imparted.

Much of the policy framework for reform has now been put in place alongside a number of important laws and decrees. Various activities have been initiated at the center and a number of pilot governance programmes established at the provincial level. However, in light of the above, the clear need for development partner assistance to improve strategic management of the reform process and strengthen the capacity of government is apparent. These steps are essential for improving service delivery at central and local levels, which in turn are imperative to achieving the goals and targets of the NSEDP and MDGs. The governance sector involves several development partners and a very diverse array of intervention. Reviews of results of development cooperation highlight successes and results. Wide impact calls for the lessons—negative lessons as well as success stories—to be shared across the country to stimulate other stakeholders to build on these lessons and mainstream them.

References

Chamberlain, J. (2007). *Participatory Poverty Assessment-II.* Vientiane: National Statistics Centre and Asian Development Bank.

Government of the Lao PDR (GoL, 2003a). *Decree 82/PM dated 19 May 2003: Decree on Civil Service of the Lao PDR.* Vientiane.

Government of the Lao PDR (2003b). *Decree 32/PO dated 28 May 2003 of the President: Amended Constitution of the Lao PDR.* Vientiane.

Government of the Lao PDR (2003c). *Law No. 02/NA dated 28 May 2003: Law on the Government of the Lao PDR.* Vientiane.

Government of the Lao PDR (2003d). *Law No. 03/NA dated 21 October 2003: Law on Local Administration of the Lao PDR.* Vientiane.

Government of the Lao PDR (2003e). *Public Service Reform, People's Participation, Rule of Law and Sound Financial Management: A Policy Paper of the Government of Lao PDR on Governance Issues.* Vientiane.

Government of the Lao PDR (2008). *Decree 99/PM dated 23 June 2008: Decree on Administrative Positions of Lao Civil Service.* Vientiane.

Government of the Lao PDR and United Nations (2008). *Millennium Development Goals: Progress Report of Lao PDR.* Vientiane.

Government of the Lao PDR and United Nations (2009). *Employment and Livelihoods: The Human Development Report of Lao PDR, 2008.* Vientiane (draft).

Keuleers, P. (2001). *The District in the Local Administration in Lao PDR: Recent Developments, Challenges and Future Trends.* Vientiane: Governance and Public Administration Reform Project (mimeo).

Keuleers, P. (2002). *Corruption in the Lao PDR: Underlying causes and Key Issues for Consideration.* Bangkok: UNDP Sub Regional Resource Facility.

Keuleers, P. and Sibounheuang, L. (1999). Central-Local Relations in the Lao People's Democratic Republic in Turner, M.(ed.). *Central-Local Relations in Asia-Pacific: Convergence of Divergence* NY: St. Martin's Press.

Phommasack, B. et. al. (2005). Decentralization and Recentralization: Effects on the health systems in Lao PDR. *South Asian Journal of*

Tropical Medical Health 36 (2): 523-528.

Stuart-Fox, M. (2004). Politics and Reform in the Lao People's Democratic Republic, *Working Paper No. 1, Program on Civil Society and Governance*. Williamsburg, VA: The College of William & Mary.

Winter, M. (2002). *Lao PDR: Fact Finding Mission Report*. Unpublished report prepared for UNCDF, Bangkok.

World Food Programme (2007). *Lao PDR: Comprehensive Food Security and Vulnerability Analysis*. Rome.

Key Government of Lao PDR websites:

Ministry of Foreign Affairs: http://www.mofa.gov.la

Ministry of Finance: http://www.mof.gov.la

National Statistics Centre, Ministry of Planning & Investment: http://www.nsc.gov.la

Public Administration & Civil Service Authority: http://www.pacsa.gov.la

Chapter 6 Malaysia

Hong-Hai Lim

Introduction

Academic and policy discourse has expanded from government to governance. However, government remains the leading actor and governmental weakness remains a major obstacle to good governance. Governmental weakness is manifested primarily in deficiencies in public administration. As the main instrument and largest component of government, public administration has to be able to meet the needs of society as expressed through the political process in order to secure wide acceptance or legitimacy for itself and the government. Improving the performance of public administration is therefore a major and continuing concern in most countries. This essay examines the ability of public administration to meet the needs of society in Malaysia through an analysis of reforms or deliberate changes for improving the performance of public administration. In Malaysia, public administration has been the target of reform since independence. Examining these reforms is useful for understanding the present state of Malaysian public administration and its remaining shortfalls in performance. Further reforms can then be identified for addressing these performance shortfalls.[1]

Public administration and reforms for improving its performance can only be properly understood in the larger context of a country's social and political system which, in turn, is exposed to outside–nowadays global–pressures that a country has to cope with. Accordingly, the paper begins with a section that provides the essential information on the sociopolitical context and public administration in Malaysia. The second section presents some basic concepts and ideas that guide the subsequent discussion of reform in Malaysia. The third section examines past reforms (i.e. until the end of 2008) and notes their nature, achievements, and deficiencies. The fourth section identifies the main outstanding performance needs and proposes reforms for addressing them. The fifth section concludes the essay with a brief discussion of the political prospects of the proposed reforms.

The Sociopolitical Context and Public Service

Malaysia is a federation of thirteen states consisting of the eleven states in the Peninsular of Malaysia and the two states of East Malaysia. The eleven states of the Peninsular of Malaysia gained independence from the British in 1957 as the Federation of Malaya. The two states of East Malaysia became independent of the British and joined the Federation of Malaya to form the Federation of Malaysia in 1963. Singapore also joined as a member state but separated from the federation two years later in 1965.

Malaysia is a multiracial society and race continues to be the major social and political cleavage in the country. The various

1) An earlier and slightly different version of this essay is translated into Mandarin for publication in *Journal of Public Administration* in China. This essay is published here with the permission of the journal.

races are officially classified as *bumiputra* (literally "sons or princes of the soil" in the Malay and official language) and non-*bumiputra*. The former category, consisting of Malays and numerous other native groups–usually called "other *bumiputra*" –concentrated in East Malaysia, enjoy constitutionally enshrined special rights, including employment in the public service. Non-*bumiputra* consist mainly of Chinese and Indians. Demographic trends since 1957 show a steady increase in the percentage of *bumiputra* and a corresponding decline in the percentage of non-*bumiputra*. The last census in 2000 shows a total population of 23 million, consisting of 53.4% Malay, 11.7% other *bumiputra*, 26.0% Chinese and 7.7% Indian.

Like most former British colonies, Malaysia has a parliamentary form of government with elections scheduled at five-year intervals, at both federal and state levels. Reflecting the society, political competition continues to be mainly inter-racial in nature and political parties are wholly or mainly based on particular races. Since independence, the federal government and most state governments have been controlled by a multiracial coalition. Since 1972, the coalition has expanded from three to about a dozen member parties and changed its name to BN (Barisan Nasional or National Front in English). It continues, however, to be dominated by the main Malay party, i.e. UMNO (United Malays National Organization). Reflecting Malay political dominance, the prime minister, deputy prime minister, and about three-quarters of other ministers at the federal level are Malays. However, the inclusion in government of parties of all races contributes importantly to government legitimacy and political stability in the country.

A major objective of government policy since 1957 is to improve the inferior economic position of *bumiputra*, especially Malays, in relation to non-*bumiputra*. The government greatly increased these "restructuring" (or affirmative action) efforts by launching the 15-year NEP (New Economic Policy) in 1971 and expanding its role in the economy to increase opportunities for *bumiputra*. This objective has essentially remained unchanged with the expiry of the NEP and its official replacement by the present National Development Policy–indeed this latter policy is usually referred to, including by government leaders, as the NEP. As a result, the educational and economic disparities between *bumiputra* and non-*bumiputra* have been significantly reduced. This has increased non-*bumiputra* demands for the policy to be gradually phased out. The need to enhance the country's global competitiveness is also pushing in the same direction.

The country's public service will now be briefly described. Malaysia is a federal system. The total public service thus consists of the civil services at the federal and state levels, including state-controlled local governments. The number of civil servants has expanded about threefold since independence, especially at the federal level and after 1970 under the NEP. Current staff strength is estimated to be around 1.3 million, which for the country's population (23 million in 2000 and presently around 27 million) is high by international standards. Malaysia's federal system is extremely top-heavy. The federal civil service currently accounts for roughly 90 percent of all civil servants and is the focus of the paper.

The public service is integrated with the political system in broadly the same way as in other parliamentary systems. The civil service is permanent: civil servants have life-long careers and serve until the age of retirement (58 years at present). The civil service is merit-based but this is importantly qualified by preference for *bumiputra*. The doctrine of political neutrality that accompanies permanency in the "Westminster model" continues to be part of official policy. However, the question has long been raised as to whether it has not been seriously compromised in practice under continuous rule by a single dominant coalition that has put considerable pressure on civil servants to be loyal to it (Puthucheary, 1978: 43-47). Nevertheless, it seems fair to say that political neutrality remains largely in place if not entirely intact among Malaysian civil servants. The activity of public administration is grouped under ministries (presently close to 30), each of which is headed by a minister who is responsible to parliament.

In terms of career structure, civil servants join particular closed service schemes at the bottom and work their way up. Since independence, the number of service schemes has been gradually reduced to less than 300 at present. These schemes are also horizontally divided into service groups, which were simplified in 1992 to the present three of Top Management Group, Management and Professional Group, and Support Group. A college degree is required for entry-level positions in the Management and Professional Group but not in the Support Group. The Top Management Group consists of those promoted to senior positions from the Management and Professional Group, mostly from the elite generalist service scheme known as the PTD (short for Perkhidmatan Tadbir dan Diplomatik; in English, the Malaysian Administrative and Diplomatic Service).

Table 6-1 provides a snapshot of the Malaysian civil service in 2005, the most recent year for which complete official data broken down by service group and race are available. The table covers civil servants at all-federal, state and local-levels of government but excludes the police and the armed forces. The police are presently about 100,000 strong while the size of the armed forces is not released for security reasons. The last row shows a total of 899,250 civil servants, of which 0.2% is in the Top Management Group, 21.2% in the Management and Professional Group and 78.6% in the Support Group.

[Table 6-1] The Malaysian Civil Service (2005)

Race	Top Management Group		Management & Professional Group		Support Group		Total
	No.	%	No.	%	No.	%	No.
Malay	1,370	83.95	155,871	81.65	535,495	75.77	692,736
Chinese	151	9.25	17,896	9.37	66,248	9.37	84,295
Indian	83	5.08	9,777	5.12	36,194	5.12	46,054
Other *bumiputra*	23	1.41	6,156	3.22	63,649	9.01	69,828

Source: Reply by Mohd. Johari Baharum, the then Parliamentary Secretary in the Prime Minister's Department, to a question in the Senate or upper house of parliament on December 7, 2005. It was reported in the Malaysian Chinese language daily, *Oriental Daily News*, December 8, 2005.

Table 6-1 also shows the racial composition or "representativeness" of the Malaysian civil service. This is an important concern to under-represented races in the plural society. Dividing a racial group's percentage in the civil service (as shown in the table) by its percentage in the country's population (in the 2000 census referred to earlier) yields a simple index for measuring over-representation or under-representation. The results are shown in Table 6-2.

[Table 6-2] Index of Representation by Race in the Malaysian Civil Service (2005)

Race	Top Management Group	Management and Professional Group	Support Group	Total
Malay	1.57	1.53	1.42	1.44
Chinese	0.35	0.36	0.36	0.36
Indian	0.66	0.66	0.66	0.66
Other *b'putra*	0.12	0.27	0.77	0.66
Others	0.25	0.51	0.59	0.57

The last column in Table 6-2 shows that Malays are over-represented to the tune of 1.44 times their population share. All other races are under-represented. Indians as well as other *bumiputra* have only 0.66 times of their population share. Chinese are the most under-represented, with only 0.36 times or just over one-third of their population share compared to two-thirds for Indians and other *bumiputra*. Looking across the columns shows that Malay control of the civil service is even greater than suggested by their overall index: their over-representation increases with service-group level, from 1.42 in the Support Group to 1.53 in the Management and Professional Group to 1.57 in the Top Management Group. The police and armed forces that are excluded are even more Malay in composition.

Improving Administrative Performance: Some Basic Concepts and Ideas

Any discussion of the performance of public administration immediately raises the question of how it is to be evaluated– or what is "good" public administration? The passage reproduced below states the three basic value-criteria that underlie the discussion of Malaysian public administration and its reform in this paper:

> Good public administration is responsive, i.e. endeavors to produce the services that we want and to do the things that we (or political leaders on our behalf) decided they should do for us. It is effective, i.e. succeeds rather than fails in producing what we want. It is efficient, i.e. produces what we want at lower rather than higher costs (to the government or to us separately). Responsiveness, effectiveness, and efficiency are widely used as basic criteria for judging public administration or its performance. Responsiveness is arguably the most basic: effectiveness and efficiency in doing

> something that is not responsive to our wants is worthless at best. Responsiveness is also more complex than effectiveness or efficiency. This is because the "we" or "public" that public officials are supposed to be responsive to often consists not of a single collective "we" but of many groups–or many "we's" and "publics" –that want different and often incompatible things. This situation suggests the necessity and importance of equitable responsiveness to all groups as a criterion or measure of performance (Lim, 2007a: 33).

Various other value-criteria, including merit, representativeness, transparency, accountability, and the level of corruption, are found in the literature. However, these can be seen as requirements for achieving, and therefore implied by, the three basic values of responsiveness, effectiveness and efficiency. Fundamentally, then, reform is undertaken for improving the performance of public administration in terms of these three basic value-criteria.

The design and choice of reforms should ideally be based on prior knowledge or at least received ideas–essentially a good conceptual framework–of available alternatives or measures for improving public administration. Such a framework is as needed for understanding past reforms as for identifying further reforms. Identifying further reforms becomes a useful exercise when past reforms still fail to produce desired levels of performance, as is evidently the case in Malaysia and many other countries. However, a systematic conceptual framework of reform alternatives and their specific contributions to improving administrative performance is not a prominent feature of contemporary administrative reform literature. Some earlier works, therefore, have to be dredged out to provide guidance.

Highly useful for this purpose is the classification by Simon, Smithburg, and Thompson (1950: 55-91) of the various influences on the behavior of individuals in organizations. These consist of influences on the individual before becoming a member of the organization, influences on the individual from inside the organization (these intra-organizational influences are divided into two categories, formal and informal), and influences on the individual from outside the organization. The organization can also be taken to mean the whole public administration or bureaucracy. Reform then covers all measures for changing the influences classified by Simon, Smithburg, and Thompson so as to ensure desired behavior and hence performance.

The Simon, Smithburg, and Thompson classification shows the broad range of influences on behavior that reform can seek to change—including, notably, the first category or pre-entry influences that do not receive enough attention because of the emphasis on post-entry influences in discussions of reform. The fourth category, namely external or environmental influences, is now generally recognized as the primary source of pressure on organizations to perform; this pressure is then transmitted down the organizational hierarchy to all members within the organization. The nature of the environment differs significantly between public and private (or business) organizations: it is mainly the political system for the former and the market for the latter. It may be noted parenthetically that the NPM (New Public Management) does not obliterate this fundamental distinction or its usefulness, but applies it more sophisticatedly to identify possibilities for choosing and mixing political and market pressures. There is also a growing realization that both the proper choice and proper use of market pressure for public purposes in NPM measures like privatization and contracting-out are dependent on public decisions that are primarily subject to political pressure.

It is also useful to see the individual behavior of public officials as directly dependent on two broad variables, namely capacity and will. Desired behavior—and performance—requires that public officials have both the capacity and the will to carry out assigned tasks. As enunciated by Madison in Federalist 51 for the purpose of constitutional design, the basic principle for ensuring performance is to match capacity and will with role or function, or in his more eloquent words, to match "constitutional means and personal motives" with "the constitutional rights of the place" (Rossiter, 1961: 321-2).

The various influences classified by Simon, Smithburg, and Thompson thus affect behavior and performance through, or because of, their effect on the capacity and will of officials to perform. The various concepts are thus importantly related as follows: reforms affect Simon, Smithburg, and Thompson's influences, which affect capacity and will, which then affects actual behavior and performance. These concepts and relationships inform the examination of administrative reform in Malaysia that follows.

Past Reforms

Administrative reform in Malaysia began soon after independence and largely took place under the leadership of three of the country's (so far) five prime ministers. These three prime ministers are Razak, Mahathir and Abdullah, the present incumbent. The summary of the reforms under Razak and Mahathir in this section is largely based on the author's earlier, more extensive account (see Lim, 2006a). Abdullah's reforms are also summarized but await more systematic scholarly scrutiny.

The specific reforms under the three prime ministers are quite diverse and to some extent reflect changing ideas on improving public administration. The specific perceived problems, or dissonances, driving reforms also vary considerably. These reflect the changing scope of public administration and the changing internal and external conditions faced by the country —as well as deficiencies inadequately addressed or even accentuated by earlier reforms. To enhance understanding and guide prescription, this section will also discern important underlying similarities or continuities in past reforms in terms of broad approaches or strategies. These reforms also appear to result from a similar underlying political calculation or "bottom line" that will be stated and used for assessing future reform prospects in the concluding section.

The Razak Reforms (1960~76)

After the 1959 electoral setback, the government set up a new Ministry of Rural Development for undertaking a massive rural development program to win back the rural and predominantly Malay support for UMNO. The ministry was headed by Razak who was the powerful deputy prime minister at that time. After some initial reforms to push the slow-moving bureaucracy to expedite rural development (Ness, 1967), Razak sought and accepted advice from two American professors to strengthen the capacity of the bureaucracy (Montgomery and Esman, 1966). The introduced reforms focused on personnel administration, the budgeting system, and administrative procedures.

These reforms reflect the scholarly debate on administrative reform at that time within so-called development administration. That debate–which seems largely forgotten nowadays–centered on two broad alternatives: the so-called balanced and unbalanced strategies (see Riggs, 1971). The unbalanced strategy refers to reforms within the bureaucracy to enhance capacity and will, but mainly the former, while the balanced strategy is even broader and includes external reforms for strengthening control institutions for making the bureaucracy perform. Proponents of the balanced strategy insisted on the prior importance of strengthening control institutions for ensuring adequate will to perform: without adequate will, capacity would be difficult to enhance and, moreover, would not be translated into significant improvements in performance. Proponents of the unbalanced strategy, on the other hand, doubted both the priority and political feasibility of strengthening control institutions.

Esman was then a leading proponent of the unbalanced strategy (Esman, 1967). Although concerned with the weakness of control institutions in Malaysia, Esman recommended the unbalanced strategy for the country and justified it as follows: "In Malaysia externally induced cultural transformation or political change were out of the question; strengthening the administrative apparatus appeared to be feasible and to offer early and assured returns in governmental effectiveness; attention to participative institutions, while complementary, was secondary in time and importance" (Esman, 1972: 8, 286-7).

The most durable and successful component of these reforms was personnel training. Esman (1972: 145) regarded changing the elite status and Malay control of the generalist PTD as politically infeasible and sought to enhance its capacity through training. He also wanted PTD officers to specialize in broad policy areas but this was effectively scuttled by the PTD-staffed central personnel agency (now known as the Public Service Department). Besides graduate-level training at foreign universities for senior officers, the government's training centre was expanded and transformed into INTAN (the Malay acronym for National Institute of Public Administration) in 1972 to provide training to all categories of staff. More problems attended other reforms. Although popular at the time, performance budgeting made heavy demands on information and skills that were inadequately met, even in the US (Dean, 1989: 5-10). Not surprisingly, its implementation in Malaysia encountered problems from the start, especially when it was rapidly introduced throughout the federal government.

After another electoral setback (and racial riots in the capital city of Kuala Lumpur) in 1969, Razak took over as prime minister in 1970 and launched the NEP in 1971. This led to the government's active intervention in the economy to increase opportunities for Malays, especially in the commercial and industrial sectors, and to step up training and assistance for Malays to take up these opportunities. Lacking faith in the existing bureaucracy and the ability of the newly introduced reforms to produce quick results, Razak rapidly increased the number of public enterprises for undertaking the government's vastly expanded role. This large-scale resort to public enterprises may or may not be endorsed by Montgomery and Esman, but it is broadly consistent with the unbalanced strategy recommended by the two scholar-consultants.

Razak passed away in 1976 but the reforms he instituted have important long-lasting effects and provide the basis for later reforms by Mahathir. Largely because of the government's expanded role, but also because of the use of the public sector to provide jobs for Malays (Ismail and Osman Rani, 1991: 39-57), the civil service expanded rapidly under Razak and even faster under his immediate successor, almost doubling from 398,000 in 1970 to 765,000 in 1982 (Rugayah, 1995: 64-5). It also became more Malay in racial composition.

Performance in terms of effectiveness and efficiency, however, was more mixed, especially in the public enterprises (Abdul Hafiz, 1992). Nevertheless, it cannot be denied that the Razak reforms were highly responsive to Malays, who understandably revere Razak as the "father of development." It is worth noting that Razak's reforms, together with the Malaysian plural society, make abundantly clear the political nature of public administration and the complexity of evaluating its performance. Not only do reforms often involve trade-offs among different values, but also these trade-offs affect different groups differently so that reforms tend to be evaluated differently by different groups in society.

The Mahathir Reforms (1981~2003)

Mahathir was widely known to be dissatisfied with the performance of the expanded bureaucracy. Upon becoming prime minister in 1981, at a time of economic slowdown, Mahathir took steps to curb public personnel growth and effectively limited it to about one percent annually throughout his 22-plus years in office. He was also quick to signal his concern with bureaucratic performance by requiring civil servants to clock-in and clock-out. Administrative reform was stepped up with Mahathir's announcement in 1991 of his "Vision 2020" plan to make Malaysia a modern industrialized country. Many of these reforms reflected the then popularized ideas of the NPM.

Mahathir was more favorably disposed than Razak towards the private sector as the engine of economic growth, with the public sector playing a supportive role. He introduced the Malaysia Incorporated policy and the privatization policy in 1983 and accelerated their implementation after 1990. The former led to the setting up of joint committees at various levels to foster closer cooperation between the public and private sectors to enhance the country's economic growth and competitiveness. The latter, which appears to be Mahathir's response to weak public enterprises, had multiple and potentially inconsistent objectives: mainly to reduce the size of the public sector and the burden of the government, to improve efficiency through competition, and to help *bumiputra*. The government has claimed varying degrees of success on all objectives. However, scholarly studies are more critical in terms of both equity and efficiency: they point to widespread political patronage or cronyism, the creation of monopolistic or oligopolistic rather than competitive markets, especially for privatized public amenities and weak regulation (Jomo, 1995; Gomez and Jomo, 1999: 75-116; Tan, 2008).

A wide range of internal administrative reforms was also introduced. These reforms fall broadly under financial administration, personnel management, and service delivery. The main financial reforms were the introduction of the so-called Modified Budget System to streamline budgeting procedures and to encourage greater decentralization in the management of expenditure, the establishment of committees at various levels to monitor financial management for integrity and rule-compliance, and the introduction of computerized accounting systems. In personnel administration, a system of merit pay (called the New Remuneration System) was introduced in 1992. Difficulties and weaknesses in evaluating performance led to its replacement in 2002 by the present system (called Malaysian Remuneration System), in which promotion is based not only on superiors' evaluation but also on passing departmental competency examinations or courses. These competency assessments, however, have proved to be a burden to departments and civil servants alike and the umbrella union of the latter is pressing for their removal. Reforms introduced to improve service delivery included total quality management, client charters, ISO certification, the use of computers to expedite and decentralize various routine transactions with clients, and various programs to foster proper values and attitudes among civil servants.

These internal reforms have attracted some scholarly scrutiny (Ho, 2002; Common, 2003). However, the most extensive accounts have come from senior civil servants who served under Mahathir (see especially Ahmad Sarji, 1996, and the collection by Muhammad Rais, 1999). These scholarly and participant accounts are highly consistent in painting a picture of mixed results or under-achievement in terms of both the implementation and contribution of these reforms. Introduced from the top in rapid succession during the 1990s, but without effective monitoring, they have been characterized by widespread and uncorrected implementation shortfalls. This situation has led one scholar to observe that Malaysian political and bureaucratic leaders "appear to have seized on administrative reform as a way of masking the shortcomings of the public sector while maintaining the appearance of strong, efficient government both to domestic and international audiences" (Common, 2003: 166).

Be that as it may, Mahathir's reforms seem to be based on a broad conception of the public sector as partner to the private sector in national development. His reforms sought to right-size or right-task the public sector, make it more supportive of the private sector, and enhance its performance. A competent and business-friendly bureaucracy–or at least one internationally perceived as such–was seen as imperative for maintaining national competitiveness under globalization.

Mahathir's reforms differ in many particulars with those of Razak and even appear intended for ameliorating the latter's reforms or their effects. However, there are also important similarities. Both leaders focused on internal reforms in accordance with the unbalanced strategy and neglected the strengthening of external control institutions. Indeed, Mahathir further aggrandized executive powers and weakened external control institutions like parliament, non-governmental organizations, the press, and even the judiciary (Milne and Mauzy, 1999: 29-49). Mahathir also continued the strong preference for recruiting Malays. This is clearly reflected in the following figures from the Public Services Commission: "While Chinese accounted for 29.7% and Indians 9.8% of civil servants in the 1980s, their numbers fell to 8.2 and 5.2% respectively in 2003." The Commission's secretary explained that this "drastic drop … was due to the retirement of the post-Merdeka (i.e. post-independence) batch of (non-*bumiputra*) civil servants, who were not being replaced" (*New Straits Times*, July 26, 2005).

Mahathir himself has provided the efforts that the general assessment of his reform efforts that the Malaysian civil service compares favorably with most developing countries but "there is still much room for improvement" (*New Straits Times*, May 8, 1999). This failed to meet public expectations, as dissatisfaction with administrative performance persisted and in some respects even increased during the later years of Mahathir's leadership. In particular, corruption in government, not only among civil servants but also among ruling party politicians, became a matter of widespread concern. Non-Malays were also increasingly concerned with their treatment by the predominantly Malay civil servants and with their under-representation in the civil service. Following a widely publicized case of police bias in handling Malay-Indian violence, Mahathir has acknowledged the need for more non-Malays to be taken into the civil service to make it "sufficiently representative" (*New Straits Times*, May 20, 2001).

The Abdullah Reforms (2004~2008)

After taking over from Mahathir in October 2003, Abdullah led the ruling coalition to a resounding victory in the 2004 general election by making reform, especially fighting corruption, the centerpiece of his campaign. Most of his reforms were introduced during the first two years of office.

The ACA (Anti-Corruption Agency) took action against a few high-ranking public officials and increased to some extent the number of persons it arrested for corruption. A royal commission was set up to investigate the police and make recommendations to improve it. An Integrity Institute of Malaysia was set up to conduct courses to promote integrity and an Anti-Corruption Academy was set up to train anti-corruption staff. Some steps were also taken towards strengthening or encouraging existing institutions of public control. In parliament, a few committees were set up for examining important national problems and for the first time the Public Accounts Committee had a deputy chairman selected from the opposition–even though, contrary to parliamentary convention, the chairman remained a government member. The press was allowed more freedom and the role of non-government organizations was acknowledged. Reforms were also initiated in the educational system to arrest the declining standards that would diminish manpower quality in all sectors. In 2007, a high-level task force called Pemudah (a Malay acronym meaning facilitator) was set up to simplify administrative procedures in order to improve service delivery to business and reduce opportunities for corruption.

However, Abdullah's anti-corruption measures were widely seen as inadequate. The early actions against high-level political and bureaucratic officials for corruption were not sustained. Placed directly under the prime minister, the ACA was widely seen as lacking in initiative and energy, but Abdullah resisted mounting calls to increase the independence of the ACA by making it responsible to parliament. The 2005 royal commission report on the police found widespread corruption and abuse of power within the force, recommending as a matter of urgency the setting up of an independent police complaints commission with the power to investigate and punish wrongdoing. However, Abdullah gave in to opposition by the police and stalled.

The government increasingly stressed the prevention of corruption through courses for changing values and simplifying procedures. However, these measures failed to produce quick results. The annual ratings of corruption by Transparency International showed, at best, no improvement for the country. The numerous media reports of wrongdoing and probable corruption by UMNO politicians that were not followed by government action only fed public disillusionment. In late 2007, the public was shocked by the appearance of a videotape taken in 2002 (when Mahathir was prime minister) showing the fixing of appointments and decisions at the highest levels of the judiciary.

Abdullah was seen as lacking the political will to act against corrupt officials. These included not only those within the mostly UMNO-supporting civil service but also within UMNO itself. Since the late eighties, many UMNO politicians were seen as improperly influencing government decisions to raise money for buying votes in party elections. Thus a major source of high-level corruption in government – as well as an obstacle to fighting it – was traced to the widespread practice of vote-buying or "money politics" within the main ruling party. Like Mahathir before him, Abdullah was reluctant to risk internal party support by cracking down on money politics and its corrupting influence on government (Vatikiotis and Jayasankaran, 2004) or to set up independent control institutions that would dilute or check his own power.

The last general election held on March 8, 2008, however, forced the government to step up reform. Although returned to power at the federal level, the ruling coalition lost the two-thirds majority it had enjoyed since independence. It also lost an unprecedented five states to a loose rival coalition, now called the PR (Pakatan Rakyat; People's Front in English). Abdullah's slow pace in carrying out promised reforms, especially his tardiness in fighting corruption, was widely seen as an important factor for the BN's loss of support (Ooi, Johan, and Lee, 2008).

The unprecedented electoral setback threw the BN into considerable disarray. Within UMNO, pressure built up against Abdullah and culminated in a hastened transition plan for him to hand over office to his deputy in March 2009. Abdullah announced that he would use his remaining months as prime minister to legislate the establishment of three needed bodies: a judicial appointments commission to address weaknesses in the appointment of judges, an anti-corruption commission (i.e. a strengthened and more independent ACA), and a special complaints commission that covers more than the police. Finally, in mid-December 2008, laws were passed for setting up the first two bodies at the beginning of 2009.

The new Judicial Appointments Commission's role of filtering and nominating candidates is useful for improving judicial appointments, notwithstanding some concern for the prime minister's control over the appointment of some commission members. However, there is more substance to the complaint that the new MACC (Malaysian Anti-Corruption Commission) is still not independent enough to be effective in rooting out corruption at high levels.

The MACC consists of civil servants. Only its head or chief commissioner may be appointed from outside the civil service; however, the civil servant who headed the former ACA has been appointed to the post. The MACC has increased powers of investigation but no autonomous powers of prosecution. The MACC Act provides: "A prosecution for an offence under this Act (that) shall not be instituted except by or with the consent of the Public Prosecutor." The Public Prosecutor is the Attorney General, the government's chief legal officer. The MACC reports –and the Anti-Corruption Advisory Committee that advises the MACC submits comments–not to parliament or a committee thereof but to a Special Committee on Corruption that reports to and advises the prime minister. All members of the MACC, the Advisory Committee and the Select Committee are to be appointed by the prime minister or by the constitutional monarch on the advice of the prime minister. Also provided for is a Complaints Committee to receive complaints (on non-criminal matters) against the MACC and to suggest improvements in its procedures. Members of this committee are also to be appointed by "the Minister" (i.e. the prime minister), or someone under him. The prime minister thus remains the dominant influence within the whole new anti-corruption setup.

Outstanding Needs and Reform Proposals

Since independence, Malaysian leaders have focused on internal reforms for enhancing individual and organizational capacity. There appears to be growing awareness that administrative performance is threatened not only by deficiencies in capacity but also–perhaps even more–by deficiencies in will. Some of Mahathir's NPM-inspired reforms during the 1990s, like merit pay (which lasted a decade) and privatization also targeted the will to perform. Abdullah introduced some reforms to strengthen external control institutions. However, all prime ministers were reluctant to reduce executive dominance and to strengthen external control institutions in ways that would significantly reduce their own control and exercise of power.

There is no doubt that capacity needs to be strengthened. Concern has persisted over the years with the ability of the civil service to attract able men and women into its ranks. In particular, there is increasing worry about the policy-formulation and management capacity of senior civil servants, and even about their grasp of international affairs and the English language that is needed to cope with the challenges of globalization. However, the major problems of corruption and racial bias are largely or wholly due to deficiencies in will. The increasing number of complaints to the Public Complaints Bureau (an executive agency under the prime minister) in recent years, mostly about the delivery of routine services, testifies more to deficiencies in will than to poor capacity among frontline staff. They also testify indirectly to deficiencies in will as well as capacity among managers. While capacity remains a concern, the clear and main lesson of almost fifty years of experience is the need to improve and sustain the will of ruling politicians and civil servants to perform. What follows is a brief explanation of further reforms that appear to be needed for improving capacity and will.

To increase the capacity of civil servants, several other measures besides continued post-entry training merit attention. Resisted in the past, greater functional and policy-area specialization within the generalist PTD appears increasingly needed. The capacity of civil servants depends importantly on pre-entry influences as well, especially the educational system, which the government should continue and redouble its efforts to improve. Better use should also be made of the country's universities for training civil servants, a point to be elaborated in the next two paragraphs. Also important is recruitment, which Simon, Smithburg, and Thompson point out is the primary means for selecting pre-entry influences or their effects. These effects are importantly reflected in merit criteria, which should therefore determine selection into the civil service. In the present Malaysian context, this requires reducing the importance of race or the preference given to bumiputra. Merit or job performance should also govern promotion in order to attract and retain capable personnel–and also to strengthen their will to perform.

The use of universities for training civil servants requires some explanation. At present, undergraduate and master-degree programs in public administration (or public management) exist in a handful of the country's universities. However, none of these programs are systematically used or preferred over non-public administration programs by the civil service for meeting its training needs, whether pre-entry or post-entry. Civil service criteria for recruiting management personnel also do not give any preference or advantage to candidates with prior preparation in public administration. This is probably an important reason why the tertiary public administration programs have not attracted many students or, it is generally believed, the academically better ones. The end result is that the vast majority of management recruits into the civil service do not have any prior training in public administration. This group probably exceeds 90% of PTD recruits if the 1995 official data reproduced in Abdullah Sanusi Ahmad, Norma Mansor, and Abdul Kuddus Ahmad (2003: 94) is still indicative.

Given the generally accepted view–also articulated by Simon, Smithburg, and Thompson (1950: 389-374)–that training in public administration improves relevant skills and knowledge (i.e. capacity) as well as appropriate values (i.e. will), the civil service should make better use of the universities for training its personnel. Programs can be jointly designed to suit the needs of the civil service. Graduate programs should then be used for the post-entry training of civil servants. Fresh graduates of undergraduate as well as graduate programs in public administration should also be given some preference in civil service hiring. These measures would help to increase student enrollment and quality in public administration programs, which would then be able to enhance their faculty and offerings. Stronger training programs would also support the above-proposed specialization within the PTD.

More important for increasing and sustaining the will to perform, however, is external pressure that is channeled through and reinforced by the institutions of public control. Before Abdullah, the government (i.e. the executive), consistently acted to increase its own powers (see Crouch, 1996: 77-95) and diminish the institutions of public control, with predictable and deleterious consequences for ministerial and bureaucratic behavior (Lim, 2002). This trend of executive aggrandizement has to be reversed. The improved balance between government and opposition after the 2008 general election has invigorated parliament. However, parliament still needs to be strengthened, not only by internal reforms to make parliamentary scrutiny more effective but also by making the electoral system fairer so that parliament would better reflect public opinion (Lim and Ong, 2006). The media and non-government organizations have to be given more freedom by reducing the government's wide powers of control over them. The effectiveness of these control mechanisms also requires more freedom of information and greater transparency in government.

In the Malaysian plural context, another needed measure relating mainly to the will of civil servants is to make the civil service more representative of the various races. While external control is crucial, it cannot completely determine the will of civil servants or eliminate the discretionary exercise of their will. Thus what Selznick (1966: 256) aptly calls the "prior commitments" of civil servants remain significant factors in shaping their behavior. These prior commitments that affect will are the result of pre-entry influences which are importantly related to social background, especially race. In addition to prior commitments to their own social group, civil servants also have more understanding of the wishes of their own social group, making them more capable of being responsive to their own social group. Thus, as the largely US literature on representative bureaucracy has argued and empirically demonstrated (see Lim, 2006b for a review), civil servants tend to be more responsive to their own racial group than to others. Although similar research evidence is not available for Malaysia, there is widespread public perception that even race-blind policies are often implemented to favor Malays. Scholarly observations also point to racial bias as a factor. For example, Shamsul (1996: 25) notes that the predominantly Malay civil servants have "inevitably become deeply ethnicised if not deeply pro-Malay" and that their usual reply to accusations of racial discrimination is that "we are simply implementing national politics." To reduce pro-Malay bias and to ensure more equitable responsiveness to all races, the civil service has to be made more representative.

It does not necessarily follow, however, that the civil service should be made strictly or proportionally representative. This is because Malays and also other bumiputra are still economically worse off than other racial groups and under-represented in the private sector, thus a measure of preference and over-representation in the civil service can be supported on grounds of overall equity. However, an argument can be made for moderating or reducing Malay over-representation from its present high level. Making the bureaucracy "sufficiently representative," in Mahathir's earlier-cited term, would reduce the presently considerable loss of capacity–considerable because merit is compromised for large numbers from the majority group, unlike countries that compromise merit for small numbers from minority groups. It would also reduce the palpable sense of injustice among under-represented races that strains race relations and threatens national unity in the multiracial country (Lim, 2007b).

The "representativeness" of the civil service is importantly determined by recruitment, which selects not only the prior capacity but also the prior value commitments or will of civil servants. The Indian member party in the BN wants a higher intake quota for presently under-represented Indians. However, a better way is simply to put more emphasis on merit criteria in recruitment. In the Malaysian context, this would make the civil service not only more capable, as noted earlier, but also more representative and hence more equitably responsive to the country's various races. There is no need to resort to the second-best method of quotas, which is indifferent to merit.

Conclusion: Prospects of Further Reform

The improvement in administrative performance through the above reforms would benefit society generally. However, the reforms would bring about important changes in the existing distribution of benefits and costs for the various races and for ruling politicians and civil servants. Whether or not they would be adopted is therefore mainly a political question. It is useful to end by briefly looking at the prospects of the two main suggested reforms, namely strengthening public control for improving the will to perform and strengthening the merit principle for improving both capacity and representativeness. These reforms, it may be noted, are not new paradigms but just long-established basics for achieving good public administration.

Malaysia's experience supports the view that administrative reform, itself involving multiple interests, is only part of a much larger process of balancing multiple shared and competing interests that ruling politicians are engaged in. These interests include the interests of groups in society. More importantly for the purpose of understanding reform, they also include the interests of ruling politicians. Ruling politicians want better administrative performance, but they also want less rather than more fetters on their exercise of power. As a result, they resist strengthening public controls that would also control them, even though these controls would improve public administration. As Wolf (2006) generally notes, "Intellectually, governments accept the value of multiple sources of power. Practically, they hate it." But most of all, ruling politicians want to remain in power. Thus, with respect to reforms for improving public administration, they would undertake those that they see as needed for–or as not risking–their continuation in power.

In Malaysia, the 2008 general election convinced ruling politicians that they had to undertake more reforms in order to remain in power. This led to Abdullah's parting reforms. The belief, as he put it, is that "with some reforms, the BN government will stay" (*New Straits Times*, October 24, 2008). The MACC is not as powerful or independent as widely hoped. The special complaints commission, to be established soon, is also likely to remain under effective government or executive control. It is hardly surprising that a political executive and bureaucracy long accustomed to enjoying power with little effective control by other institutions would try to limit change to what they think is the necessary or unavoidable minimum, even when ostensibly introducing reforms.

Thus it appears unrealistic to expect that the government would quickly introduce additional reforms that would strengthen the institutions of public control, namely parliament, non-governmental organizations and the mass media. However, public expectations of government performance have been raised. If more citizens come to see stronger control institutions as important for achieving what they want and if the rival political coalition remains united to provide voters with a viable alternative and hence the means for making their wishes more effective, pressure will build up for the BN government to undertake reforms for strengthening the institutions of public control.

The prospects for the other main proposed reform, namely greater emphasis on merit in hiring and promotion, would appear to be no less problematic. This reform promises more effective and efficient public administration for all, but it would impose costs–i.e. diminished jobs and particularistic responsiveness–on the presently favored bumiputra, especially Malays who form the majority of the population or voters to politicians. Unless enough Malays are willing to accept it, Malaysian ruling politicians are unlikely to strengthen the merit principle in the public service–or, for that matter, in most other areas of government operation.

Nevertheless, there are some grounds for hope. The Malays may be more open to the merit principle and a more representative bureaucracy as their representation in other sectors and economic well-being improve, and also as they become more concerned with the costs, or benefits forgone, of not undertaking this reform. Some of these costs seem poised to increase with globalization. Politicians or more specifically political leadership–even more precisely, of the transformational kind (Burns, 1978) – can play a catalytic role. And Malaysia's senior politicians have performed–and are performing–some of this role with their constant reminders of the need to enhance national competitiveness in the global marketplace. Indeed, in a recent Bloomberg television interview (see *New Straits Times*, October 25, 2008), Najib, who is due to take over from Abdullah in March 2009, explicitly stated that he would like to be a transformational leader and do away with "elements" of the NEP and that the Malays are ready to compete with other races on equal terms.

References

Abdul Hafeez Shaikh (1992). "Malaysia's Public Enterprises: A Performance Evaluation," *ASEAN Economic Bulletin* 9 (2): 207-218.

Abdullah Sanusi Ahmad, Norma Mansor and Abdullah Kuddus Ahmad (2003). *The Malaysian Bureaucracy: Four Decades of Development*, Petaling Jaya: Prentice-Hall.

Ahmad Sarji (1996). *The Chief Secretary to the Government, Malaysia*, Petaling Jaya: Pelanduk Publications.

Burns, James MacGregor (1978). *Leadership*, New York: Harper and Row.

Common, Richard (2003). "Malaysia: A Case of 'Business as Usual'?" in Anthony B. L. Cheung and Ian Scott (eds.), *Governance and Public Sector Reform in Asia*, London: RoutledgeCurzon.

Crouch, Harold (1996). *Government and Society in Malaysia*, St. Leonards, New South Wales: Allen and Unwin Australia.

Dean, Peter N. (1989). *Government Budgeting in Developing Countries*, London: Routledge.

Esman, Milton J. (1967). "The Ecological Style in Comparative Administration," *Public Administration Review* 27 (3): 271-278.

Esman, Milton J. (1972). *Administration and Development in Malaysia*, Ithaca: Cornell University Press.

Gomez, E. T. and K.S. Jomo (1999). *Malaysia's Political Economy*, 2nd ed., Cambridge: Cambridge University Press.

Ho, Khai Leong (2002). "Reinventing the Bureaucracy? Malaysia's New Administrative Reform Initiatives," *The Journal of Comparative Asian Development* 1 (1): 87-104.

Ismail Salleh and H. Osman Rani (1991). *The Growth of the Public Sector in Malaysia*, Kuala Lumpur: Institute of Strategic and International Studies.

Jomo, K. S. (ed.) (1995). *Privatizing Malaysia*, Boulder: Westview Press.

Lim, Hong-Hai (2002). "Public Administration: The Effects of Executive Dominance," in Francis Loh Kok Wah and Khoo Boo Teik (eds.), *Democracy in Malaysia: Discourses and Practices*, Richmond, UK: Curzon Press.

Lim, Hong-Hai (2006a). "Malaysia: Distilling the Lessons of Forty Years," in K. L. Ho (ed.), *Re-thinking Administrative Reforms in Southeast Asia*, Singapore: Marshall Cavendish.

Lim, Hong-Hai (2006b). "Representative Bureaucracy: Rethinking Substantive Effects and Active Representation," *Public Administration Review* 66 (2): 193-204.

Lim, Hong-Hai (2007a). "Improving Administrative Performance in Malaysia: The More Difficult Next Steps," *Policy and Society*, 26 (2): 35-59.

Lim, Hong-Hai (2007b). "Ethnic Representation in the Malaysian Bureaucracy: The Development and Effects of Malay Domination," *International Journal of Public Administration* 30 (12-14): 1503-1524.

Lim, Hong-Hai and Ong Kian Ming (2006). "The 2004 General Election and the Electoral Process in Malaysia," in Aurel Croissant and Beate Martin (eds.), *Between Consolidation and Crisis: Elections and Democ- racy in Five Nations in Southeast Asia*, Berlin: Lit Verlag.

Milne, R. S. and Diane K. Mauzy (1999). *Malaysian Politics under Mahathir*, London: Routledge.

Montgomery, John D. and Milton J. Esman (1966). *Development Administration in Malaysia: Report to the Government of Malaysia*, Kuala Lumpur: Government Printer.

Muhammad Rais Abdul Karim (ed.) (1999). *Reengineering the Public Service: Leadership and Change in an Electronic Age*, Subang Jaya: Pelanduk Publications.

Ness, Gayl D. (1967). *Bureaucracy and Rural Development in Malaysia*, Berkeley and Los Angeles: University of California Press.

New Straits Times. Various dates. An English-language newspaper in Malaysia.

Ooi Kee Beng, Johan Saravanamuttu, and Lee Hock Guan (2008). *March 8: Eclipsing May 13*, Singapore: Institute of Southeast Asian Studies.

Puthucheary, Mavis (1978). *The Politics of Administration: The Malaysian Experience*, Kuala Lumpur: Oxford University Press.

Riggs, Fred W. (ed.) (1971). *Frontiers of Development Administration*, Durham: Duke University Press.

Rossiter, Clinton. (ed.) (1961). *The Federalist Papers*, New York: Mentor.

Rugayah Mohamed (1995). "Public Enterprises," in K. S. Jomo (ed.), *Privatizing Malaysia*, Boulder: Westview Press.

Selznick, Philip (1966). *TVA and the Grass Roots: A Study in the Sociology of Formal Organization*, New York: Harper and Row.

Shamsul, A. B. (1996). "The Construction and Transformation of a Social Identity: Malayness and Bumiputraness Re-examined," *Journal of Asian and African Studies*, no. 52: 15-33.

Simon, Herbert A., Donald W. Smithburg and Victor A. Thompson (1950). *Public Administration*, New York: Knopf.

Tan, Jeff (2008). *Privatization in Malaysia: Regulation, Rent-seeking and Policy Failure*, Abingdon: Routledge.

Vatikiotis, Michael and S. Jayasankaran (2004). "Softly, Softly Go Reforms," *Far Eastern Economic Review*, June 3: 20-23.

Wolf, Alison (2006). Comment in *The Times Higher Education Supplement*, October 20: 13.

Chapter 7 Myanmar

Tin Hla Kyi

Introduction

Myanmar is the largest country in mainland Southeast Asia, stretching 2,000 km from north to south with a total land area 676,577 sq. km (261,228 sq. miles). It is an agricultural country. The agriculture sector accounts for over 40% of gross domestic product (GDP) and provides employment to about 65 percent of the labor force. Moreover, about two-thirds of the processing and manufacturing sector is agri-based and agricultural products dominate exports. The total population of Myanmar, estimated to be 55.4 million in 2005, comprises many races with some 130 ethnic groups spreading over 14 states and divisions. The majority of Myanmar's people are Bamars, but the Shan, Kayin, Kachin, Mon, Rakhine, and other races also constitute a significant proportion of the total population. Before the Second World War, Myanmar was under British Colonial rule. Myanmar gained independence from the British on January 4, 1948. After attaining independence, the political economy of Myanmar changed from a Parliamentary Democracy period (1948~1962) to Socialist period under military rule (1962~1988) and finally to a Market-oriented period under military rule (1988 to the present). This paper intends to look at public administration and public governance in Myanmar during these periods.

Brief Overview of Development of Government Structure and Administration

After gaining independence, the Myanmar Government changed from the Union Government during 1948~1958 to the Caretaker Government in 1958~1960, then back to the Union Government from 1960 to 1962. From 1962 to 1974, the Revolutionary Council Government governed Myanmar, followed by the Peoples' Council Government from 1974 to 1988. In September 1988, the government changed hands and the State Law and Order Restoration Council Government governed until 1997, the year the State Peace and Development Council Government, which still governs Myanmar, was established.

At the time of gaining independence, under the new constitution introduced in 1947, Myanmar was set up with Myanmar proper (divided into 7 divisions): (Rakhine, Tanintharyi, Ayeyarwaddy, Bago, Magway, Mandalay, and Sagaing) and four states (Shan, Kachin, Kayah, and Chin). Then on January 3, 1974, when Myanmar again adopted a new constitution and was named "The Socialist Republic of the Union of Myanmar," Myanmar was divided into 7 states (Kachin, Kayah, Karen, Chin, Mon, Rakhine, and Shan) and 7 divisions (Sagaing, Tanintharyi, Bago, Magway, Mandalay, Ayeyarwaddy, and Yangon).

After independence, new administrative functions were distributed among a large number of ministries: functional ministries and territorial ministries. The functional ministries are those that deal with the matters reserved under the constitution to the Union Government and the territorial ministries deal with the affairs of the four states and the Chin Special division (Kyaw, 2004: 22-23).

The basic structures of administrative ministries are generally constant throughout this post-independence period. During 1958~1960, some ministries were newly constituted for the political situation in line with the 1947 constitution. During 1962 ~1988, some ministries were reformed in line with the new administrative system and the socialist ideology. And, after 1988, new ministries were formed in line with market orientation and the building of a peaceful, modern, and developed nation.

Executive Service and Role of Administrator

After independence, the officials of the administrative service on behalf of the Government were responsible for law and order and the welfare of the state. At that time, the State governments concerned administered the executive service of the States, and the Frontier Areas Administration Department administered the executive service of frontier areas. In 1963, Under the Revolutionary Council Government, executive service officials of each division, district, subdivision and township were responsible for peace, tranquility, and the welfare of the public, supervised by Security and Administrative Committees at different levels.

In 1974, under the new constitution, the central committee of the Peoples' Council held the centralized power of the state while different levels of the people's councils in ward, village-tract, township, state, division, and the union, carried out region-wide administration. In 1988, the Armed Forces took state power and formed the State Law and Order Restoration Council (SLORC) to assume the responsibilities of the state. Since then the executive service and officials under the supervision of the Ministry of Home Affairs have been responsible for the realization of the three main national causes of the people, namely Non-disintegration of the Union, Non-disintegration of the National Races, and consolidation of the National sovereignty of the state.

The State Law and Order Restoration Council also formed

administrative bodies at different levels, gave authorized powers to departments exercising administrative power under the adoption of law No. 8/88, and reorganized the General Administration Department (GAD) which was under the Ministry of Home Affairs. At the same time the country had become peaceful as a result of cooperation between the Government and the people. Toward the emergence of a well disciplined democracy, the SLORC has been engaging since 1992 in transforming the current administration system into a civil administration where public service personnel could undertake their responsibilities in accordance with existing civil rules and regulations.

The Current Status of Public Administration and Public Governance

Myanmar is governed by the State Peace and Development Council (SPDC) which was formed on November 15, 1997. The SPDC was constituted with chairman and other members under proclamation No. 1/97, dated November 15, 1997. The SPDC has worked to transform the country's political, administrative, economic, and social structure in accordance with the needs of the people and changing times. To carry out these changes, the SPDC has adopted the following political, economic and social objectives as guidelines.

The four political objectives are: (1) stability of the State, community peace and tranquility, prevalence of law and order, (2) national re-consolidation, (3) emergence of a new enduring State Constitution, and (4) building of a new modern developed nation in accord with the new State Constitution. The four economic objectives are: (1) development of agriculture as the base and all-round development of other sectors of the economy as well, (2) proper evolution of the market-oriented economic system, (3) development of the economy inviting participation in terms of technical know-how and investments from sources inside the country and abroad, and (4) the initiative to shape the national economy must be kept in hands of the State and the nation's peoples.

The SPDC controls various state authorities. The head of the state of the Union of Myanmar is the chairman of the SPDC. The chairman is not only the head of the state but also the commander in chief of the defense services. The sovereignty of the state consists of the legislative, executive, and judicial authority. Legislative authority is exercised by the SPDC at present. The cabinet and regional Peace and Development Councils (PDCs) have been vested with the executive authority and the Chief Judge vested with judicial authority by SPDC.

Central Organs of the State

The following central organs of the state are assigned duties laid down by SPDC: the Government, the Supreme Court, the Attorney-General, the Auditor-General, and the Civil Service Selection and Training Board (CSSTB). The SPDC has constituted the Government with ministers including prime minister and deputy ministers. The Myanmar government is structured in a ministerial format: all activities conducted by the government come under the purview of line ministries. The Structure of Government is shown in Figure 7-1. The ministries are in turn organized on the basis of department and enterprises, departments mainly carry out regular and supervisory functions, whereas enterprises engage in actual operation of factories, firms, financial institutions, transport services, etc. The cabinet receives close guidance from the SPDC which is the supreme authority exercising state power in Myanmar. Each ministry is headed by a minister who is assisted by a deputy minister. The minister and deputy ministers are political appointees. The

[Figure 7-1] The Structure of Government of the Union of Myanmar under the State Peace and Development Council

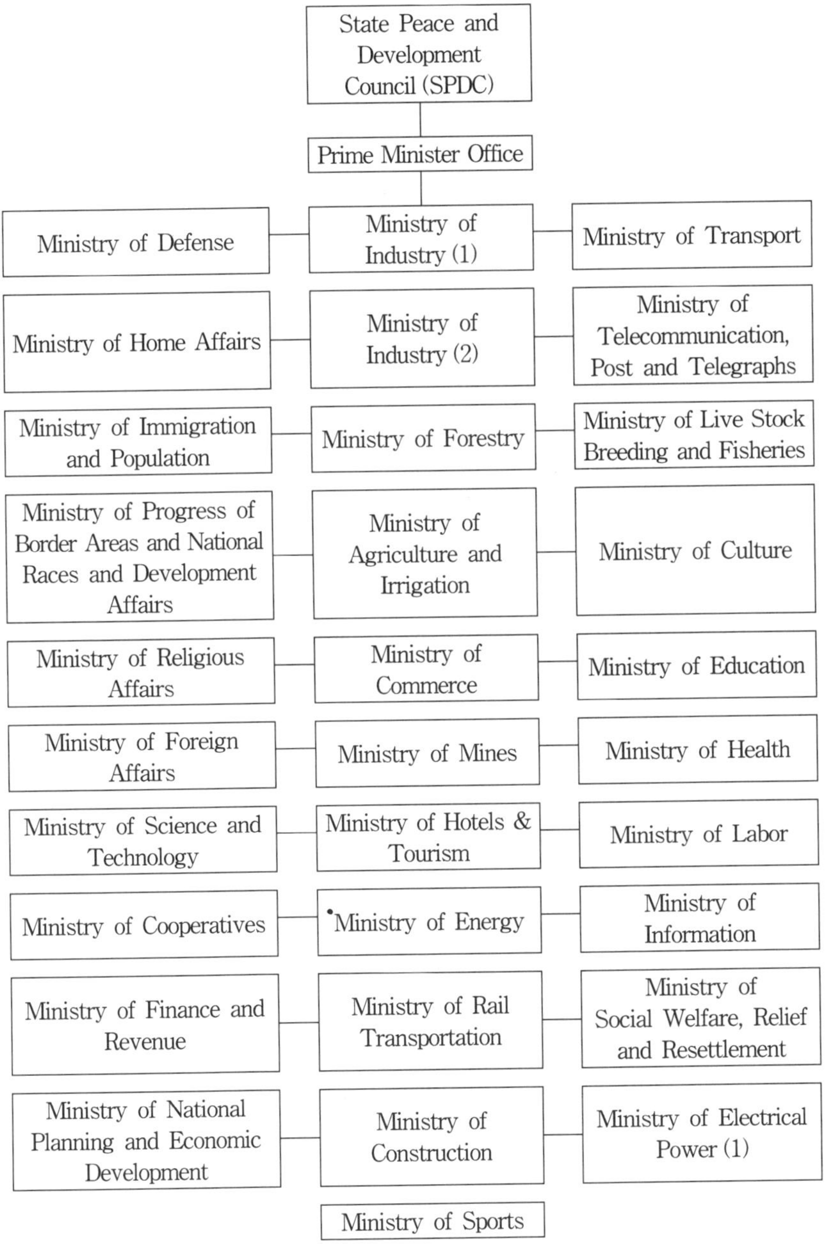

Source: Kyaw (2004).

departments are headed by Director-General (DG) and the enterprises by Managing-Director (MD). They are appointed by the SPDC.

Structure of the Union of Myanmar and the Local Government

Local areas of the Union of Myanmar are organized as follows: (1) villages are organized into village-tracts, (2) wards are organized into towns, (3) village-tracts and towns are organized into townships, (4) townships are organized into districts, (5) districts are organized into divisions, (6) divisions are organized into union. The different levels in the administrative structure of the Union of Myanmar, therefore, are as follows: (1) wards or village-tracts, (2) townships, (3) districts, (4) divisions, and (5) the union. At present, the Union is composed of 7 states and 7 divisions, 65 districts, 326 townships, and 16,217 wards and village tracts.

To carry out local administration, the SPDC has formed Peace and Development Councils for each State and Division, District, Township, Ward and Village-tract. In 2006, SPDC reformed local Peace and Development Councils for each State and Division, District, Township, Ward and Village-tract with General Administration Department, Myanmar Police Force and Planning Department personnel. The main functions and duties of new Peace and Development Councils at different levels are: (1) to accomplish policies and duties laid down by SPDC, (2) to supervise, examine, direct, and co-ordinate respective government organizations and enterprises in the effective and rapid exercising of their powers, vested by the ministries according to law, regulation, rule, procedure and directive, and (3) to carry out their public work as defined by the existing laws.

Ministry of Progress of Border Areas and National Races and Development Affairs (PBANRDA)

To conduct regional development tasks, the government enacted the Development Committees Law on April 1, 1993 under Order No 5/93, and the Border Areas and National Races Development Law on August 13, 1993 under Order No. 11/93. To make these measures more effective all over the country, save the municipal areas in Yangon and Mandalay, the government brought to life the Ministry of Progress of Border Areas and National Races and Development Affairs by Order No. 15/94 on January 30, 1994.

The Central Committee for the Development of Border Areas and National Races is headed by the Chairman of the State Peace and Development Council, and the Work Committee by the Secretary-1 of the State Peace and Development Council. Seventeen work subcommittees and regional work committees were also formed to supervise the implementation of tasks more effectively.

The PBANRDA Ministry is now undertaking tasks for regional prosperity and development tasks along with its three departments in order to pump progress to rural and border areas which lagged behind in development. The three departments are: the Progress of Border Areas and National Races Department, the Education and Training Department, and the Development Affairs Department. The ministry is responsible to undertake development affairs tasks in 286 townships, excepting 33 townships in Yangon municipal areas and 5 townships in Mandalay municipal areas.

Administration of Municipal Areas

The two largest cities in Myanmar, Yangon and Mandalay, have development committees to undertake development tasks. They are the Yangon City Development Committee (YCDC) for the development of thirty-three townships in the Yangon municipal areas, and the Mandalay City Development Committee (MCDC) for the development of five townships in the Mandalay municipal areas. These committees are under the direct supervision of the SPDC Chairman.

The Functions and Duties of Ministry of Home Affairs (MOHA) and General Administration Department (GAD)

Under SPDC, the Ministry of Home Affairs is an institution which was established with the aim of creating a stable and modern state to ensure security, prevalence of law and order, and peace and tranquility. MOHA is carrying out four pioneer tasks: (1) uplift of morality and spirit decorps, (2) constant training program, (3) staff welfare, and (4) correct administrative system for the nations one that meets five efficiencies criteria (morality, discipline, loyalty, unity, and competency).

Similarly the General Administration Department is responsible to MOHA: (1) to maintain law and order, (2) to preserve community peace and tranquility, and (3) to incite area development in accordance with prescribed laws and orders. Besides, at state and division levels, all administrative officers of state and division GAD are secretaries of PDCs concerned. At district level, all administrative officers of district are chairmen of PDCs concerned. At township level, administrative officers of township are the chairmen of the local PDCs. These local administrative units have, in practice, authority to decide on security, administrative, economic and social affairs of the unit concerned. Officers of the state/division, sub-state, sub-division, districts and township General Administration Departments therefore have to carry out the following duties: (1) tasks entrusted by the SPDC, (2) general Administration duties and functions entrusted by the MOHA, and (3) duties and functions delegated by other Ministries. The SPDC and the Ministry concerned set the formulation of public policies according to the existing laws, regulations and procedures.

The Central Organ of Civil Service

The basic requirement essential for the preservation of efficient and honest civil service personnel are those who are impartially selected, competent, politically neutral and imbued with spirit of service to the community. To obtain civil service personnel with these qualities, the SPDC has formed the Civil Service Selection and Training Board (CSSTB). It is the central organ of the civil service in Myanmar and is under the direct control of the chairman of the SPDC. It is placed at a ministerial level under the control of SPDC. A chairman and full-time members are appointed by the SPDC for a stipulated term. Most of the members are civil service pensioners well experienced in civil service.

There are four control services under the Board. They are Civil Services Selection and Training Department (CSSTD), the Civil Service Affairs Department (CSAD), the Central Institute of Civil Services (CICS) (Phaunggyi), and the Central Institute of Civil Services (CICS) (Upper Myanmar), and University for Development of the National Races of Union (UDNR). All these agencies give support for productivity and quality improvement to civil services.

Civil Service Structure of Departments and Enterprises

Civil service personnel are divided into 6 officer posts and 6 other ranks. The Director General and Managing Director are the highest ranking civil service officials in Myanmar. The strength of the Civil Service in Myanmar in 2002 was approximately 46,400 officers and 850,000 in other ranks. These figures did not include teachers, the police and armed services personnel, medical and nursing personnel. If all these categories were included, total personnel under government payroll would be about 1.2 million, representing about 2.4% of the total population (Zaw Moe Lwin, 2008: 30). At present, government activities in the fields of education, health, culture, information, development of border areas, village community development, greening of arid zones, construction of roads, bridges, and railways are all expanding and this has increased the scope and strength of the civil service in Myanmar.

Economic Reforms

After 1988, public sector reforms were carried out in line with a market-oriented economy. Among them, major economic reforms carried out since 1988 can be summarized as follows: (1) introduction of Foreign Investment Law-enhancing development in all sectors except those for the state; (2) industrial reforms-restitution of small and medium-sized establishments; transfer of management autonomy to state-owned economic enterprises (SEEs), allowing more private sector participation through the relaxation of restrictions on private investment, promotion of cottage industry, and promotion of privatization; (3) land and agricultural sector reforms-initiating institutional changes such as the establishment of land commission to ensure optimum use of land resources, and abolishing price controls; (4) reduction of compulsory delivery quota for paddies, reduction of subsidies, leasing of land for private investment as well as foreign direct investment and measures for production expansion; (5) fishery and aquaculture sector reforms-granting of fishing rights to foreign fishing vessels, marine fisheries, fresh-water fisheries, and aquaculture; (6) mining sector reforms-building legal framework, allowing private sector participation in mining; (7) tourism sector reforms-allowing private sector participation in hotels and tourism business; and (8) reform of frontier areas administration-pacification and promotion of development of minority races in frontier areas.

The overriding objective of these sector-wise reforms was, as mentioned earlier, "development of agriculture as the base and all-round development of other sectors of the economy as well." The emphasis on agricultural development was an important departure from the past. Likewise, although no specific mention has been made in the reform agenda, the greening of hills and mountains in the Dry Zone in central Myanmar to arrest the process of desertification was worthy of note. Then again, although some mention has been made of the development of minority races in frontier (or border) areas, the magnitude of the efforts made to promote the economic and social development of the border areas was such that it must also be regarded as new and deserves to be noted (Myat Thein, 2001: 176-177).

Public Administration Education and Training

Training of government personnel can make a major contribution to greater administrative effectiveness. Training is one of the important tasks in Myanmar Civil Service. Such tasks are performed by the Central Institute of Civil Service (Phaunggyi), the Central Institute of Civil Service (Upper Myanmar), and the University for Development of National Races (Sagaing) under the control of CSSTB.

Central Institute of Civil Service (Phaunggyi) and Central Institute of Civil Service (Upper Myanmar)

Inaugurated on January 1, 1965, the Central Institute of Civil Service (Phaunggyi) now runs regular courses and special refresher courses concurrently. Regular courses are conducted for a period of fourteen weeks along with special refresher courses lasting two to six weeks according to the classification of training. The Central Institute of Civil Service (Upper Myanmar) was inaugurated on February 7, 1999. The formation and functions of that institute are the same as that of CICS (Phaunggyi).

Regular training courses conducted by the Institute are: the Basic Course for Senior Civil Officers, the Pre-service Course for Newly Selected Senior Civil Service Officers, the Basic Course for Junior Civil Service Officers, the Supervisory Course for Office Superintendents and Branch Clerks, and the Basic Course for Senior Clerks. Special refresher courses are also run by the institute for faculty members of universities and colleges, doctors, state/division, district, township Law and Order Restoration Council members, police officers, Red Cross executives, officers of Development Affairs Department, trainers of military personnel, judicial officers, officers of the Immigration and Manpower Department, and basic education teachers.

Institute of Development Administration (IDA)

Aiming at building a modern developed nation, Myanmar has visionary schemes on training. As the current socio-economic situation in Myanmar changes rapidly, it is necessary to train local administration officers continuously so that they may handle any problems associated with new trends. In order to train local administration officers to possess management skills, mental and physical fitness, high efficiency and good moral conduct, all of which being the basic needs in development of human resources, the GAD has under the guidance of Ministry of Home Affairs, opened Institute of Development Administration (IDA) on July 2003.

Training courses offered include an induction training course for assistant township officers, an advanced training course and a treasury course for assistant township officers, efficiency enhancement course for district and township officers, seminars and workshops for state and division administrative officers, instructors' training course, and an efficiency enhancement course for staff. Moreover, regional and international seminars and workshops pertaining to administration are held from time to time to discuss and share the knowledge and experiences of civil service affairs.

Institutes of Economics

There are three Institutes of Economics in Myanmar offering Master of Public Administration (MPA) Programs: Yangon Institute of Economics, Monywa Institute of Economics and Meiktila Institute of Economics. The Yangon Institute of Economics is also offering a Bachelor of Public Administration (BPA) program. The main objective of the Public Administration program is to equip students with administrative knowledge and skills and to produce well-trained public administrators who are qualified to work effectively and responsibly in planning, organizing, directing, coordinating and controlling of government and society in accordance with national economic and social development plans. One requirement for the MPA degree is a research paper on any public issue topic. Up to the present, these three Institutes of Economics have produced 582 MPA graduates.

Future Prospects and Conclusion

Ratified and promulgated by the National Referendum on May 29, 2008, the new State Constitution of the Republic of the Union of Myanmar will certainly result in a new administrative structure for the nation. The new constitution states that: (1) the Union is delineated and constituted by seven regions and seven states and the Nay Pyi Taw prescribed as Union territory shall be under the direct administration of the President; (2) the Head of the Union and the Head of Executive of the Union is the President; (3) the Region or State Government is formed in the region or state and the Chief Minister (Prime Minister) is the Head of Regional Government or State Government; (4) the Head of the General Administration Department in the respective self administered region or state concerned shall serve as secretary of Region or State Government; and (5) administration at district and township level shall be carried out with state service personnel. The current administration system is being transformed into a civil administration system, and administrative bodies at different levels are expected to take full responsibility in the future administrative machinery. Civil service personnel are expected to play active roles as participators, regulators, and advocators in the building of a modern and developed Myanmar nation.

Myanmar is at the threshold of an important event in its history. The State Constitution of the Republic of the Union of Myanmar was ratified and promulgated by the National Referendum on May 29, 2008, and next year in 2010, free and fair elections for Pyithu Hluttaw (Legislation Bodies) will be held and a new State leader, a new government, and new central organs will be formed by the Hluttaw. New policies and measures are expected and these will put heavy demand on the skill and competency of the Myanmar civil service. The increased complexity of economic and social change and administrative management will make the task of administration more challenging. Administrative decentralization is needed, as is the promotion of decentralization, while active citizen participation is also essential. The government, citizens, and career officials must work together in building a peaceful, modern, and developed nation.

References

Basu, Rumki (1994). *Public Administration: Concepts and Theories*, 3rd ed., New Dehli, India: Sterling Publishers.

Civil Service Selection and Training Board (2004). *Journal of Myanmar Civil Service* 1 (2) C.I.C.S (Phaunggyi) Press.

General Administration Department. Undated. *Report on Institute of Development Administration*, Ministry of Home Affairs.

Kan Shein, Dr. (2003). *Development Plans for Myanmar Civil Service*, Paper presented at the workshop on Capacity Enhancement of Myanmar Civil Service, Yangon, Myanmar.

Khin Maung Myint (2003). *Civil Service Training and Career Development in Myanmar*, Paper presented at the Workshop on Capacity Enhancement of Myanmar Civil Service, Yangon, Myanmar.

Khin Maung Myint, and Kan Shein, Dr. (2002). *Civil Service in Myanmar*, Paper presented at the workshop on Capacity Enhancement of Myanmar Civil Service, Yangon, Myanmar.

Kyaw (2004). *Changes in Territorial Administrative Structures and Role of Public Administration in Myanmar*, unpublished MPA Research Paper, Yangon Institute of Economics.

Ministry of Information (2008). *Constitution of the Republic of the Union of Myanmar*.

Myat Thein (2001). *Economic Development of Myanmar*, Singapore: Institute of Southeast Asian Studies.

Myint U. (2004). *Human Resource Development for Local Administration Officers in Myanmar*, unpublished MPA Research Paper, Yangon Institute of Economics.

Nyi Nyi Lwin Soe (2004). *Local Administration in Myanmar*, unpublished MPA Research Paper, Yangon Institute of Economics.

Phyu Phyu Sint (2002). *A Study on Administrative Competence in the Union of Myanmar*, unpublished MPA Research Paper, Yangon Institute of Economics.

Schiavo-Campo, Salvatore and Pachampet Sundara (2000). *To Serve and To Preserve: Improving Public Administration in a Competitive World*, vol. 1, Asian Development Bank.

Wai Myint (2003). *Civil Service Structure and Function in Myanmar*, Paper presented at the workshop on Capacity Enhancement of Myanmar Civil Service, Yangon, Myanmar.

Win Maung (2008). *Civil Service Training in Myanmar*, unpublished MPA Research Paper, Yangon Institute of Economics.

Yin Yin Moe (2006). *A Study on Civil Service Commission and Personnel Affairs Being Imposed in Myanmar*, unpublished MPA Research Paper, Yangon Institute of Economics.

Zaw Moe Lwin (2008). *A Study on Structure and Functions of Myanmar Civil Service*, unpublished MPA Research Paper, Yangon Institute of Economics.

Ministry of Home Affairs
HYPERLINK "http://www.moha.gov.mm" http://www.moha.gov.mm
Ministry of Progress of Border Areas and National Races and Development Affairs
HYPERLINK "http://www.myanmar.gov.mm" http://www.myanmar.gov.mm
Ministry of Education
HYPERLINK "http://www.myanmar-education.edu.mm" http://www.myanmar-education.edu.mm
Ministry of Finance and Revenue
HYPERLINK "http://www.myanmar.com/finance/" http://www.myanmar.com/finance/
Ministry of National Planning and Economic Development
HYPERLINK "http://www.myanmar.com/ministry/nationalplanning" http://www.myanmar.com/ministry/nationalplanning
Civil Service Selection and Training Board
HYPERLINK "http://www.csstb.gov.mm" http://www.csstb.gov.mm
www.csstb.myanmar.com.mm

Chapter 8 Philippines

Alex B. Brillantes, Jr. and Maricel T. Fernandez

Introduction

Development and reform in public administration and public governance today have been immersed in a dynamic and fascinating, yet complex, milieu. While political and administrative reforms continue to saturate bureaucracy as general themes, a crop of innovative and emerging paradigms have fashioned notably in recent years to assume significance and to create an impact in the mainstream praxis (theory and practice) of public administration and public governance.

This paper provides an overview of the political and administrative experience of the Philippines by highlighting some features of administrative reforms that were articulated, advocated, and implemented by the successive presidents in the country in response to the idiosyncratic Filipino experience and expectations, and in adapting to the multi-faceted milieu of public administration and governance throughout history. This paper highlights the Philippine experience, taking cognizance of some of the major issues that beset Philippine Public Administration today: the continuing efforts to rationalize, reorganize, or reengineer and even decentralize the bureaucracy, foster democratic governance, and promote accountability and combat corruption (which are common themes germane to most countries). The paper also chronicles the development of the discipline of Public Administration in the Philippines, recognizing the role of the National College of Public Administration and Governance (NCPAG) of the University of the Philippines as a pioneer institution in public administration education and its significant role in the mushrooming of other academic institutions offering the same field.

Overview of the Politico-Administrative Experience of the Philippines

This part presents an overview of the historical context of politics and public administration in the Philippines.[1] The Philippines is an archipelago of over 7,000 islands divided into three major geographical areas, namely, Luzon, Visayas, and Mindanao. It stretches from the south of China to the northern tip of Borneo. The country has over a hundred ethnic groups and a mixture of foreign influences that have shaped a distinct Filipino culture. Before the Spanish explorers discovered the Philippines in 1521, Indo-Malays and Chinese merchants had settled there. The Spanish conquerors, or "conquistadores," first established a colonial government in Cebu in 1565 and transferred the seat of government to Manila in 1571.

The *Spanish-American* War, which started in Cuba, changed the history of the Philippines. On May 1, 1898, the Americans and the Filipinos attacked the Spanish Navy in Manila Bay. Faced with defeat, the Philippines was ceded to the United States by

1) This section of the paper was created using the information drawn from the Republic of the Philippines website accessible at HYPERLINK http://www.gov.ph/aboutphil/general.asp, *HYPERLINK "http://geocities.com/philippinepresidents 『 http: //geocities.com/philippinepresidents; HYPERLINK "http://www.country-watch.com, and" http://www.countrywatch.com,and http://www.philippinehistory.org/*

Spain in 1898 after a payment of US$ 20 million to Spain in accordance with the "*Treaty of Paris,*" hence, ending the three hundred thirty-three years of Spanish regime. On June 12, 1898, Filipinos led by Emilio Aguinaldo declared independence. This declaration was opposed by the U.S., who had plans of taking over the colony, which lead to a guerrilla war against the Americans. In 1901, Aguinaldo was captured and declared allegiance to the United States. In the same year, *William Howard Taft* was appointed as the first U.S. governor of the Philippines.[2]

Under American rule, initiatives were undertaken to build representative institutions in a democratic government and to prepare the Philippines for eventual independence. In 1907, the first legislative assembly in the Philippines was elected and a bicameral legislature was established, largely under Philippine control (ADB, 2005). The U.S. passed the *Jones Law* in 1916 establishing an elected Filipino legislature with a House of Representatives and a Senate. In 1934 the Tydings-McDuffie Act passed by the U.S. Congress established the Commonwealth of the Philippines with the provision of the position of President and promised Philippine independence by 1946. In the May 14, 1935 elections, *Manuel L. Quezon* won the position of President of the *Philippine Commonwealth.*

The process of democratization in the Philippines was rapid compared with other Western colonies in Asia. The interruption of the transition period by the Japanese occupation of the country in 1942, during World War II, did not delay the birth of the country's freedom. In accordance with the Tydings-McDuffie Act of 1934, the Republic of the Philippines was born on July 4, 1946. Philippine Independence Day was celebrated on July 4, until 1962, when a presidential directive changed the date to June 12, to commemorate the Filipinos' declaration of

---

2) Drawn from http://www.philippinehistory.org.

independence from Spain on June 12, 1898.

Ferdinand Marcos was elected president in November 1965. He was the longest running president of the Philippines with 21 years in power. In September 1972, he declared Martial Law, citing growing lawlessness, insurgency, and rebellion that threatened the survival of the Republic. During that period, democratic rights were violated and freedom was suppressed. Democratic institutions were largely under the control of Marcos (ADB, 2005); however, in 1986, Marcos was overthrown through a People Power Revolution that forced him into exile in Hawaii. *Corazon Aquino,* the wife of exiled and murdered opposition leader Benigno Aquino, was installed as President through a snap election. It was during Mrs. Aquino's time that the 1987 Constitution was enacted and implemented—concrete evidence of the country's democratization.

Since then, the Philippines has had a series of popularly elected presidents beginning with Fidel V. Ramos (1992~1998) and followed by the former actor Joseph Estrada (1998~2001). Estrada's term was interrupted by another People Power Revolution in 2001 and Gloria Macapagal-Arroyo, as the Vice-President, completed his remaining term and, in May 2004, ran for re-election against Fernando Poe, Jr., another popular actor and friend of Estrada. Arroyo was eventually proclaimed the President. Since then the Arroyo administration has been pushing the cudgels for charter change which has been interpreted by the opposition as a way to prolong her stay in power.

The Philippine Civil Service

Since the country went through a long period of colonization by Spain and the United States,[3] its political and administrative systems were dominantly patterned after its colonizers. Political economist and historian Onofre D. Corpuz (1957) asserts that the Spanish colonial government introduced the bureaucracy as a social institution consisting mainly of Spaniards. He added that the colonial administration was "bankrupt in constructive policy, as the bureaucrats were corrupt in their motivations and either incompetent or oppressive in their actions" (Corpuz, 1957: 129). Accordingly, Endriga (1997) echoes the same contention and claims that the Spanish colonial rule bequeathed four things to the Philippines. First, the idea that everything should be rigidly run from Manila-others would consider this as the "Imperial Manila." Second, the emergence of bureaucratic techniques best summed up by the Spanish expression "obedezco pero no cumplo" (I obey but don't comply). Third, is a profound distrust of government on the part of the indigenous people, and fourth, the notion that it is somehow patriotic to subvert the bureaucracy.

The American occupation on the other hand was a significant phase in the evolution of modern colonial policy and administration of the Philippines. The political institutions of the country were in accordance with the democratic and republic character of political institutions in the United States. The civil service system introduced to the Philippines is said to be a "finished product" where efficiency, economy, and merit were dominant values. These values were reflected in Act No. 5 (Civil

---

3) In 1898, the US grasped control in what American Secretary of State John Hay called a "splendid little war," sparked by American claims that the Spaniards had attacked the battleship USS Maine in Havana harbor. Spain ceded control of the archipelago to the US under the Treaty of Paris in December 1898. Initially applauded, the US occupation developed into a lengthy battle with the local population. The US decided to pull out in 1916 but fears that the situation could descend into civil war meant it was to be a further 30 years before sovereignty was returned to the Filipinos. In 1941, Japan attacked the Philippines, sparking a three year long occupation. The US returned in 1944; in 1945 the Japanese surrendered, and, one year later, the islands were granted full independence under the name of the Republic of the Philippines.

Service Act) passed by the second Philippine Commission in 1900 (Endriga, 1985). This Act formally established the civil service in the country.

If the Philippine Civil Service was patterned from the American model in terms of form and substance, its application, according to Heady (1957: 45), is more accurately described as an excellent fusion of East and West, with local flavor transforming considerably its original Weberian principles (Endriga, 1997). The Bureau of Civil Service (BCS) was established November 31, 1900, with the mandate that the "greatest care should be taken in the selection of officials for civil administration." To head the various executive and line agencies, the Philippine Commission preferred American civilians or military men who had been honorably discharged. All recruits, both American and Filipino, were to be "men of the highest character and fitness" who could conduct their duties unaffected by "partisan politics" (Philippine Commission, 1900: 121).

In 1916, the Civil Service Law was embodied in the new administrative code. The BCS was, however, to continue under the control of an American director until Jose Gil was appointed in 1920 as the first Filipino Director of Civil Service. American leadership, coupled with Filipino cooperation made possible good government service throughout the period of 1899~1920. The period 1913~1921 marked the rapid "Filipinization" of the Civil Service. In 1913, there were 2,623 Americans and 6,365 Filipinos in the government services. By 1921, the services consisted of only 614 Americans as opposed to 13,240 Filipinos.

The 1935 Philippine Constitution firmly established the merit system as the basis for employment in government. The following years also witnessed the expansion of the bureau's jurisdiction to include the three branches of government: the national government, local government, and government corporations (CSC website). On July 4, 1946 the Philippines was left on its own after the US granted its independence. The early republic, according to Corpuz (1955 as cited in Alfiler, 1999), was characterized as one vulnerable to nepotism and exposed to the spoils system. Among the other features that marked the early Philippine bureaucracy, was included its highly centralized nature (attributed by the influence of Spanish colonization), a civil service whose systems and procedures were patterned after that of the American civil service (upon its establishment after American colonization), and a bureaucracy highly vulnerable to attacks from politicians from the executive and legislative branches of government who meddled with the merit system.

The Bell mission of 1950, which studied the conditions of the newly-independent country noted, among many other things, that the government inherited a "reasonably well-organized administration and a well-trained civil service" (Endriga, 1985: 145). The report made a general recommendation that "a special effort must now be made to improve the public administration in order to give the people confidence in the government. It is particularly important at this time because the economic development program will of necessity place even greater responsibility on public administration. The success of the development program may depend more on the efficiency and honesty of the public service than on any single factor" (Endriga, 1997).

On June 19, 1959, the Republic Act 2260, otherwise known as the Civil Service Law, was enacted. This was the first integral law on the Philippine bureaucracy, superseding the scattered administrative orders relative to government personnel administration issued since 1900. This Act converted the Bureau of Civil Service into the Civil Service Commission (CSC) with department status. In 1972, following the declaration of martial law, President Ferdinand Marcos promised the most extensive and wrenching effort at reform in the history of the Philippine republic. He implemented Presidential Decree No. 1, which activated the Integrated Reorganization Plan (IRP) initially set up by the Reorganization Commission, thereby setting in motion the most extensive reorganization scheme ever in the Philippine government (Endriga, 1985). During the time of Aquino, the government had to contend with a bureaucracy that had become militant about guarding its own interest and was slowly venturing out to make executives more responsible. Its more articulate and critical elements rallied against "unequal treatment, the lack of political neutrality, and irresponsible performance" (Cariño, 1992: 135).

Today, CSC's mandate is derived from Article IX-B of the 1987 *Constitution*, which was given effect through Book V of Executive Order No. 292 (The 1987 *Administrative* Code). The Code essentially reiterates existing principles and policies in the administration of the bureaucracy and recognizes, for the first time, the rights of government employees to self-organization and to conduct collective negotiations under the framework of the 1987 Constitution.[4)]

An interesting pattern in the politico-administrative system of the Philippines is the fact that all administrations since 1946 have placed high on their agenda the reorganization of the bureaucracy upon their assumption of office. Among the more dramatic and visible reorganizations implemented were those by President Elpidio Quirino in the 1950s (through the Government Survey and Reorganization Commission), the Presidential Commission on Reorganization and the implementation of the Integrated Reorganization Plan (through Presidential Decree Number 1 of Marcos upon the proclamation of martial law), the Reorganization Plan of Corazon Aquino in 1986 (by the Presidential Commission through Government Reorganization), the reengineering and reinventing of the bureaucracy of

4) For more details see CSC website HYPERLINK http://csc.gov.ph.

President Ramos in the late nineties, the Presidential Commission for Effective Governance of Estrada, and finally the rationalization program of Gloria Macapagal-Arroyo.

With all these, the Philippine bureaucracy has essentially been shaped and influenced by the different periods it underwent, including a colonial heritage and legacies inherited from different administrations and innovations. Now, with over a hundred years of history, the civil service system continues to respond to the challenges and demands of nation-building and development, yet continues to be adversely affected by the political system of the country. Among the major contemporary initiatives of the civil service system is the formulation of a Civil Service Code that essentially would attempt to define a Philippine civil service system resulting from, and operating within the context of, the unique Philippine politico, administrative, and cultural history.

The Central Government Structure

Today, the political system of the Philippines occurs within an organized framework of a presidential, representative, and democratic republic, with the president as both the head of state and the head of government within a pluri-form, multi-party system. The president is elected by popular vote to one 6-year term and may only be removed from office by impeachment. The president cannot run for re-election unless they become president through constitutional succession and serve as president for no more than four years.

The Philippine bureaucracy has three branches namely, the legislative (the law-making body), which is vested in a bicameral Congress that consists of the House of Representatives (composed of 219 congressmen elected in the each district of the country and 21 party list representatives) and the Senate (composed of 24 senators); the executive (law-enforcing body) which is vested in the president; and the judiciary (the law-interpreting body) which is vested in the Supreme Court and lower courts as may be created by law. These three equal branches operate under the doctrine of separation of powers and a system of checks and balances (Nolledo, 1996 as cited in ADB, 2005).

The Philippine President enjoys several powers such as the power to contract or guarantee foreign loans on behalf of the country, with the prior concurrence of the Monetary Board, and he may enter into treaties or international agreements that become effective only with the concurrence of the Senate. The President is also considered as the commander-in-chief of the armed forces. He may suspend the privilege of the writ of habeas corpus and place the country or any part thereof under martial law under limited conditions prescribed by the Constitution of the Republic of the Philippines that also include mechanisms for congressional revocation and Supreme Court review of the factual basis thereof (ADB, 2005).

The heads of executive departments comprise the Cabinet. As the head of the executive branch of the government, the President may hire and fire his cabinet members. Unlike the nominated Cabinet who, with the consent of the Commission of Appointments, are appointed by the President, the vice-president may be appointed to the Cabinet without any need for such appointment to be confirmed by the Commission on Appointments.

The fundamental purpose, structures, and functions of the departments in the executive branch, the Constitutional Commissions, and other major government offices are stipulated in the Administrative Code of 1987. It also laid down the powers, functions, and responsibilities of the department secretaries and the heads of the departments. So far, this is the latest material after it was first issued in 1917. The Constitutional Commissions of the Republic of the Philippines include among others, the Civil Service Commission (CSC), Commission on Elections (COMELEC), and Commission on Audit (COA).[5]

The Local Government Structure

The 1987 *Constitution* provides a three-layered structure of local government. The first layer is the "province," comprising the largest unit in the political structure of the Philippines. It consists, in varying numbers, of "municipalities" and, in some cases, of "component cities." Its functions and duties in relation to its component cities and municipalities are generally coordinative and supervisory. Another level consists of cities and municipalities that are a subsidiary of the province. Municipalities consist of a number of "barangays" within its territorial boundaries. Cities have three different classifications: the highly urbanized, the independent component cities that are independent of the province, and the component cities which are part of the provinces where they are located and subject to their administrative supervision. Barangays comprise the third layer of local governments. A barangay is the basic and the smallest political unit into which cities and municipalities in the Philippines are divided. Barangays are created by ordinances passed by city or municipal "sanggunians" (councils). Cities, municipalities, and provinces are created by laws enacted by Congress. The creation of a local government or its conversion to another type is based on three criteria: income, population, and land area. In terms of income, the local government units-provinces, cities and municipalities-are divided into first to sixth classes.[6]

5) For more details, see the Organizational Structure of the Philippine Government HYPERLINK COA website accessible at http://lcweb2.loc.gov/frd/cs/philippines/ph04_01b.p.

6) For more details, see the income classification for provinces, cities and municipalities at http://www.nscb.gov.ph.

The Local Government Code of 1991

The history of the development of the politico-administrative system of the Philippines shows that a number of variations of decentralization within the context of local autonomy for sub-national governments have been initiated. However, it was only in 1991 with the enactment of the *Local Government Code* (through Republic Act 7160) that an immense process of devolution kicked off. The *Code* is considered as the most radical and far-reaching policy to deal with the decade-old problem of a highly administrative system in the country (Brillantes, 2003). The *Code* fundamentally transformed the nature of power relationships between the central government and the thousands of local governments in the Philippines through the devolution process by transferring the responsibility of delivering basic services such as health, social services, environment, and agriculture, etc. to the local government units.

Current Status of the Philippine Public Administration and Public Governance

The Philippine bureaucracy is the single biggest expense item in the Government Appropriations Act (GAA). For the fiscal year 2007 at least 30% goes to salaries. If you set aside debt service, 42% goes to salaries. Unfortunately, the public generally perceives bureaucracy as a liability rather than an asset. This explains why, according to David (2007: 7), "the bureaucracy has always been a 'non-entity' whether from the perspective of the public, or the politicians, or even the bureaucracy itself." However, the bureaucracy is influenced by different factors such as the political parties, civil society organizations, and other varieties of institutions like media, religion, family, etc. The major institution that holds all these together is the bureaucracy (David, 2007).

Growth of the Bureaucracy

The Philippine civil service today has a total workforce of 1,475,699. In terms of major subdivisions, there are 1,000,495 or 67.86% from the National Government Agencies, 370,227 or 25.09% from the local government units (LGUs) and 103,977 or 7.04% from the Government-Owned and Control Corporations (GOCCs) and Government Financing Institutions (GFIs). NGAs share the largest complement in the government workforce and these are subdivided into the different branches of government: the executive with the biggest pie of 94.97% or a total of 951,120 employees, the judiciary with 26,931 or 2.68%, the constitutional bodies with 17,606 or 1.58%, and the least number of employees, the legislative with only 0.58% of the total workforce in the national government.

[Table 8-1] Distribution of Government Personnel According to Branch of Service

Branch of Service	Number of Employees	Percentage
Executive	951,120	94.97%
Judiciary	26,931	2.68%
Legislative	5,838	0.58%
Constitutional Office	17,606	1.76%
Subtotal	1,001,495	67.86%
LGUs	379,227	25.09%
GOCC/GFI	103,977	7.05%
Grand Total	1,484,699	100%

Note: Data drawn from CSC (2008). The computation of the percentages is provided by the authors.

In terms of levels in the civil service, there were a total of 1,316,166 (89%) career employees and only a few non-career personnel (159,533; 11%). See Table 8-2 below. The continuous

[Table 8-2] Distribution of Career and Non-Career Personnel

Career (1,316,166 persons; 89%)	Non-career (159,533 or 11%)
1st level (28.39%)	Executive (0.5%)
2nd level (70.37%)	Elective (13.0%)
3rd level (1.24%)	Coterminous (11.0%)
Executive (0.71%)	Casual (62%)
Highly specialized (0.53%)	Contractual (13%)

Source: David (2007).

[Table 8-3] Distribution of Career Personnel

Type of Position	Positions
First level (28.39%)	Clerical, the trades, the crafts, the custodial service positions
Second level (70.37%)	Professionals, the scientists, the technical people
Third level (1.24%)	
Executive (0.71%)	Managers, or career executives
Highly specialized (0.53%)	Highly technical positions including ambassadors, people in the foreign service, and the scientific career systems.

Source: David (2007).

effort of professionalizing the bureaucracy can be manifested in the large number of career service employees, comprising 89% of the total government workforce. Career service is divided into the following Table 8-4. As shown in Table 8-3, there are only 159,533 in the non-career service or 11% of the entire bureaucracy.

As a repository of records on government personnel, CSC continually puts into effect measures towards record management (Philippine Panorama, 2002). Table 8-5 shows the distribution of personnel by 10 year intervals. There was no available data from GOCCs in 1964 and 1974. The underlying reason for this is that personnel in government corporations

[Table 8-4] Distribution of Non-Career Service Personnel

Type of Position/Rank	Positions
Executive (0.5%)	Appointed at the pleasure of the President, including Cabinet members, heads of GOCCs
Elective (13.0%)	
Coterminous (11.0%)	
Casual (62.0%)	
Contractual (13.0%)	

Note: The estimated data shown in Tables 2,3, and 4 were drawn from the paper presentation of Karina David in a Public Lecture Series held at UP NCPAG on December 14, 2007.

[Table 8-5] Distribution of Personnel Every 10 Years

Year	Total	NGA	GOCC	LGU
1964	272,845	201,401		71,444
1974	280,167	194,735		85,432
1984	991,445	667,114	134,453	189,878
1994	1,225,676	796,795	112,858	316,023
2004	1,475,699	1,001,495	103,977	370,227

Note: Data for the year 1964, 1974 and 1984 are derived from The Bureaucracy, in Government and Politics of the Philippines, edited by Raul P. de Guzman and Mila A. Reforma, 1988, Oxford University Press. The data excludes employees from schools, state colleges and universities. Data for the year 2004 is from the Inventory of Government Personnel by the Civil Service Commission.

were only absorbed into the regular civil service in 1973 (de Guzman, Brillantes, and Pacho, 1988). The distribution of personnel for every decade starting from 1964, and the number of employees from the NGAs and LGUs scales up one notch while the number of workforce in GOCCs decreases every ten years. In 1994, there were only 112,858 employees from 134,453 employees in GOCCs, thereby trimming down 21,595 employees from the GOCCs. In 2004, GOCC employees were further reduced into 104,977 employees.[7)]

In terms of local governments, as of September 2008, the National Statistics Coordinating Board (NSCB) lists 17 regions, 81 provinces, 136 cities, 1,495 municipalities, and 41,995 barangays in the Philippines as of September 2008. The country also has special local government units-Autonomous Region of Muslim Mindanao (ARMM) (RA 6734, RA 9054) and Metro Manila Development Authority (MMDA) (RA 7924).[8)]

Major Issues and Concerns on Public Administration and Public Governance

Governance has become a global agenda and a rallying theme for the management and conduct of public affairs in the new millennium. Bad governance is said to be the main reason why many countries, especially in the Third (or "Developing") World, continue to fall short of their pursuit for development. Development is a defining element in this modern era and many governments recognize that the quest for development is not a one-man job. The bureaucracy cannot do it alone; thus, governance has expanded the meaning of government and has introduced a new paradigm where managing people is not only the task of government, but one that requires a synergy of efforts by various stakeholders. It endeavors a "multi-stake-holder process, and a function of the many ways that individuals and institutions, both public and private, manage their common affairs" (Kim et al., 2005: 647).

Governance and good governance indicators such as

---

7) Data for the year 1964, 1974 and 1984 are derived from The Bureaucracy, in *Government and Politics of the Philippines*, edited by Raul P. de Guzman and Mila A. Reforma, 1988, Oxford University Press. The data excludes employees from schools, state colleges and universities. Data for the year 2004 is from the Inventory of Government Personnel by the Civil Service Commission.

8) RA 7924 is An Act Creating the Metropolitan Manila Development Authority, Defining its powers and functions, providing funds and for other purposes.

participation, transparency, accountability, and predictability, among others, serve as a heuristic strategy; however, the application of such varies from country to country. In the Philippines, the need for reform and for good governance has been recognized in different sectors and numerous efforts are being pursued. The participation of civil society in the delivery of basic services to the public and in the advocacy of significant reform initiatives has contributed to a redefinition of governance in the Philippine context. Governance processes have traditionally been the sole domain of government, however, fundamental limitations, like the lack of resources (both personnel and financial), excessive red tape, and even graft and corruption, have made government an institution generally unable to adequately deliver. Hence, it is within this context that governance in the Philippines has been redefined to include the private sector, NGOs, people's organizations, and civil society in general (ADB, 2005).

Public administration and public governance in various developing countries have been confronted with tougher challenges and demands in the new millennium. "Demands for better service are increasing and various public sector reforms, such as decentralization, greater managerial discretion, and increased reliance on market or quasi-market mechanisms have been introduced" (ADB, 2002: 603). The Philippines still has its share of issues and concerns in public administration and public governance. The country has been struggling with various areas of concerns from reorganization, decongesting the central government, and the ever-present challenge of addressing corruption and promoting accountability in government.

Continuing Reorganization

Over the years, many techniques and strategies have been practiced to advance government performance in many developing countries. In the Philippines, actions have ranged from Development Administration in the 1950s to 1960s, New Public Administration in the 1970s, New Public Management in the 1980s to 1990s, and Reinventing Government in the 1990s to PA as Governance in the 1990s to the present.

Philippine public administration has always seen "re-organizing" as a tool is central to the entire initiative in the continuing search and design for more responsive structures and process. Indeed, among the initial initiatives of any president-from Roxas in the 1940's to Arroyo in 2002-upon assumption to office is the declaration to "reorganize" the bureaucracy with the end-goal of attaining the three Es-economy, efficiency, and effectiveness (Brillantes and Fernandez, 2008). These values have been recycled into contemporary buzzwords such as "streamlining" the bureaucracy, "downsizing" or "rightsizing," implementing a "lean and mean" structure, and others.

Administrative reform was introduced in 1972 (during the time of President Marcos) with the establishment of Presidential Decree (PD) No. 1, the Integrated Reorganization Plan, which was the result of a two-year effort of the Reorganization Commission. The IRP provided mechanisms for decentralizing and reducing the bureaucracy and standardizing departmental organization. The IRP also sought to introduce structural changes and reforms to strengthen the merit system, as well as to professionalize the civil service system. However, stakeholders who were to benefit by the program were not involved. The program was the handiwork of a few trusted allies of Marcos (ADB, 2005).

Aquino's administration has been credited for restoring civil liberties, initiating the formation of a new constitution (the 1987 Constitution), and the restoration of Congress. She also introduced the Presidential Commission on Public Ethics and Accountability and the Presidential Commission on Good

Governance (PCGG). These initiatives, however, fell short of the public expectations. Paradoxically, "while layoffs were justified in the name of downsizing the bloated government, the number of civil servants and political appointees increased considerably" (ADB, 2005: 11). Under the Ramos administration, a blueprint for "reengineering" the bureaucracy in 1995 was created. Estrada's administration, on the other hand, introduced the Rationalization Program of 2001 through Presidential Committee on Effective Governance (PCEG). It was also during this time that Executive Order No. 165, "Re-Engineering the Bureaucracy for Better Governance Program," was laid down, aiming to strengthen and streamline the bureaucracy.

The present administration of Macapagal-Arroyo administration continued the program to streamline the bureaucracy, but has yet to adopt an overall agenda for reform. In the Medium-Term Philippine Development Plan (MTPDP) 2001~2004, the present administration adopted the "Reengineering the Bureaucracy for Better Governance Program" of the Estrada administration. PCEG was likewise reactivated upon Arroyo's assumption to office. It serves as the ad-hoc body that shall be the focal point of administrative reforms in the civil service. On October 4, 2004, the Department of Budget and Management (DBM) and the Civil Service Commission (CSC) pursued the Rationalization Program as mandated in EO 366. This executive order directs all departments/agencies of the executive branch to conduct a strategic review of their operations and organizations for purposes of focusing government purposes on its vital functions and channeling government resources to these core public functions, and improving the efficiency of government services, within affordable levels, and in the most accountable manner (EO 366). Obviously, the rationale of the program is effectiveness, efficiency, economy, and accountability.

[Table 8-6] Overall Status of the Rationalization Program ([Net of Entities Exempted], As of April 30, 2008)

Status	Depts	OEOs/Other Agencies	GOCCs	Total No.	%
Plans Submitted to DBM	17	27	36	80	75%
1. Approved					
1.1 Attached agencies	2	16	9	27	25%
2. Evaluation completed but	5*			5*	
not yet approved	3			3	3%
3. Under evaluation	8	10	19	37	34%
3.1 Complete submission	3		4	7	7%
3.2 Partial submission	1	1	4	6	5%
4. Plans returned for revision					
Plans for Submission to DBM	3	1	24	28	26%
Total	20	28	60	108	100%

Source: DBM (2008).

Table 8-6 shows the overall status of the implementation of the rationalization program in the Philippines as of April 30, 2008. Four years after the implementation of EO 366 in 2004, only 17 out of 26 department agencies of the government, 27 OEOS/ other government agencies, and only 36 out of more than 100 GOCCs in the country have submitted their rationalization plans. Out of the 80 submitted rational plans, only two department-level offices and nine GOCCs were approved; three departments have been evaluated but are not yet approved. Out of the 44 plans (complete and partial submissions) that are under evaluation, eight departments and 19 GOCCs have completed their submission while three departments and four from the GOCCs have made partial submissions. There were also plans returned for revision-one from a department agency and four from the GOCCs. DBM is awaiting submissions from three departments and 24 GOCCs.

According to David (in DGF, 2005), the rationalization program has abolished 102 agencies which have existed since the 1950s and has transferred 23 agencies from the Office of the President to other departments. Among those departments, agencies which have completed their rationalization programs were Department of Health, Department of Social Welfare and Development, Office of the Press Secretary, Department of National Defense and from the GOCCs, the National Development Company, Garment and Textile Export Board, and Sugar Regulatory Commission, to name a few.

The attempt to reorganize, reengineer, and restructure the bureaucracy is palpable in the programs and projects of the different Philippine Presidents. Different administrations may assign various terms but everything boils down to the following overriding goals of rationalization, namely, efficiency, effectiveness, economy and even transparency and accountability. This is also an attempt to face the challenges of overlapping functions, lack of acceptance and commitment by affected entities, red-tape and corruption inherited from past administrations. The risks of trimming down the bureaucracy, according to the former Chairman of the Civil Service Commission (CSC), Karina Constantino-David, is losing good people and retaining those who have nowhere else to go. Another challenge is how to minimize the use of discretion. Streamlining the bureaucracy has always been accused of being saddled with political intervention (David in DGF, 2005).

Decentralizing the Bureaucracy

Decentralization became a popular strategy among both developed and developing nations in the 1960s. It "came on the heels of the development administration bandwagon that gained currency in the late 1950s" (Reyes, 1993: 251). It is a trend that has occurred in many parts of Asia: in Indonesia, in 1998, and in Pakistan, Korea, Japan and the Philippines in 1991. This is another major initiative that can be observed in the continuing attempt to design and develop a more responsive public administration in the country.

The devolution strategy in the country is said to have three phases which started in the passing of the Local Government Code of 1991. Phase 1 (1992~93) involved the transfer of functions that varied by type of local government. Phase 2 (1994 ~96) gave LGUs time to adjust to their formal responsibilities (Brillantes, 2003). Phase 3 (1997 onward) expected a more stable system to focus on building capacity, with technical assistance from national agencies. Currently, the decentralization process is in the final phase. Although this phasing is said to have not been systematically followed with problems that continue to persist (World Bank, 2005), the Philippine decentralization has also been described as "going smoothly," with intergovernmental fiscal systems institutionalized, workers transferred from central ministries to local governments without significant disruptions, and service delivery functions taken up by local government officials with reasonable effectiveness (World Bank, 2005).

Issues and Challenges in Decentralization and Local Governance

There are a lot of issues and lessons learned for the past seventeen years of decentralization in the country. Although there are a number of best practices in local government, records also show that there are a lot of shortcomings and pitfalls in local governments.

A series of Rapid Field Appraisals conducted by the Local Development Assistance Program (LDAP) and later the Governance and Local Democracy (GOLD) Program through independent consultants reveals some of the major findings of their study conducted from 1992~1998.[9] These include lack of

9) The conduct of RFAs was supported by the United States Agency for International Development(USAID), the Department of Interior and Local Government, the

financial resources, lack of technical capacities/capabilities of LGUs, too many politics, problems in inter-governmental relations, a perceived absence of a central coordinating body, and devolved agencies at both the central and local levels continued to be very slow in responding to the operational demands of decentralization. Other issues and concerns include local fiscal matters like the inequitable computation of Internal Revenue Allotment (IRA), the issue of recentralization of devolved services (health: management of local hospitals) and environment (cadastral survey), abolition of the Sangguniang Kabataan (SK) (Youth Federation), integration to social services as part of its components, untapped corporate powers of LGUs, among others.

Accountability, Graft and Corruption

"Public administration and politics have generally both become the whipping boy of a disenchanted public over the poor performance of government" (Reyes, 1993: 241). Politicians suffer from public displeasure over poor government performance. Horror stories of graft and corruption, red-tape, mismanagement, rigidity and other bureaucratic failings have become common. Pervasive corruption cripples the Philippine economy and hinders efficient governance. Corruption inhibits growth and development, distorts access to services for poor communities, undermines public confidence in the government's will and capacity to serve the public, deters trade and investments, reduces revenues, increases costs, and propagates wasteful allocation and use of scarce resources.

Coronel (2000) considers corruption in the Philippines as a daily fare in the Philippine newspapers. It also "provides meat for the congressional exposés that keep the political mill grinding" (Coronel, 2000: vii). In a survey conducted by

---

leagues of local government of the Philippines, and other stakeholders.

Transparency International (TI), the Philippines is perceived as more corrupt in 2008 than in 2007. The 2008 Corruption Perceptions Index (CPI) showed that the Philippines got a score of 2.3 in 2007—down by 0.2 points from 2.5 in 2007. This year's score is the lowest for the country since 1995 when the first CPI was devised as a tool for a country's resolve to fight corruption. The Philippines ranked 141st—along with Cameroon, Iran and Yemen—and was behind most of its ASEAN neighbors but fared better than other than ASEAN countries like Timor-Leste (145th with a grade of 2.2), Laos (151st with a rating of 2.0), Cambodia (166th with a score of 1.8), and Myanmar (178th with a score of 1.3). Singapore got the fourth highest score from among 180 countries with a 9.2 rating, while Malaysia got 5.1 to land on the 47th place. Thailand is in the 80th spot with a rating of 3.5 while Vietnam is in the 121st place with a score of 2.7; Indonesia, which ranked lower than the Philippines last year, was in 126th place with a rating of 2.6.[10)]

The prevalence of corruption effects negative consequences to institutions and to the people at large. The undermining of the rule of law and violating political legitimacy are included among the social costs of corruption. Disadvantaged people are deprived of fair treatment, which increases poverty. Corrupt practices jeopardize the welfare of the people. Tolerating corruption encourages negative and poor bureaucratic behavior of anyone in the service. In effect, it ruins public trust and confidence in the government. Corruption undermines the merit and fitness system and inhibits civil servant motivation to uphold integrity. Finally, corruption leads to poor quality programs, projects and services, and ineffective, inefficient and un-accountable administration.

10) See HYPERLINK http:// www.transparency.org).

Public Administration Education in the Philippines

There was a strong "American flavor" (Pilar, 2008: 308) to the Philippine Public Administration as a discipline. As a field of study, it was brought to the country under a bilateral agreement with the United States through the Bell Report on June 15, 1952. With the assistance of the University of Michigan, the Institute of Public Administration (IPA) was established at the University of the Philippines (UP).

The College has changed its name four times, from Institute of Public Administration (IPA) to School of Public Administration (SPA) to College of Public Administration (CPA) and now the National College of Public Administration and Governance (NCPAG). Conscious of its role in nation-building, the College has expanded its scope from governmental management to the broader concerns of governance, including the roles of the private sector and civil society. Today, NCPAG is a center for research, academic instruction, and in-service training and consultation services. It houses the Center for Public Administration and Governance Education (CPAGE), Center for Local and Regional Governance (CLRG), the Center for Policy and Executive Development (CPED), and the Center for Leadership and Community Development (CLCD).

After putting up the requirements of the Bell Mission, Danilo R. Reyes (2003) accounts for 35 bachelors' and 33 masters' degree candidates of Public Administration in the school year 1953~1954 (Reyes, 2003: 55-58). Eventually, IPA became a graduate school in the 1960s and it was later named as the College of Public Administration (CPA). The College began to create its niche in public administration education and its programs have always been benchmarked by other schools in the nation as well.

The College was later named as the National College of Public

Administration and Governance (NCPAG) and it has continually enriched the public administration discipline in theory, content and methodology, through periodic review and fine-tuning of its academic courses, thereby ensuring their continuing relevance to the needs of the times. Its substantive concerns encompass: (1) improvement and reform of management in its traditional domain, the civil service, (2) the recognition and enhancement of the public roles and management approaches of other organizations involved in governance, and (3) the creation and strengthening of partnership and/or collaborative engagements among state institutions, private sector and civil society organizations. Its teaching-learning techniques span the whole spectrum, from concept to application, covering the development and assessment of participation and community-based process, the integration of service-learning and volunteerism, and the application of high-end technologies and/or their combinations. It has published the *Philippine Journal of Public Administration* since 1957, which is a quarterly publication of international circulation and stature (Alfiler and Nicolas, 2007: xv-xvi).

The programs of the College enjoyed wide acceptance and support not only from national but international agencies. Its services included professional and policy advice as well as technical assistance to a wide variety of local, national and international institutions. It was a resource not only to the Asian region but also to the regions within the country. The success of NCPAG has inspired other institutions to offer the same courses in public administration.

Considered as both a professional and scholarly discipline, Public Administration was generally offered in the Philippines mostly at the graduate level. PA as a field of study has flourished all over country with many academic institutions all over the country offering degree programs in PA and/or its equivalent. By 1971, there were a total of 15 colleges and universities offering public administration. In 1986, De Guzman's accounts more than sixty (60) universities, colleges and schools offering PA degree program (De Guzman, 1986). A study in 2004 revealed that after almost two decades this number of PA degree offering institutions more than tripled. Based on the 2003~2004 listing from the Commission on Higher Education (CHED),[11] there were about 263 PA degree offerings both in the undergraduate and graduate levels in 219 public and private institutes, schools, colleges and universities all over the country (Ricote, 2004: 4-10).

According to Pilar (2008) the escalating number of public administration institutions throughout the country was abetted by at least two mechanisms. The first was the UP Management Education Council (UPMEC) that developed an interdisciplinary graduate course in management, Master of Management (MM). The said course offered opportunities for specializing in business, educational or public management (with the assistance of the Colleges of Business Administration, Public Administration, and Education). It allowed for specialized education according to the disciplines, yet providing common courses (e.g. Research, the Ecology of Administration, and Human Behavior in Organization (HBO). UPMEC provided the forum for developing textbooks in these common courses. The MM program was delivered to regional units of the University of the Philippines System in Baguio, Clark, Los Baños, Tacloban, Iloilo and Cebu. It was this program that became the vehicle for NCPAG to extend technical assistance to other schools offering the MPA program, the precursor of ASPAP. The growth and advancement of Philippine PA study and practice through the years can also be largely attributed to the linkages and collaborations between and among PA education institutions in the country and in the Asian

11) See HYPERLINK http://www.ched.gov.ph.

region, all with the UP-NCPAG at the forefront (Ricote, 2008).

Apart from being a pioneer, NCPAG serves as a think-tank and a capacity-builder. It has organized in 1979 the Association of Schools of Public Administration in the Philippines (ASPAP)-a non-stock national organization of college and universities in the Philippines offering public administration/management education programs. ASPAP currently has 120 member schools covering the country's regions from Northern to Southern Philippines. The organization has been spearheading programs geared toward the development and improvement of public administration/management education through the conduct of public lectures on public administration, "roving" seminars on instructional methodologies, evaluation of curricular programs, and distribution of knowledge products to member schools (ASPAP website). UP-NCPAG houses the ASPAP Secretariat which functions under the administrative supervision and guidance of the ASPAP Board composed of the representatives from all ASPAP regional chapters. There are sixteen chapters all over the country including the National Capital Region (NCR), Autonomous Region of Muslim Mindanao (ARMM), Cordillera Administrative Region (CAR) and the CARAGA Region. Along with the UP-NCPAG, the ASPAP is the principal Philippine PA organization consistently pursuing the critical tasks of developing and strengthening the field of PA in the country[12] (Ricote, 2008).

Also, NCPAG, through the initiatives of Carlos Ramos and Raul P. De Guzman in 1960 (both served as dean of the college), co-founded the Eastern Regional Organization for Public Administration (EROPA), an organization of states, groups and individuals in the general area of Asia and the Pacific. This is an international organization which consists of State members in the Region, institutions in the area such as institutes or schools

12) See HYPERLINK http://www.aspap.org.ph for more information about ASPAP, Inc.

of public administration, universities, agencies and municipal corporations and individuals whose achievements in the field of governance and public administration are recognized. This initiative is in response to a collective goal of developing countries to promote regional cooperation in improving knowledge, systems and practices of government administration to help accelerate economic and social development. It was the first organization in the region to be devoted to the development of public administration in order to advance the economic and social development of countries in Asia and the Pacific. EROPA has been accredited by the United Nations Online Network of Regional Institutes for Capacity Building in Public Administration and Finance (UNPAN) as one of the latter's Online Resource Center (ORCs). The organization also publishes *Asian Review of Public Administration (ARPA)*.[13)]

There are presently ten State Members in the Organization. These are: India, Indonesia, Islamic Republic of Iran, Japan, Republic of Korea, Nepal, and People's Republic of China, Philippines, Thailand, and the Socialist Republic of Vietnam. As of December 2003, membership in EROPA (academic and government) has a total 112. Individual membership (academicians and public administration practitioners) has a total of 489 (EROPA website).

The governance framework embraced by public administration, not only in the Philippines but in the rest of the developing world starting in the 1990s, also ushered in another collaborative venue growth and expansion for Philippine PA study and research. The Network of Asia-Pacific Schools and Institutes of Public Administration and Governance (NAPSIPAG), initiated through a technical assistance project of the Asian Development Bank (ADB), was officially established in a launching conference

13) See HYPERLINK "http://www.eropa.gov.ph" www.eropa.gov.ph.

in Malaysia in 2004. Similarly, the UP-NCPAG plays a major role in NAPSIPAG as a member of its steering committee (Ricote, 2008).

The NAPSIPAG was essentially established to respond to the need of public administration and governance professionals in the region to explore innovations, breakthroughs, best practices and solutions to issues such as poverty alleviation, peace administration, human rights, etc. It holds an annual international conference where faculty and scholars from various schools and institutes of PA in the region convene to present their public administration and/or governance papers, research, cases and innovations on a particular topic or theme.[14)]

Fields of PA in the Philippines

The study of Public Administration in the Philippines did not follow the conventional path and has evolved independently from political science. Various fields have grown out of the study of public administration in the country from the traditional subfields of organization and management, public personnel administration, public fiscal administration, and local government, new subfields have emerged, namely, policy analysis and program administration, public enterprise management, voluntary sector management, spatial information management.

NCPAG's pioneering work in voluntary sector management as a field of specialization which has developed expertise over the years through its institutional linkages, its research on the profit sector and its immersion in civil society organizations has been widely recognized. It has been at the forefront in conducting pioneering research studies in areas like negative bureaucratic behavior in the country and in Asia (referred to as graft and corruption during the Martial law period), with its research

---

14) See HYPERLINK "http: www.intanbk.intan.my/napsipag."

interest in this area being sustained by looking at the broader issues of accountability and ethics in public service. Other research interests include administrative policies, processes and reforms to include administrative culture, reorganization and management studies, red tape and decentralization studies, political policies, processes and reforms such as decision-making, leadership, citizenship, election processes, participation, and re-democratization; regulatory management such as studies on public enterprises, competition policy; program/sector studies such as health, population, agriculture, agrarian reform from the perspective of a general policy or program implementation or both; and overarching policy issues such as disaster management, poverty alleviation, social reform agenda, minimum basic needs, women's and children's concerns (Alfiler and Nicolas, 2007: xvii).

Public Administration Research in the Philippines

Cariño (2007) reveals in her paper the research interests of Filipino scholars in different fields of public administration. Most research dealt with traditional public administration; personnel administration, organization and management, fiscal administration, agency studies and the Philippine Administrative system; new public administration, which includes ethics and accountability, public service values, alternative delivery systems, public policy and program administration were also offered and research in the governance tradition like democracy and bureaucracy, citizen participation, decentralization among others.

Challenges in Public Administration Education

In 2004, the Commission on Higher Education (CHED) and the Fund for Assistance to Private Education (FAPE) conducted a national comprehensive evaluation of graduate education in the

Philippines (EGEP) throughout sixteen regions of the country. Findings of the study revealed that only one school has an outstanding ranking. A small minority (1.93%) of the PA graduate programs is categorized as "superior," while alarmingly more than half (57.9%) were rated "fair, low or poor."

The FAPE study highlights the fact that while PA offerings have burgeoned all over the country, which is an attestation that the PA discipline has already established itself in Philippine higher education, a lot remains to be done (Ricote, 2008). From the results, Pilar (2008: 310) expressed that the findings appeared to "exhibit robustness along several measures" like the increasing enrollment. The recommendations of the FAPE study are basically the same concerns raised by De Guzman in 1986, i.e. to improve the quality of public administration in the country. The following has to be considered: (1) getting faculty members who have both academic qualifications and administrative experience, (2) the production and use of indigenous teaching materials, (3) the use of innovative teaching methods and techniques, and (4) the formulation of more relevant models and analytical concepts.

Regulation and Accreditation of PA Programs

In his study, Ricote (2008) concludes that the regulation and accreditation of PA programs in the country is still far-reaching. While there exists accrediting institutions the Association of Christian Schools and Colleges Accrediting Agency, Inc. (ACSC-AAI), the Philippine Accrediting Association of Schools, Colleges and Universities (PAASCU), the Philippine Association of Colleges and Universities Commission on Accreditation (PACU-COA) and the Accrediting Agency of Chartered Colleges and Universities of the Philippines, there remains an increasing concern as to how these various accrediting bodies build-up, update, and strengthen the applicability and relevance of their individually-defined methodologies of quality assessment. Or do they have commonly-defined standards that would warrant comparability among them? Or is there a body that assures this and/or makes sure this is consistent with the very intention of accreditation? He also argues that classifying PA programs according to accreditation levels, presumably based on proven measures of quality standards, obviously does not necessarily solve the increasing number and continued operation of "fair," "low" and "poor" PA programs which continue to attract students, precisely because of their "less rigid" and/or "flexible" requirements.

The other major concern of PA degree offerings in the country is its lost identity. The discipline of public administration has been characterized as one with a continuing "identity crisis." To a certain extent, it was that "identity crisis" that served as theme that led to the emergence of the New Public Administration movement in the 1970s. Rutgers (1998) argued in "Paradigm lost: Crisis as Identity of the Study of Public Administration," that public administration lacks an "epistemological identity." In the Philippines, Reyes (2003) revisited the so-called "identity crisis" of public administration initially raised by various scholars of the discipline in his various writings (Brillantes and Fernandez, 2008).

Pilar (2008) identifies Philippine PA with the social sciences. It is bolstered by the fact that it has been accorded membership in the Philippine Social Science Council (PSSC) along with history, anthropology, psychology, sociology, political science, economics, and linguistics and even ahead of other "applied" fields such as demography and mass communications. PSSC membership requires a strong academic (teaching and research) program and the publication of a professional journal with the alumni or professional association (Pilar, 2008: 308). PA is also identified with other commonly offered degree programs such as Teacher Education and Business Administration. There is a tendency that this will result in a "passing and superficial" look at PA as a field of study without a clear delineation of its distinct character and temperament compared to other "generic" fields of management and/or administration (Ricote, 2008). One thing is sure though, Public Administration is multi-disciplinary in nature and can blend with any other disciplines. These and a few other concerns about the current policy and practice of accrediting and classifying PA degree offerings all over the country, justify the need to revisit accreditation as a mechanism to measure and define quality standards.

Prospects for the Future and Conclusion

Philippine public administration as a field of study and practice has undergone a number of "identity crises and conceptual challenges from within and without. It has been buffeted by reforms and movements to broaden its concerns, to emulate private management, to adopt new technology, and to recognize a disaggregated and de-centered (yet globalized) world in which the state and government are just two of the important actors" (Ocampo, 2008: 91). The Philippine civil service is indeed an institution of paradoxes. It is an institution of continuity amidst instability, finding the ability to deliver amidst perceptions of ineptitude, corruption and red tape. The civil service will continue to face more challenges and newly demanding tasks but there are several ways forward.

Karina David, former chair of the Civil Service Commission (CSC), was blatant in saying that although the CSC has a degree of autonomy it, being a constitutional body, is "invariably influenced, assisted, or impeded by the administration" (David, 2004: 3). Upon her assumption to office, David diagnosed the current state of affairs of the civil service and revealed some of its weaknesses. First, the civil service is a "monster" of an organization with complex substructures and no identified coordinating unit. This is the very reason why the efforts (including money) of the government are often wasted. Second, inefficient systems and procedures exist because people in the government are primarily concerned with adherence to rules rather that with the attainment of desired results. Third, the bureaucracy is prone to red tape and is without a deeply imbedded culture of customer satisfaction. Fourth, appointments, from executive positions, to job orders and contracts of service, continue to be vulnerable to patronage politics. Fifth, mechanisms to make people accountable for their actions are almost non-existent. Sixth, the function of human resource management (HRM) in government is not accorded due importance (David, 2005: 4-8).

The above gaps became a backdrop for the CSC in coming up with an intervention to respond to the challenges. This intervention includes seven major paradigm shifts in the relationships, behavior, and values in the bureaucracy: (1) shifting the role of civil servants from followers to sources of expertise and institutional memory for government; (2) creating a bias for service values in the recruitment of civil servants; (3) fostering a visionary role for the third level bureaucracy; (4) insulating appointments and promotions in the third level from politics and the discretionary exercise of presidential prerogative; (5) shifting of management style in government units from the hierarchical authoritarian supremacy to a participatory and consultative system of management; (6) a reorientation toward assistance to clients rather than rigid regulation in the operating environment of government; and (7) shifting in essential relationships of the Civil Service with other branches of the government (David, 2004: 811).

David's predecessor, former Civil Service Chair Corazon de

Leon, employed a six point strategy towards a vision of building human resources for good governance. She believed that good governance is the foundation of sustainable development and strong civil servants make good governance possible. For these reasons, she adopted a six-point strategy which included the following: (1) ensure that the government attracts, develops, motivates, and manages a service-intensive corps of public servants; (2) set and maintain policies and standards of merit for performance-based, disciplined, and accountable governance; (3) empower employee organizations and agencies to develop and institutionalize worker friendly human resource management systems that promote professionalism, integrity, and productivity; (4) initiate, develop and propagate programs that will ensure continuous learning, value orientation, professional growth, and career advancement; (5) strengthen our capabilities to become a resource center for governance innovation and human resource development; and (6) build strong partnerships with other resource centers (both local and foreign), decentralize front line operations, and acquire appropriate and updated technologies.

Earlier still, former Civil Service Chair, Patricia Sto Tomas, offered six key result areas for a revitalized public sector. These were: (1) effective and efficient administration of justice, (2) better public service, (3) professionalized bureaucracy, (4) empowered government unions, (5) improved external relations, and (6) the provision of appropriate and adequate management and support services. Using current CSC Chairman Ricardo Saludo's MERCI as a battle cry is an initial step in the right direction. MERCI stands for morale, efficiency, responsiveness, courtesy, and integrity. These values appropriately build upon the gains of previous CSC administrations, address the imperatives as incorporated in the proposed Civil Service Code, and also recognize the principles of good governance. But MERCI may conceivably be pushed a little further and be expanded to MERCI-PIPP, where PIPP stands for "Partnerships and Insulation from Political Partisanship."

The history of public administration and political development in the Philippines gave us a glimpse of what transpired in the past and how these experiences contributed or diminished the institutional capacity of the Philippine bureaucracy. It also showed us that some of the characteristics of the present bureaucracy have their enduring characteristics and have persisted for so long despite criticisms and even disapproval. Like most public organizations, how the Philippine bureaucracy functions is determined largely by its goals and priorities (the bigger challenge here is continuity and sustainability of programs, projects and activities), processes which the people expect them to utilize, the amount of power they are vested with, the level of accountability that they exercise, and the outputs they are expected to deliver (Alfiler, 1999). The Philippine bureaucracy will continue to face tougher challenges as the government gets worse or gets better. As Corpuz (1957: 248) put it, "the bureaucracy will be as big as the as the tasks of society; it will be as complex and fascinating as the nation itself; it will be afflicted with the Filipino's weaknesses, but it will benefit from their virtues. If only administration and politics can blend together well, there could be a good harvest for public administration and governance."

The experience of the local governments are replete with rich lessons in practical ways, however, there are a number of lessons that can be drawn in the paper. The long road to achieving the real essence of local autonomy is paved with problems and issues, including the lack of financial resources, unclear and uncoordinated policies, control of the national government, and unfunded mandates, among others. The next step is for the central government and the local government to orchestrate their efforts to come up with synchronized goals to realize their collective interests in nation-building, or perhaps to fully devolve the services immediate to the needs of the local governments. This is the very essence of the principle of subsidiary.

Public administration education in the Philippines is barely 56 years old and it still has a long way to go. The schools of Public Administration in the Philippines must prepare for various challenges of globalization which have brought more choices to students wishing to enroll in practical courses like nursing and care giving. With the assistance of international networks like EROPA and NAPSIPAG, academic institutions in the country shall continue to improve public administration instruction and research to produce the best and the brightest students in public administration. In the future, these students will be the occupants of important positions in the bureaucracy.

References

Alfiler, Ma. Concepcion P. (1999). *Philippine Administrative System.* Quezon City: University of the Philippines Open University.

Alfiler, Ma. Concepcion P. and Eleanor Nicolas (2007). "Philippine Administrative System. Quezon City: University of the Philippines Open University. "*In Public Administration Plus Governance Assessing the Past, Addressing the Future.* Quezon City: UP National College of Public Administration and Governance.

Asian Development Bank (2005). *Country Governance Assessment.* Manila, Philippines: ADB.

Asian Development Bank (2000). "Civil Society and Non Government Organizations." In *To Serve and to Preserve Improving Public Administration in a Competitive World.* ADB.

Brillantes, Alex B. (1987). "Decentralization in the Philippines." In *Philippine Journal of the Public Administration* vol. 31 (2). Quezon City: UP National College of Public Administration and Governance.

Brillantes, Alex B. (1995). "Development Administration in the Philippines." In Ledivina V. Cariño, ed. *Conquering Politico-Administrative Frontiers, Essays in Honor of Raul P. de Guzman*. Quezon City: UP College of Public Administration.

Brillantes, Alex B. (2003). *Innovations and Excellence*. Quezon City: Center for Local and Regional Governance. National College of Public Administration and Governance. University of the Philippines Diliman.

Brillantes, Alex B. and Maricel T. Fernandez (2008). "Is There a Philippines Public Administration, Or Better Still, For Whom is Philippines Public Administration." *Philippine Journal of Public Administration* 52 (2-4). (April-October).

Cariño, Ledevina V. (1992). *Bureaucracy for Democracy. The Dynamics of Executive-Bureaucracy Interaction During Governmental Transitions*. Philippines: UP College of Public Administration, International Center for Economic Growth and Philippine Institute for Development Studies (PIDS).

Cariño, Ledevina V. (1995). "Development Administration in the Philippines." In *Conquering Politico-Administrative Frontiers, Essays in Honor of Raul P. De Guzman*. UP College of Public Administration and the University of the Philippines Press.

Cariño, Ledevina V. (2007). "From Traditional Public Administration to the Governance Tradition: Research in NCPAG, 1995~2002." In *Public Administration Plus Governance Assessing the Past, Addressing the Future*. Quezon City: UP National College of Public Administration and Governance.

Cariño, Ledevina V., Iglesias, Gabrielle R., and Ma. Fe Mendoza (1998). "Initiatives Taken Against Corruption: The Philippine Case." A paper prepared for the Programme for Accountability and Transparency (PACT) of the Management Development and Government Division, United Nations Development Programme.

Coronel, Sheila S, ed. (2000). *Betrayals of Public the Trust: Investigative Reports on Corruption*. Quezon City: Philippine Center for Investigative Journalism.

Corpuz, Onofre D. (1975). *Bureaucracy in the Philippines*. Quezon City: UP Institute of Public Administration.

Civil Service Commission (2004). *Inventory of Government Personnel*.

Available online at http://www.csc.gov.ph/cscweb/2004IGP_stat.pdf. (Retrieved May 8, 2008).

De Guzman, Raul P. (1986). "Is There a Philippine Public Administration?." *Philippine Journal of Public Administration* 30 (4).

De Guzman, Raul P., Alex Brillantes, and Arturo Pacho (1988). "The Bureaucracy." In *Government and Politics of the Philippines*. Oxford New York: Oxford University Press.

David, Karina (2004). "The Civil Service Commission: Rebuilding the Integrity of the Bureacracy." In Domingo, Ma. Oliva, ed. *The Civil Service Commission and the Commission on Audit: Self Assessments and Alternative Views and Assessments (2001~2004)*. Third UP Public Lecture Series on the Philippine Presidency and Administration, vol. 3. Quezon City: University of the Philippines.

David, Karina (2005). "Combating Corruption in the Philippines: Are we Plundering Our Chances or Doing it Better?," Diliman Governance Forum *Working Paper Series No.* 2.

David, Karina (2007). "Self Assessment: Civil Service Commission," A UP Public Lecture Series held at UP NCPAG.

Diliman Governance Forum (2005). "Reinventing, Reengineering and Reorganizing the Bureaucracy in the Philippines: Why We Should be More Hopeful." *Working Paper Series No. 1*. Quezon City: UP-NCPAG.

Elliott, Gary (2008). "Antidote for Philippine Corruption available at http://philippines.suite101.com" Philippines.

Endriga, Jose N. (1997). "Comparative Studies of National Civil Service Systems Country Paper: The Philippines." Paper prepared for presentation at *Civil Service Systems in Comparative Perspective*, School of Public and Environmental Affairs, Indiana University, Bloomington, Indiana, 5-8 April.

Endriga, Jose N. (1985). "Stability and Change: The Civil Service in the Philippines." *Philippine Journal of Public Administration* 29 (2) (April): 132-154.

Galing Pook. Foundation (2001). "Promoting Excellence in Urban Governance." *Kaban Galing*.

Heady, Ferrel (1957). "The Philippine Administrative System: A Fusion of East and West." *Philippine Journal of Public Administration* 1 (1) (January): 27-45.

Kim, Pan Suk et al. (2005). "Toward Participatory and Transparent Governance: Report on the Sixth Global Forum on Reinventing Government." *Public Administration Review* 65 (6), (November-December): 646-654.

Manila Times (2008). *The civil service they wish our country would have one day.* 31 August. http://www.manilatimes.net/national/2008/aug/31/yehey/top_stories/20080831top2.html

Nolledo, Jose (1996). *The 1991 Local Government Code with Basic Features.*

Pilar, Nestor N. (2008). "Philippine Public Administration: From Classical, to New Public Administration, To New Public Management." *Philippine Journal of Public Administration* 52 (2-4).

Philippine Commission (1900). *Report of the Philippine Commission.* Washington, DC: GPO.

Philippines, Republic of (1987). Constitution *of the Republic of the Philippines.*

Philippines, Republic of (1991). Republic Act 7160. *The Local Government Code of 1991.*

Philippine Panorama (2002). "The Civil Service Commission: Redefining Service Delivery in Government." *Philippine Panorama.*

Reyes, Danilo R. (2003). "The Study of Public Administration in Perspective: A Passing Review of the Development of the Discipline." In Bautista et. al, eds. *Introduction to Public Administration: A Reader.* Quezon City: UP National College of Public Administration and Governance.

Reyes, Danilo (1993). "The Identity Crisis in Public Administration Revisited: Some Definitional Issues and the Philippine Setting." In Bautista et al., eds. *Introduction to Public Administration: A Reader.* 1st Edition. Quezon City: UP College of Public Administration.

Reyes, Danilo R. (1993). "The Tensions in the Troubled Bureaucracy: Reform Initiatives in Public Organizations and Service Delivery Systems." *Philippine Journal of Public Administration* 37 (3).

Ricote, Eleazar E. (2004). Poverty Alleviation and Role of Public Administration in the Philippines. *Paper Presented in the Launching Conference of the Network of Asia Pacific Schools and Institutes of Public Administration and Governance (NAPSIPAG).* Kuala Lumpur,

Malaysia.

Ricote, Eleazar E. (2008). "Philippine Public Administration as a Field of Study Enduring and Emerging Areas, Challenges and Prospects." *Philippine Journal of Public Administration*, 52 (2-4).

Sto Tomas, Patricia A., and Mangahas, Joel V. (2002). "Public Administration and Governance: How Do They Affect Government Efficiency and Effectiveness?," A paper presented at the International Conference on Public Administration Plus Governance; 21~23 October 2002, Manila Hotel, Philippines.

The Fund for Assistance to Private Education (2004). A Quality Assessment of Three Graduate Programs: Teacher Education, Business Education and Public Administration. *Evaluation of Graduate Education in the Philippines (EGEP)*. Manila: Commission on Higher Education.

World Bank (2005). *East Asia Decentralizes Making Local Government Work*. Washington DC.

Major Websites Related to Public Administration and Public Governance in the Philippines

National Statistics and Census Board: http://www.nscb.gov.ph

Civil Service Commission: http://www.csc.gov.ph

Eastern Regional Organization of Public Administration: http://eropa.org

Commission on Higher Education: http://ched.gov.ph

Transparency International: http://www.transparency.org

Association of Schools of Public Administration in the Philippines, Inc.: http://www.aspap.org.ph

National College of Public Administration and Governance: http://www.up-ncpag.org.

Network of Asia-Pacific Schools and Institutes of Public Administration and Governance:

http://www.intanbk.intan.my/napsipag

Commission on Audit: http://www.coa.gov.ph

Chapter 9 Thailand

Toni Ivergard and Brian Hunt

Introduction

The shape, structure, and functions of the modern day Thai public administration began in the mid-late nineteenth century (Bunnag, 1977). Two monarchs, King Mongkut (1804~1868; r1851~1868) and his son King Chulalongkorn (1853~1910; r1868 ~1910), are widely regarded as vanguards of the modernization of the country (Baker and Phongpaichit, 2005: 47ff). The reforms of King Chulalongkorn, the fifth monarch of the Chakri dynasty, are known as the Chakri Reformation (see: Samudavanija, 1997). From the 1870s, the monarch began centralizing the bureaucracy into a pyramid structure. From the 1890s onward the government infrastructure was overhauled and streamlined and moved towards a professional bureaucracy of trained civil servants (Mead, 2004). Appropriately, the Thai word for civil servant is kharatchakan, servant of the king. In the early 1900s, a Civil Service School was established in Bangkok and, from 1890 to 1919 the numbers of salaried officials at the lower ranks grew from 12,000 to 80,000 (Phongpaichit and Baker, 1997: 251). The Civil Service Act of 1928 represented another step in professionalizing the bureaucracy; henceforth, civil servants were hired on merit rather than through patronage (Bowornwathana and Poochareon, 2005). However, empirical research conducted in the 1970s discovered "inbreeding" in a career in government service, such that younger generations of civil servants followed parents and older family members into the profession, and that family background mattered (Dhiravegin, 1975: 1). Thai public administration structures and bureaucrats are parts of "the state within the state" (Samudavanija, 2002: 66; also see: Boworn-wathana, 1994). Against this cultural background, impetus for change has come from "outside and approval from above" (Siffin, 1966: 247). Thailand's current monarch, King Bhumibol Adulyadej (Rama IX of the Chakri dynasty) continues the traditions of his grandfather and great-grandfather by taking a keen interest in issues of national and social development.

In the past, there existed a rather strong village democracy with an informal administration lead by a headman (descriptions of the workings of village democracy can be found in: Keyes, 1979; Moerman, 1979; Young, 1979; Nelson, 1998). In the later years of his reign, King Chulalongkorn revived the concept of local government at the village level. Under the provisions of the Siam Local Administration Act of 1897 each hamlet was presided over by an elder or headman (Pu Yai Baan). The elders of a collection of hamlets elected a senior elder (called a Kamnun) who was responsible for overseeing their collective hamlets. Those seeking office as a Kamnun must already hold the position as a Pu Yai Ban. This role as a sub-district headman still exists today (Nelson, 1998: 33). Until 1991, post-holders stayed in office until they reached the prescribed retirement age of civil servants at age 60, although this was amended by the Local Administration Act to a period of five years (Nelson, 1998: 54). Kamnun are regarded as both local representatives of the central government and of the people who elected them to office (Nelson, 1998: 54-55). As the central bureaucracy has grown in size and strength, the roles of the village headman have slowly faded (Moerman, 1979; Nelson, 1998; Nartsupha, 1999).

Recent Social and Political Change in Thailand

On October 27, 1997, amid continued fallout from the 1997 Asian financial crash, Thailand gained a new constitution. Thailand's sixteenth constitution in the sixty-five years since the inception of constitutional monarchy in June 1932, this was variously called "The People's Constitution" and "The Anti-corruption Constitution." This constitution represented a change of direction in the governance of Thailand. It established the ground rules for "participatory democracy in which citizens have greater opportunities to chart their destiny" (Klein, 1998: 4). The new constitution emphasized public participation and encompassed issues pertaining to human rights. In the period since 1997 there have been many positive changes in the Thai public administration, including moving from its traditional role of provider of public services to facilitator of national human and social development (Teokul, 1999). There has also been an increase in public participation in the political processes, a wider interpretation of civil society, and the rise of professional politicians (McCargo, 2002: 59; Connors, 2003; Ockey, 2004). The Eighth National Plan (1997~2001) was drafted by people from "all walks of life and from all regions" (Teokul, 1999: 365).

Developing the Competencies of Public Administrators: The Rightsizing Project

From 1992~1993 the Office of the Thai Civil Service Commission (OCSC) engaged in a collaborative research and training project. Collaborating partners provided technical assistance and financing. The project conducted a comparative study of the public administration workforce through close analysis of socio-economic data up to and including the year 1990. An intended feature of the project design was to develop the decision-making skills of public administration officers using actual data about public administration work and institutions. However, a frustrating element of the project was the difficulty of obtaining reliable comparative data in sufficient quantity to study changes over time and differences between countries. A subsequent study aimed to redress this deficiency. The project "Right Sizing of the Thai Public Sector," focused on the implementation of Human Resource (HR) planning at the regional level. The Office of the Thai Civil Service Commission (OCSC) hosted this study, with external support and part-funding by the World Bank. One of the current authors again was project consultant and composed the final report (Ivergard, 2003).

In rightsizing the Thai public administration infrastructure, the main issue is not the total size (number) of resources. Rather, the key issue is how these resources are distributed and utilized. Resources include both the human resources (such as suitably qualified and experienced dentists, doctors, and teachers) and physical resources (such as equipment, clinics, and resource materials). Of crucial importance is the geographic distribution of the public administration workforce. Thailand is a country with a concentrated capital city, Bangkok. Greater Bangkok (including its environs) is home to almost 20 percent of the total population. Current data suggests that of a total national population of over 62 million the population of Bangkok is approaching 12 million. This figure may be an underestimation as not everyone working and residing in the capital cares to register with the relevant authorities (A thriving black economy ensures that people have places in which to hide and reasons for wishing to remain out of sight of officialdom.)

In spite of some worthy initiatives and concerted effort for improvements over the past few years, there remains a sizeable inequity in the distribution of public administration personnel. Greater equity in resource availability can still be made in the healthcare and, to some extent, the education sectors. Bangkok and the surrounding urban and semi-urban areas are very well resourced with personnel while many rural areas suffer an acute shortage of public services. The gap between Bangkok and the rest of the country is also increasing, particularly in the area of public health. For example, official (1998) data from the Ministry of Public Health suggests that residents in the Bangkok Metropolitan Area (BMA) have access to 8,212 physicians out of a national total of 17,510 (Ivergard, 2003: 49). For a country like Thailand such inequity is a major problem. And, somewhat ironically, methods chosen to alleviate the problem are likely to aggravate it. For example, compulsory work contracts oblige young, inexperienced, healthcare professionals to work, often alone, in outlying regional locations. This is less than optimally efficient. Not only does this system misuse human resources and neglect the continued need for supervision, it is also dangerous for patients as well as for the medical professionals themselves.

Accelerating Modernization: The Civil Service Act of 2008

In 2008 a new Civil Service Act was promulgated by King Bhumibol. This act aims to improve or accelerate the pace of modernization within the government bureaucratic infrastructure. The intention is to mobilize civil servants' commitment so that the organizations of the public administration can more readily support national development. The 2008 Civil Service Act focuses on developing the relevant human resources in competencies to manage and operate the mechanisms of public administration. The spirit of this re-focusing is shown in Tables 9-1 and 9-2. These tables indicate the main differences between the traditional Thai public administration organizations and the

[Table 9-1] Changes in Structure and Culture

Traditional	Reformed
Centralized infrastructure	Decentralized infrastructure
Work to satisfy the boss	Work to satisfy the population
Empire building	Rightsizing
Work focus on efficiency	Work focus on effectiveness
Bureaucratic orientated	Productivity/service orientated
Hierarchical structure and work processes	People (customer) orientated process (service minded management)

Source: adapted from Nophakoon (2008).

intended reformed configuration of these organizations.

Table 9-1 lists the proposed changes in structure and culture. Key issues are a higher degree of decentralization, a focus on involvement of citizens, and a size of the public administration infrastructure to fit its needs of service delivery (i.e. rightsizing). The new structure focuses on effectiveness and on service delivery, and is people-oriented. Table 9-2 contrasts the traditional and reformed work processes in public administration. The intention is to shift the focus of administrative work towards more flexible, people-oriented approaches based on rational decision-making.

In the areas of work process reform, the emphasis is on flexibility and empowerment of individuals. The intention is to reward high-value performance and team-working. This envisages a rational, goal-oriented organizational culture which has a system of performance-based budgeting. These changes are expected to promote a culture of entrepreneurship. The workplace will also become highly competitive. Each of these components is a radical change from past mindsets and practices.

The Deputy Secretary-General of the office of the Thai Civil Service Commission, Somphoch Nophakoon, has provided a

[Table 9-2] Changes in Work Processes

Traditional	Reformed
Work governed by rules, regulations and Standard Operating Procedures (SOPs)	Flexibility, empowerment, and individual initiative
Lack of adaptability, change and risk taking	Performance based rewards, team working, and cooperation (networking)
Rigid culture, many customary practices	Rational culture and goal orientation
Incremental budgeting practices	Rational/performance based budgeting
Mindset of being "bureaucrats" or "technocrats"	Developmental cultures of entrepreneur and/or opportunistic approach
No competitive atmospheres at work	Strong competition with others and him/herself (performance improvement)

Source: adapted from Nophakoon (2008).

[Figure 9-1] Four Pillars Supporting Development

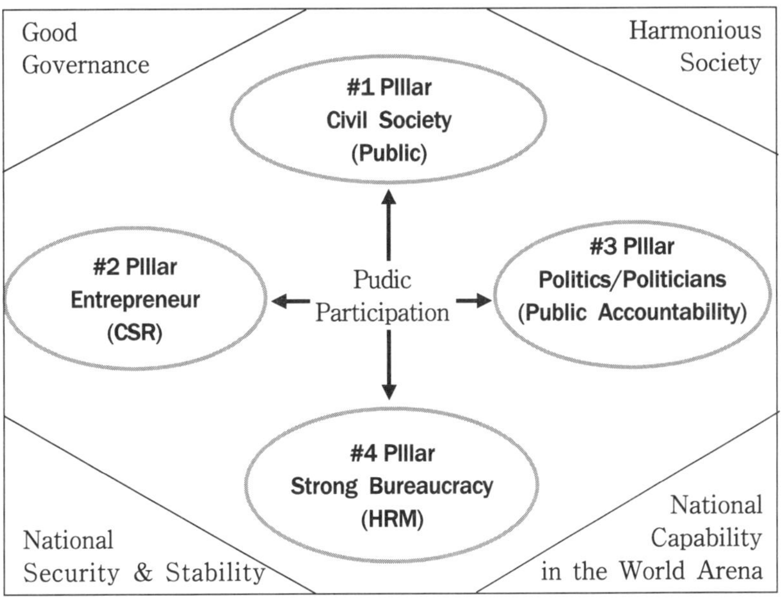

Source: adapted from Nophakoon (2008).

vision of the future of the Thai public administration. This is comprised of four pillars and is strongly supported by good governance, a harmonious society, national security and stability, and national capabilities and trust in the world arena. These key pillars of society uphold the delivery of public services to the nation. This vision is illustrated in Figure 9-1.

Naturally, this vision requires changes in the public management work process. Traditional approaches have been inward-looking and organizational-centric. Production of public goods and services has been a factor of supply, in turn driven by resource allocation somewhat disconnected from external realities. Figure 9-2 shows the envisaged changes in the public management infrastructure and its work.

The traditional work process configuration has been from 1 →2→3. That is, the process is driven by existing processes and procedures in the administrative mechanisms. In the near future the new public management of Thailand is expected to

[Figure 9-2] Focus of Changes in New Public Management in Thailand

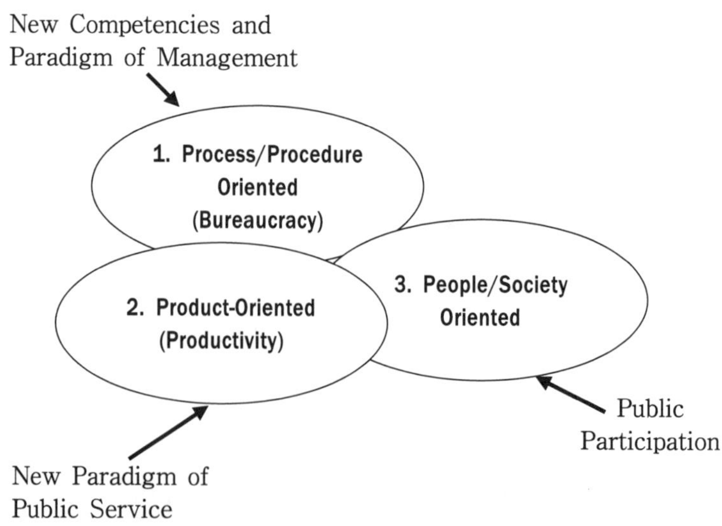

Source: adapted from Nophakoon (2008).

reverse this process of change to 3 → 2 → 1. In other words, the new configuration would be demand-driven. The starting point for reform would be society at large and people-oriented processes of change, including public participation. Pressure from this direction would drive the public administration towards a production-oriented way of working and provide the new paradigm for the provision of public services. The final step will be processes and procedures based on new competencies of public administration employees and new paradigms of public administration management.

Delivering Public Services: Myriad Moments of Truth

In his classic book *Service Management*, Richard Normann (1984) defines the concepts "Service" and "Service Management." To a large extent, service is a social and psychological phenomenon which occurs in the interaction between people (the service provider and the consumer). From the perspective of provider and receiver, "… perceived quality is realized at the moment of truth" (Normann, 1984: 21). In Richard Normann's (1984) model of service, it is essential to set an organizational-wide framework for the management of good service. Critical issues are management systems and processes, sufficient and appropriate internal resources, and an organizational culture that can be (or become) customer focused. These issues become even more critical in a public administration where key tasks involve the creation and delivery of public services. For managers, key concerns are communication, competencies (inherent or to be trained), and processes that are not contrary to customer service and quality. It is helpful to have a clearer idea of the composition and completion of the moment of truth– especially as those involved are likely to perceive the process and outcome differently. This issue is highly relevant for the work of public services in which state organizations are tasked to deliver quality service at a manageable (justifiable) cost.

In public administration work there can be a service focus paradox which gives rise to a conflict between two sides of service. On the one side is the need to provide good service to end users. Each instance of service provision is a moment of truth. As recipients of service, consumers have a symbiotic relationship to the service provider. On the other side is the need to provide key functions of the public administration, for example related to community care, law enforcement, and the judiciary. Delivery of public services incorporates a number of stake-holders who play various roles including predicting what public services are required and to what levels of quality. This role is traditionally undertaken by government departments who may or may not also engage in specific service delivery.

Invariably, there will be a continued need for public administrators, and there will always be a need for managing the moment of truth in the context of public service delivery. The myriad moments of truth show the complexities of managing the delivery of public services. Each moment of truth is fundamentally unique but each has features in common. As described above, at each moment of truth a front-line employee provides service in a real-time situation. Ideally, in this situation the wants and needs of consumers are to be satisfied. In reality, there are often shortfalls in the quality of service delivery. The moment of truth allows the consumer an opportunity to evaluate service quality by comparing expectations (based on hearsay, recommendation, or prior experience) with the reality. The service provider can treat each moment as an opportunity for immediate consumer feedback. Innovations in service often emanate from encounters with consumers at the moment of truth (see, for example, Beaujean et al., 2006).

The delivery mechanisms for public services are often

monopolistic. A lack of comparative service delivery makes it difficult for the consumer of the public service to evaluate quality. This is one feature of public service that is invariably more complex (and more difficult to manage) than service delivery by private (commercial) organizations. One possible means to address this issue in public administration is to create competitive systems within public administration. In this unconventional model, parallel service providers are established within the public administration. The user/citizen thus has choices about which service to use based on on-going data reporting quality and performance measurement. Local government agencies can allocate different benefits to the service providers according to performance and user/citizen preference (measured over time).

The concept of the moment of truth also has relevance in an automated version of service provision. While the majority of moments of truth continue to be face-to-face, service delivery facilitated by technology can bypass the personal encounter. Here, at the moment of truth, the consumer has to relate to a technological interlocutor (a machine) instead of meeting a human service provider. The moment of truth will fall flat if the technology interface is difficult to understand and is perceived as "unfriendly" by the user/consumer. Thus, usability is a key concept in the design of a technology interface with people (Hunt et al., 2004). Incorporating the moment of truth into technology design would help obviate this. In e-government, where a large proportion of the total population of a nation should be able to access the automated government services, high usability becomes even more critical. If not, the users may become disheartened with the public services.

Public Administration: the Potential of Automation

Technology is capable of delivering quality the first time, every time, but technology is reliant on a human element. Human actors tire, need rest breaks, and have "bad" days. For an organization, the goal is to focus on the service tasks and ensure systems are in place to use feedback for purposes of improvement. Effectively managed, the organization and its processes can expect satisfied customers. The importance and the social and psychological characteristics of "moments of truth" create a demand for a different type of management to be successful and efficient. Critical to success is the internalization of thc "good service concept" in all parts of the service organization. Organizational leadership in public administration organizations have a responsibility to create and put in place the internalization of good service. Management must demonstrate the same high quality service to all its personnel as the service it expects to be provided to its external customers. This is not an easy task, and is a goal that many organizations fail to achieve.

There are examples where public service delivery utilizes technology for self-service. In many countries, a marked success story has been the electronic provision of revenue services *via* the internet to access relevant information, guidance, and documents. In a developing economy such as Thailand, the e-revenue service has been lauded as a successful transition towards providing service electronically to citizens (see Ivergard et al., 2003). Other areas of automation are related to what is often called e-citizen or efforts to improve and facilitate the process of democracy in the society. Local direct participation can become a reality in decision-making, can become an everyday reality, and can bring the citizen closer to the processes of public service provision (Ivergard and Hunt, 2005).

This means a creation of a new type of moment of truth which, until now, has been unavailable in the traditional representative parliamentary democratic system. Instead of elaborate time-consuming representative processes the citizen can access on-line and be a part of real-time decision processes (Sandberg et al., 2004). Another area where technology is applied to public service is e-learning (Ivergard and Hunt, 2005). The phenomenon of e-learning is a complex application of the moment of truth. The phenomenon has two distinct levels. At the one level is the on-line provision of training to public administration officers and employees. Here the focus is development, training, upgrading of skills and development of new skills. At the second level is the interface between the citizen and the public provision of education, advice, and support for citizens.

The Private Sector as a Model for Public Administration

There is a great need for creative thinking in the establishment of alternatives for the provision of public service delivery. In some areas of public administration work, it is relatively straightforward to copy models from the private sector. In other areas it is much more difficult, not to mention politically charged. It is comparatively easy to privatize public organizations which engage in similar activities to those found in the private sector. A basic condition for this similarity should be that they are driven by similar structures of incentives; for example, there ought to be a natural competitive market for the service. In other areas, this similarity is neither apparent nor obvious. Typical examples of the latter are: court of law, the police force, prison service, national defense, basic education, health services, and public infrastructure. Using education as an example helps illustrate the difficulties. In an ordinary competitive marketplace, the well-informed customer can theoretically choose between many alternatives by assessing the price-quality differential. Before paying for the goods or service, a customer can often try out alternative offerings. In education, this is not possible as the time-lag between service delivery/use and benefit is often measured in lengthy time periods such as months or years. Payment is usually in advance of the services and, given the postponed personal and public benefits of education, the quality of the services cannot be experienced or judged beforehand. Obviously there is still scope for private initiatives in education. The historical record shows that many innovations in education have occurred in the private sector. Similarly, privatization in the education sector must seek to stimulate new ways of education practice.

In essence, there are valid rationales for making public organizations to be more like the private sector. However, the differing natures and perspectives of these two types of organization bring different problems in service delivery. In many aspects of service delivery (whether public or private sector) there seems to be inherent difficulties in nurturing a creative climate and culture of high level of service. This is especially so in the provision of public services.

In the reforms after the 1997 crisis, Thailand had very ambitious plans for outsourcing special parts or large sectors of public services. However, the outcome was very limited and, if this strategy is to be followed, there is more that can be achieved. International experiences clearly indicate that outsourcing of public enterprises, particularly in areas of energy and telecommunications, can be of great national economic benefit. The outsourcing model also brings benefits in the form of improved service for customers and working conditions and remunerations for personnel. The Swedish public enterprise Vattenfall used to be a national producer and distributor of energy. Today it is one of the largest European energy companies with a very high profile in CSR, environmental protection, and CO_2 trading. The company is also involved in some of the most advanced searches for alternative energy sources, e.g. very deep underground storage of CO_2 and also wave power production in the North Sea. In telecommunications there are many success stories from Europe, particularly Scandinavia and UK. Thailand has been discussing reforms in these areas but without much evident progress. Another area which has been discussed as potential for outsourcing are different labour market measures (e.g. skills training for the unemployed), but again, progress has been scant.

Future Challenges for the Thai Public Administration

Among the many challenges facing the Thai bureaucracy is to move away from a highly centralized structure to one where the state administrative mechanisms are more decentralized (see: Simananata and Aramkul, 2002; Bowornwathana, 2006). Efforts to do so have been made in the past (see, for example, Fry, 1983). In 1975, following the 1973 civil disorders, the government of Kukrit Pramoj introduced a program of decentralization with the aim of developing the economies of provincial districts (*tambol*). Called, in English, the Tambol Development Program, the aim was to encourage villages to be self-sufficient and engage people in local decisions under the leadership of a district council (Fry, 1983; Mutebi, 2004). Under current initiatives, regional officers are encouraged to shoulder more responsibility, especially in decisions such as infra-structure planning and investment that directly affect their region.

Since the 1980s, downsizing the size of the public bureaucracy has been a Thai government policy (Bowornwathana, 2000: 394). Various administrations, e.g. Prem Tinsulanonda (1980~1988) and Anand Panyarachun (1991~1992), have tried to control the size of the bureaucracy by restricting the numbers of employees (Malee, 2003). Another key concern is the reform of the "cultural and public values" of public officials (Painter, 2004: 379). Following the 1997 Asian financial crisis, the World Bank and IMF stipulated as part of its loan package that the Thai government undertake reforms to its public bureaucracy (Bowornwathana, 2000). Inroads were made by the government of Thaksin Shinawatra which was deposed in a military coup on September 19, 2006. Programs were set up to provide provincial governors with CEO-type training as a step towards creating executive government (Mutebi, 2004; Painter, 2006). Further issues include reforming work routines and building capacity (Malee, 2003). There have been initiatives to reform the budgetary processes and restructure the processes of personnel management (Painter, 2006: 35ff).

In developing HR competencies in the Thai civil bureaucracy, the rightsizing simulation model provided the backdrop of future possibilities and the data gathering acted as part of the planning process. A widespread organizational infrastructure is likely, in fact, to be a number of different systems and cultures: not one organization, but many. Indeed, the Thai bureaucratic infrastructure has been described as "highly fragmented" (Nelson, 1998: 32). Over time and distance, work practices and rationales may diverge from expected norms. Again this is a feature of the Thai bureaucracy with its central hub in the capital city Bangkok and many regional outstations. In an attempt to match words with actions, we would like to see more radical change in the Thai public bureaucracy as a contributory component towards reforms in the public bureaucratic system and its infrastructure. The direct involvement of local level public officials is likely to help ensure that the change is of more relevance to daily work, is more enduring over time, and, ideally is more focused on the needs of users of the public services. Participative reforms, including action research, could be expected to lead speedily to more radical improvements in public administration.

Reforming a public administration infrastructure is an area where a government must take initiatives and provide initial funding. With this done, the work of design, construction, management, and quality assurance can be carried out by private sector organizations. This situation is not dissimilar to other parts of the public administration. Each part of the sector needs its own model. It is inappropriate to merely replicate the infrastructure from one part of the system and expect it to work effectively in other situations. From this perspective, it is especially difficult to find acceptable solutions for such public services as law enforcement, prisons, and national defense.

Earlier in this chapter we illustrated and described an ambitious and elegant vision for the future of the Thai public administration. To achieve this vision, it is a necessity that all parties involved in the Thai society contribute in a powerful process of alignment of effort. It is also a necessity for all stakeholders to understand that this is a long-term process which will take decades to accomplish, so long as there is a continuation of focus and effort.

Acknowledgements

Each author contributed equally to this chapter. The authors gratefully acknowledge the invaluable assistance of Somphoch Nophakoon, Deputy Secretary General of the Office of the Civil Service Commission (OCSC) and the staff of OCSC who cooperated in some of the projects described in this chapter. We also thank the large numbers of Thai officials who participated in the various projects described here. Without their enthusiasm, commitment, and effort, the projects would not have been possible and this chapter would not have been written. Apart from the publications that we cite, we were able to consult a number of internal documents. These helped us put isolated events into perspective-in effect, helping us to see the large picture. Needless to say, the ideas and opinions expressed in this chapter are our own.

References

Baker, Chris and Phongpaichit, Pasuk (2005). *A History of Thailand,* Cambridge, Cambridge University Press.

Beaujean, M., Davidson, J., and Madge, S. (2006). "The Moment of Truth in Customer Service," *McKinsey Quarterly,* 1: 62-73.

Bowornwathana, Bidhya (1994). "Administrative Reform and Regime Shifts: Reflections on Thai Polity," *Asian Journal of Public Administration,* 16 (2): 152-164.

Bowornwathana, Bidhya (2000). "Governance Reform in Thailand: Questionable Assumptions, Uncertain Outcomes," *Governance: An International Journal of Policy and Administration* 13 (3): 393-408.

Bowornwathana, Bidhya (2006). "Autonomisation of the Thai State: Some Observations," *Public Administration and Development* 26, 27-34.

Bowornwathana, Bidhya and Poocharoen, Ora-Orn (2005). "Managing Reforms: The Politics of Organizing Reform Work," *Public Organization Review: A Global Journal* 5: 233-247.

Bunnag, Tej (1977). *The Provincial Administration of Siam, 1892-1915,* Kuala Lumpur, Oxford University Press.

Connors, Michael Kelly (2003). "Goodbye to the Security State: Thailand and Ideological Change," *Journal of Contemporary Asia* 33 (4): 431-448.

Dhiravegin, Likhit (1975). "The Power Elite in Thailand: a General Survey with a Focus on the Civil Bureaucrats," *Asian Journal of Social Science* 3 (1): 1-15.

Fry, Gerald W. (1983). "Decentralization as a Management and Development Strategy: A Thai Case Study," *Asian Journal of Public Administration,* December, 5 (2): 44-53.

Hunt, Brian, Burvall, Patrick and Ivergard, Toni (2004). "Interactive Media for Learning (IML): assuring usability in terms of learning content," *Education + Training* 46 (6+7): 361-369.

Ivergard, Toni (2003). *Rightsizing? Rightsizing and Simulation Model,*

Final report to the Office of the Civil Service Commission (OCSC), Bangkok, February.

Ivergard, Toni, Hunt, Brian and Rodsutti, Michita (2003). *E-learning and E-government in the Thai Public Sector*, paper presented at the International Ergonomics Association XVth Triennial Conference, August 24th~29th, Seoul, Korea.

Ivergard, Toni and Hunt, Brian (2005). "Towards a Learning Networked Organization: Human capital, compatibility and usability in e-learning systems," *Applied Ergonomics* 36: 157-164.

Keyes, Charles (1979). "Local Leadership in Rural Thailand," chapter 1 (section III) in Clark D. Neher (ed.), *Modern Thai Politics: from Village to Nation*, Rochester, Vt., Schenkman Books (revised edition, 1983).

Klein, James (1998). "The Constitution of Thailand 1997: A Blueprint for Participatory Democracy," The Asia Foundation Working Paper Series, Number 8, March.

Malee, Surapong (2003). "Reform, Routines and Capacity Building: Civil Service Policy Change in Thailand," *International Public Management Journal* 6 (3): 343-369.

Mead, Kullada Kesboonchoo (2004). *The Rise and Decline of Thai Absolutism*, Abingdon, RoutledgeCurzon.

McCargo, Duncan (2002). "Security, Development and Political Participation in Thailand, Alternative Currencies of Legitimacy," *Contemporary Southeast Asia*, April, 24 (1): 50-67.

Moerman, Michael (1979). "A Thai Village Headman as a Synaptic Leader," chapter 2 (section III) in Clark D. Neher (ed.), *Modern Thai Politics: from Village to Nation*, Rochester, Vt., Schenkman Books (revised edition, 1983).

Mutebi, Alex (2004). "Recentralizing while Decentralizing: Centre-Local Relations and 'CEO' Governors in Thailand," *The Asia Pacific Journal of Public Administration* 26 (1): 33-53.

Nophakoon, Somphoch (2008). "Case of the Thai Civil Service Act of 2008: Lessons Learned," paper presented at the regional conference Halong City, Vietnam, September 25th~26th.

Nartsupha, Chattip (1999). *The Thai Village Economy in the Past*, Chiang Mai: Silkworm Books (English translation by Chris Baker and Pasuk Phongpaichit).

Nelson, Michael, H. (1998). *Central Authority and Local Democratization in Thailand*, Bangkok, White Lotus Press.

Normann, Richard (1984[2000]). *Service Management: Strategy and Leadership in Service Business*, Chichester, UK, John Wiley and Sons (3rd edition).

Ockey, James (2004). "State, Bureaucracy and Polity in Modern Thai Politics," *Journal of Contemporary Asia* 34 (2): 143-162.

Painter, Martin (2004). "The Politics of Administrative Reform In East and Southeast Asia: From Gridlock to Continuous Self-Improvement?" *Governance: An International Journal of Policy, Administration, and Institutions* 17 (3), July: 361-386.

Painter, Martin (2006). "Thaksinisation or Managerialism? Reforming the Thai Bureaucracy," *Journal of Contemporary Asia* 36(1): 26-47.

Phongpaichit, Pasuk and Baker, Chris (1997). "Power in Transition: Thailand in the 1990s," chapter 2 in Kevin Hewison (ed.), *Political Change in Thailand: Democracy and Participation*, London, Routledge.

Samudavanija, Chai-Anan (1997). "Old Soldiers Never Die, They are Just By-passed," chapter 3 in Kevin Hewison (ed.), *Political Change in Thailand: Democracy and Participation*, Routledge Books.

Samudavanija, Chai-Anan (2002). "State-identity Creation, State-building and Civil Society," chapter 3 in Craig J. Reynolds (ed.), *National Identity and its Defenders: Thailand Today*, Chiang Mai, Silkworm Books.

Sandberg, K. W., Ivergard, T. K. B., and Vinberg, S. (2004). "E-service to Citizen and Companies in Rural Areas," *International Journal of the Computer, the Internet and Management*, 12 (2) (Special Issue: Proceedings of the International Conference on eLearning for Knowledge-based Society, August, 2004): 213-223.

Siffin, William J. (1966). *The Thai Bureaucracy: Institutional Change and Development*, East-West Center Press, University of Hawaii, Honolulu.

Simananata, Sima and Aramkul, Aim-On (2002). "Decentralization of Recruitment in Thai Civil Service," *International Recruitment and Selection Strategies*, unpan1.un.org.

Teokul, Waranya (1999). "Social Development in Thailand," *ASEAN Economic Bulletin* 16 (3): 360-373.

Young, Stephen B. (1979). “The Northeastern Thai Village: A Non-Participatory Democracy,” chapter 3 (section III) in Clark D. Neher (ed.), *Modern Thai Politics: from Village to Nation*, Rochester, Vt., Schenkman Books (revised edition, 1983).

Chapter 10 Singapore

M. Shamsul Haque

Introduction

Since the early 1980s, there have been significant changes in the nature of the state and its governance worldwide. These unprecedented changes or reforms are largely guided by the assumption of state failure and market superiority, the objective of replacing the role of the state by non-state actors, and the agenda of transforming public governance based on market-oriented principles, policies, and standards (Clarke and Newman, 1997; Haque, 2002a). The existing literature tends to characterize these paradigmatic changes often in terms of neo-liberal ideology, new economic policy, and new public management (NPM). Despite the advocacy of such a market-driven perspective for several decades, the current global economic crisis–which demonstrates the severe vulnerability of the market system requiring a massive rescue operation through state intervention–should encourage scholars, experts, and practitioners to reexamine such a parochial perspective.

In studying these contemporary developments in governance and public sector management, East and Southeast Asian countries represent one of the most relevant and appropriate regions–because some of these countries are globally known for economic success stories achieved predominantly through a state-centric framework, and they have recently experienced severe financial crisis in the aftermath of their market-led reforms. Within the region, Singapore is an interesting case due to its widely known rapid development and highly competitive economic performance led by the state, which has also embraced market-driven reforms despite its well recognized public sector efficiency. It is also useful to examine the Singapore case because it is often cited by international agencies as an exemplar for developing countries to learn from its economic success, administrative efficiency, corruption control, electronic governance, and so on (Lam, 2000; Wirtz and Chung, 2001).

However, there is a relative lack of comprehensive education and in-depth studies in public governance and administration in Singapore. In terms of education in public administration, the number of institutions and the scope of academic degrees are quite limited. There are two institutions under the National University of Singapore (NUS) – including the Lee Kuan Yew (LKY) School of Public Policy and the Department of Political Science – which respectively have a Master's degree program and a graduate major or specialization in pubic administration. The scope of mainstream course offerings in this field, however, is less adequate compared to similar academic schools and departments in the USA. A similar situation can be observed in the case of Minor in Public Administration at Nanyang Technological University (NTU). Although the Civil Service College covers diverse components of public administration, it is mostly guided by need-based practical training rather than in-depth academic studies.

With regard to research and publications, the overall status is even weaker in terms of the number of scholars focusing directly on public administration in Singapore. For example, the LKY School has only a couple of faculty members dealing with topics related to public administration or public policy in Singapore, and their topics are also on very narrow policy issues such as social security, pension, and immigration. Similarly, at NTU, there are hardly any scholars working on mainstream public administration in this country except some limited research on the political dimension of policy-making. Some scholars affiliated with the Department of Political Science at NUS have been more actively engaged in studying some major topics in Singapore's public administration, including administrative reform, bureaucratic corruption, policy changes, and so on. In terms of overall quality, however, most of these studies have often been too descriptive (compilations of reports or documents without adequate analysis), and too narrow and technical (focusing largely on micro-administrative matters without relating to macro-level governance). The existing studies are also less relevant to the newly emerging framework of public governance and administration in Singapore guided by market-driven principles, structures, and strategies.

This article attempts to examine and analyze the formation and transition in the macro-level state and governance as well as the micro-level public administration in Singapore. More specifically, after a brief historical overview, it examines the formation and framework of the state and governance in Singapore (including state formation, political structure, state-market nexus, state-society relations, politics-administration linkage, and administrative apparatus), explicates the major domains of reforms in public administration (such as public policies, roles, structures, and organizations), and explains some contemporary challenges and future prospects related to public governance and administration in Singapore.

Formation of the State and Governance in Singapore

Singapore is a small city state with a geographical size of only 692.7 sq km and a population of 4,492,150 (World Factbook, 2007). It has been able to remain politically stable and harmonious despite its multi-ethnic, multi-religious, and multi-lingual composition, including Chinese (76.8%), Malays (13.9%), and Indians (7.9%) in terms of ethnic background (World Factbook, 2007; Haque, 2004). In spite of such a geographic limitation, heterogeneous population, lack of natural resources, and other constraints, Singapore has become one of the most developed city-states. Within a period of four decades, its per capita GDP (PPP) reached US$49,900 (8th in the world) and the value of its foreign reserve and gold increased to US$160 billion (8th in the world) (World Factbook, 2008). These economic achievements have been based on the initiatives and efforts pursued largely by the state. This section examines the formation and framework of such state governance in terms its political system, its linkages with economy and society, and its administrative apparatus.

First, one of the major determinants of the nature of the state and governance in postcolonial countries is their long colonial history. In the case of Singapore, British colonial rule, which lasted for 140 years (1819~1959), significantly shaped its politics, administration, and economic outlook (Lam, 2000). After emerging as an autonomous entity within Malaysia in 1963, and its separation from Malaysia in 1965, Singapore continued with the British colonial legacy in the formation of its overall governance. In particular, after gaining autonomy from the colonial rule, Singapore adopted the British system of parliamentary government led by the People's Action Party (PAP). The PAP has ruled the country since 1959 with an absolute majority of more than 90% of the elected parliamentary seats (currently 82 seats out of 84) (Lam, 2000; Wirtz and Chung, 2001). In line with the overall parliamentary model of governance, the parliament in Singapore uses various standing committees to carry out its duties, including the House Committee, the Committee of Selection, the Public Accounts Committee, the Estimates Committee, and so on (Tay, 1999).

For the executive branch, the president (now elected directly by people for six years) is the ceremonial head of state that appoints the prime minister and other ministers from the majority party, appoints top officials like judges and advisory board members, and can exercise veto power over the appointment of high-ranking civil servants (Wirtz and Chung, 2001; Cima and DeGlopper, 1989). However, the primary executive power lies with the prime minister and other cabinet ministers who are collectively responsible to the parliament (PWC Consulting, 2002). Currently, in addition to the prime minister, there are two deputy prime ministers, one senior minister, and other cabinet ministers in charge of ministries such as Education, Health, Community Development, Youth and Sports, Defense, Foreign Affairs, Home Affairs, Information, Communications and the Arts, Law, Manpower, Environment and Water Resources, National Development, Transport, and Trade and Industry.

One unique feature of Singapore's parliamentary government is that the PAP has ruled the country for four decades without any strong formidable opposition from other smaller and weaker political parties, including the Workers' Party, the Singapore Democratic Alliance, and the Singapore Democratic Party. As a result, despite the provision of multi-party elections, the political system has been characterized as the so-called one-party-dominant system found in other Asian countries like Malaysia and Japan (unlike the Western model of democracy with occasional changes in government), which may have ensured the stable political atmosphere needed for continuing specific economic policies and programs (Lee, 2001; Vasil, 2000; Chua, 1997).

Second, with regard to the linkages between the state, economy, and market, it is largely the state led by the ruling party, which has played a dominant role in the overall economic management of Singapore. As found in other post-colonial countries, the end of colonial rule and a relative absence of private entrepreneurs created the need for the post-colonial government in Singapore to be actively involved in almost all socioeconomic sectors, including housing, education, utilities, finance and banking, telecommunications, airlines, tourism, transport, and so on. The wider involvement of government became more imperative for Singapore after the separation from Malaysia in 1965 due to the challenge it faced in establishing a viable sovereign state on such a small territory (without any natural resources) and pursuing nation-building with such a small but heterogeneous population, which led to the creation of a series of state agencies, public enterprises, and planning institutions.

Although the period after decolonization saw the process of experimentation with the liberal democratic model as well as some facets of socialist ideology in Singapore, the government immediately embraced a more pragmatic approach to economic development with the state as the dominant player in this development process (Vasil, 2000). In fact, survival, pragmatism, and rapid development became major tenets of the state's policy priority and orientation (Lee, 2001; Kong, 2000). For Yeung (2000a), as a result of this emphasis on development based on the active involvement of government agencies and institutions, the state in Singapore is often interpreted as a developmental state. For instance, in the 1960s, the government established a series of state enterprises or statutory boards such as the Housing and Development Board (HDB), Economic Development

Board (EDB), Public Utilities Board (PUB), Central Provident Fund (CPF), Jurong Town Corporation (JTC), Development Bank of Singapore (DBS), and Port of Singapore Authority (PSA) (Low and Haggard, 2000). In addition, in 1974, the government created Temasek Holdings Ltd. (THL) through which it could manage and invest in hundreds of Government-Linked Companies (GLCs). Such investment through THL expanded to major sectors like banking, telecommunications, technologies, airlines, technologies, power, port, and media; and by 2000, these GLCs came to account for 10 percent of Singapore's total output (Yeung, 2000a; Low and Haggard, 2000; LaMoshi, 2002).

Unlike other developmental states assisting the emergence of private investors and entrepreneurs, the unique feature of the state in Singapore is its greater emphasis on foreign multinational corporations (MNCs) and local GLCs rather than domestic private enterprises in pursuing economic development (Low, 2000). In recent years, however, this active involvement of the state has undergone certain changes. In discussing the major phases of state formation in Singapore, it is observed by Kong (2000) that the recent era has seen a greater emphasis on how to transform Singapore into a business hub, attract knowledge-intensive investment, and enhance the competitiveness of local companies to venture into the regional markets. All these initiatives necessitated a shift from state-centered to market-driven policies and strategies.

Third, in terms of the relationship between the people and public governance established through service delivery, despite the interventionist nature of the public sector in Singapore, the provisions for welfare services have been quite limited. However, on a closer examination, it is possible to identify some welfare-like provisions maintained by the government. In the case of housing, the government established the HDB in order to provide low-cost public housing to citizens—such state-provided housing now covers more than 86 percent of the population (Lee, 2001; Lam, 2000). In the health sector, the primary responsibility of health care lies with individuals and families in Singapore (unlike the typical welfare state), and the government is a "provider-of-the-last-resort" (Low, 2001b). The government introduced the Medisave Scheme in 1984 to enable citizens to pay for their medical care (Khan, 2001: 11). In the education sector, the government tried to upgrade facilities in Chinese schools and promote English education, and education became a central concern for the state as it put greater emphasis on the production of human resources (Lam, 2000: 401; Low, 1998: 85). The state invested quite heavily in education in order to accelerate economic growth, and the budget allocation for the sector has remained considerably high (Khan, 2001: 6; Lam, 2000: 406).

In terms of social safety nets, the scope of service provisions has been limited. For instance, there is hardly any unemployment benefit for jobless people, and it is assumed that it is better to assist unemployed people to find jobs instead of providing them free unemployment benefits (Cheung, 2000: 4). However, there are certain indirect forms of welfare assistance in Singapore, including: (1) Public Assistance Scheme for old or disabled citizens who are unable to work and support themselves; (2) Short Term Financial Assistance for short-term help in a difficult time; (3) Medifund for those who need help to pay medical bills; and (4) Back-to-work Child Care Scheme to pay for child care and children's education (Cheung, 2000: 5-7). However, the most established and widely practiced social security system is the Central Provident Fund (CPF) applicable to all citizens and permanent residents. The CPF system requires both the employers and employees in the public and private sectors to contribute specified percentages of salaries to the employees' CPF accounts, and about 50 percent of the population (citizens and permanent residents) in Singapore are such CPF account holders (Browning, 2000). The percentage of salaries contributed to such state-run personal CPF savings (which is the main source of financing housing, health care, and old-age security) may often change and vary between employees and employers depending on the government's policy shifts in response to the prevailing economic situation (Browning, 2000; Low, 2000).

Fourth, an important dimension of governance, more central to the theme of this chapter, is the framework of politics-administration relations as well as the nature of public administration in Singapore. In line with the parliamentary form of government discussed above, public bureaucracy in Singapore "is organized along Westminster lines as a career civil service subordinate and loyal to the government of the day and has been somewhat similarly rewarded for its loyalty" (Painter, 2004: 369). The origin of this model began during the colonial rule with the establishment of the Public Service Commission in 1959. The formation of this administrative system has been characterized by political neutrality, permanent tenure, centralized structure, loyalty-based attitude, and so on (Low and Haggard, 2000; Haque, 2002b).

However, the British legacy of the Administrative Service (which originated as the Malayan Civil Service) represents some degree of administrative elitism in the form of "mandarin" class (Bellows, 1985) with its considerable involvement in the policy-making process, especially in terms of its role in formulating and managing major development projects and directing economic development (Low, 2000; Jones, 2002). More importantly, since the 1980s, a considerable number of political leaders (including prime ministers and other cabinet ministers) have entered politics with civil service or defense personnel backgrounds (Bellows, 1985: 61; Hamilton-Hart, 2000: 196). This trend is much less problematic than the politicization of public administration by recruiting civil servants based on political affiliation or connection. In this regard, the Singapore government has always emphasized the principle of meritocracy (focusing on qualification, performance, and potential) and the importance of efficiency and competitiveness in public service recruitment and promotion (Quah, 1996; Jones, 1999).

In terms of scope, the *public service* in Singapore encompasses the civil service, the legal service, the police force, and the armed forces; the public sector includes all ministries and statutory boards; and the civil service covers all ministries but excludes the armed forces, state-owned enterprises, and statutory boards (DBJ, 2001; PWC Consulting, 2002). In any case, currently there are 15 ministries (including prime minister's office) and 62 statutory boards in Singapore, which are essential units of overall public administration in Singapore. Although the country does not have elected and autonomous local government institutions that constitute the significant part of public administration in most countries, the government has created a series of "parapolitical" institutions (also known as "grassroots" organizations) since the 1970s—including the Community Centres, the Residents Committees, the Citizens Consultative Committees, the Town Councils, and the Community Development Councils. The main functions of these organizations, in general, are to provide feedback to the government, disseminate policy information, enhance racial harmony, and assist community development. The members and chairmen of these centres are appointed by the government, many of them are members of the ruling party, and some of them (especially the chairmen of the Town Councils and Community Development Councils) are parliamentary members from the ruling party. As a result, these organizations fall between the political and administrative realms of Singapore.

In terms of number, there were 114,500 public sector

employees in 2002, with 63,300 working as civil servants and 51,200 as statutory board employees (PWC Consulting, 2002). According to the Singapore Department of Statistics (2008: 47), the total number of such government employees was 60,240 in 2002, which gradually increased to 62,792 in 2005 and to 65,832 in 2007. The civil service represents the British tradition of the prominence of the generalists belonging to the Administrative Service (Jones, 1999). The whole civil service is classified into four divisions: Division I includes the generalist administrative and professional grades; Division II covers the executive and supervisory grades; Division III comprises the clerical, technical and other support grades; and Division IV includes workers involved in manual or low-level routine work.

Public Administration in Singapore: Issues and Changes

As mentioned at the beginning, in recent years, there have been considerable changes in the nature of state governance and public administration based on certain market-oriented principles, structures, and standards. In Singapore, although the political domain has not undergone any considerable change (with regard to the form of government, one-party dominant system, and politics-administration relations), there have emerged some major reforms related to the macro-level government policies and public sector roles, indicating a reconfiguration of the state-economy-market linkages. More noticeable changes have occurred, however, in the public service itself, especially in its structure, management, finance, and so on.

First, compared to the relatively rigid control over economic management under the developmental state in earlier decades, the government has recently pursued more market-friendly initiatives like deregulation, divestment, and liberalization, and allowed the private sector to participate in various sectors that were traditionally managed by the state (Haque, 2002b; Low, 2000). Based on the recognition of the current global and national atmosphere, the state began to show some signs of retreating from economic control by creating the Public Sector Divestment Committee (PSDC) in 1986 and privatizing certain GLCs (Low, 2000; Phua, 1991). The main agenda of the PSDC was to provide guidelines and time-frame for divestment, determine the related terms and conditions, and formulate programs for divesting state-managed companies. It planned in 1987 to divest about 600 companies and 40 statutory boards over a ten year period through methods such as deregulation, privatization, and liberalization (DBJ, 2003: 6). Some of the divested state enterprises include the DBS, National Iron and Steel Mills, Sugar Industry of Singapore, Singapore Textile Industries, Singapore Food Industries, Petroleum Corp of Singapore, the PSA, and Singapore Telecommunications (DBJ, 2003: 6). The government has also liberalized other sectors (e.g. finance, banking, and insurance industry) by allowing more foreign ownership and relaxing market restrictions (Low, 2000); and contracted out certain services for various enterprises like the HDB, the Land Transport Authority, and so on (DBJ, 2003).

It has been observed, however, that compared to some other countries, the process of privatization and liberalization has been relatively slow and state-managed in Singapore since in certain instances, the privatized assets or shares have remained under government control (Low and Haggard, 2000). For Low and Haggard (2000), through the major GLCs, the state has been able to retain its economic management, ownership, and control to a great extent. Despite this relatively slow pace of market-led reforms in Singapore, the initiatives toward divestment, deregulation, liberalization, and contracting out represent a considerable shift from the earlier developmental-state model exercising greater regulation and control over the country's economic management.

Second, in line with the global shift in the role of the state in economy and society, Singapore has experienced certain major changes in the role played by the state. As discussed above, the state pursued a leading role in socioeconomic affairs through its various institutions, which encompassed major sectors such as the sugar and textile industries, electricity, transport, housing, communications, and so on (Yeung, 2000a). Beyond the economic sphere, such a role also affected sociopolitical arenas such as trade unions and community or grassroots organizations (created and supervised by the government) (Low and Haggard, 2000). Although this expansive role of the state still continues, in line with the current international trend, the government has adopted some reform measures that indicate certain moderation or easing of such an interventionist role played by the state in this country. In any case, an early change in the state's economic role was reflected in the government's initiative to shift from its direct economic intervention based on a rigid bureaucratic structure to a more indirect commercial form of organizations such as public corporations and companies (Lam, 2000: 404). Recently, the government has introduced the aforementioned pro-market policies (divestment, deregulation, and liberalization) that also represent a gradual retreat of the state's economic role and the increasing role of local and foreign private investors in various sectors (Shameen, 2000).

In addition, since the early 1990s, the government has been interested to redefine the role of public bureaucracy as a facilitator of market forces rather than a regulator of business enterprises (Lam, 2000; Low, 2000). Although the state was usually business-friendly in the past despite its extensive intervention in various sectors discussed above, more recently it has become quite proactive to enable the business sector to play a more leading role–examples include the government's effort to ease business licenses, import and export procedures, corporate taxes, and so on (RBAP, 1999). This gradual move toward a greater role played by the market forces has not been reversed even after the Asian financial crisis in the late 1990s, and the government has continued to emphasize the integration of its national economy with the global market (Lam, 2000). However, it is observed that the overall pace of withdrawing the interventionist role of the state has been relatively slow in Singapore. For Shameen (2000), Singapore needs to do more in terms of further privatization and deregulation of entities such as HDB, TV network, Singapore Power, and so on.

Third, certain reform measures adopted in Singapore have direct implications for its public service ethos. Since the early 1980s, the government has been trying to adopt an employee-centered public management, which has eventually culminated into the so-called PS21 (Public Service for the 21st Century) initiative introduced in 1995, which resonates other initiatives like Singapore 21 and Manpower 21 (Lee, 2001). However, PS21 represents a more serious attempt on the part of the government to transform the way the public service functions and serves people—its main thrust is on institutional ethos such as innovation, well-being, quality, and customer service. There are four major specific components of PS21, including: (1) Staff Well-being (staff welfare, recognition, appreciation, and challenge); (2) ExCEL or Excellence through Continuous Enterprise and Learning (continuous improvement and teamwork to be realized through measures like the Work Improvement Teams); (3) Quality Service (to satisfy customers through courtesy, accessibility, responsiveness, and effectiveness); and (4) Organizational Review (i.e. organizational innovation, use of IT, connecting with citizens, and cutting red tape) (Lim, 2005).

The PS21 initiative is led by the Prime Minister's Office and the Central Steering Committee (members include the Permanent Secretaries of various ministries), and four functional committees corresponding to the above four functional components, including the Staff Wellbeing Committee, the ExCEL Committee, the Quality Service Committee, and the Organizational Review Committee. Each of these four committees has representatives from all ministries and is led by a Permanent Secretary. There are PS21 Offices at various hierarchical levels of all ministries and statutory boards. The principles of PS21 are repeatedly highlighted by the government, and it has implications for other structural and managerial reforms in the public sector.

Fourth, with regard to organizational structure and management, the government has "corporatized" and converted various departments and statutory boards into so-called autonomous agencies for greater managerial autonomy and operational flexibility, which can be observed in the cases of the Inland Revenue Authority of Singapore, Public Works Department, Land Transport Authority, Port of Singapore Authority, Changi International Airport Services, Singapore Power, Civil Aviation Authority, and so on (Tay, 1999; Haque, 2002b). In these "corporatized" autonomous entities, the top managers are assigned with considerable autonomy in financial, personnel, and other operational matters. It was mentioned by the minister of finance in his 1997 budget speech that the government had converted 102 ministry headquarters, departments, and statutory boards into autonomous agencies in 1997; and emphasized that almost the entire civil service and all state-funded statutory boards were to be operated as autonomous agencies based on this framework of autonomy and flexibility, which was needed to facilitate quick change and encourage efficiency and performance (Budget Speech, 1997).

In particular, with regard to finance and budget, the

government introduced the so-called Block Vote Budget Allocation System in 1989 that provided ministries with needed authority to manage their budgets. Under this system, once approved by the parliament, a ministry may exercise autonomy to manage the budget in terms of transferring funds between its programs (Jones, 1999). The government also adopted a computer-based information tool, known as the Singapore Government Management Accounting System (SIGMA) in 1992, which helped practice a more detailed cost calculation of programs and activities, and thus, facilitated the realization of financial autonomy provided by the Block Vote Budget Allocation System (Jones, 1999). In 1994, the government took another step to introduce the Budgeting for Results initiative. It requires ministries to come up with precise performance targets (reflecting the costs and outputs or results of their intended activities and programs), and once the budget estimates are approved, they can enjoy procedural autonomy as long as they meet the performance targets (Low, 2001a; Jones, 1999). All these structural reform initiatives adopted recently in Singapore represent some form of businesslike "managerialism" in its public service.

Fifth, in line with the above trend in organizational restructuring for more autonomy and flexibility, there has also emerged greater decentralization in public personnel management in Singapore, especially with regard to the transfer of certain recruitment and promotion authority from the Public Service Commission (PSC) to various ministries, departments, and statutory boards. In the past, the PSC was in overall charge of human resource planning, recruitment, and promotion for all public officials, which began to be shared with the Public Service Division (PSD) on policy ground, and then with the Education Service Commission (ESC) and the Police and Civil Defense Services Commission (PCDSC) for functional reasons (the ESC and PCDSC were dissolved in 1998). However, a more significant change was adopted in 1995 when the government decided to create the so-called Personnel Boards at different levels with a view to devolve major personnel functions and responsibilities (e.g. appointments and promotions) from the PSC to these Personnel Boards. The main objective was to provide public managers more authority to manage their employees, although the PSC would remain in charge of Superscale officers (Grade D and above) as well as disciplinary matters such as demotion or dismissal (Tay, 1999).

The personnel matters related to all other public officials are now handled by the Personnel Boards, which are hierarchically arranged in the following order: (1) one Special Personnel Board (chaired by the Head of Civil Service with a Permanent Secretary, Prime Minister's Office) in charge of Superscale officers up to E1 and timescale officers in the Administrative Service; (2) six Senior Personnel Boards (each chaired by a Permanent Secretary), each in charge of Division I officers from a group of ministries (except timescale officers in the Administrative Service); and (3) 24 Personnel Boards (at least one Board for each ministry, chaired by a Superscale officer in that ministry), each dealing with Division II, III, and IV employees (Tay, 1999). In terms of the mode of public sector recruitment, there is a growing trend to offer contract-based appointment or fixed-term jobs rather than permanent tenure, and the government has been encouraging qualified business executives to join the public service even at some higher ranks (Lee, 2001; Haque, 2002b).

This trend of businesslike flexibility can also be noticed in a recent compensation reform based on the corresponding private sector salaries. Based on the assumption that without adequate salaries for top political and administrative officials (in comparison with their business sector counterparts), there could be a worsening situation of brain-drain from the public sector to the private sector; the government adopted salary revisions based on private sector standards. A set of salary benchmarks was adopted for ministers and senior civil servants in 1994 by comparing their salaries to the corresponding salaries paid for the six private sector professions, including bankers, accountants, engineers, lawyers, local manufacturing companies, and multinational corporations (Tay, 1999). These salary revisions may be examined further to assess whether the public and private sectors are comparable.

Major Impacts and Challenges

Since 1959, with the established mode of governance and administration in Singapore (encompassing the parliamentary form, the one-party dominant system, efficient and loyal bureaucracy, extensive state intervention, limited welfare provision, and so on), the country has done well in creating wealth, reducing poverty, expanding literacy, building infrastructure, maintaining racial stability, and developing a viable sovereign state, although there are critics who characterize such governance system as illiberal. However, the question worth exploring here is about the potential implications of recent reforms in governance, especially the recent adoption of market-driven policy options (divestment, deregulation, liberalization, contracting-out) and the state's tendency to replace its socioeconomic role with a greater role played by the private sector. First, in many countries, such reforms have allegedly created adverse impacts on the state's capacity due to shrinking revenue sources, budget cuts, and the reduction in public employment. In the case of Singapore, however, such impacts are unlikely to be drastic because the state still maintains considerable ownership and control through its numerous enterprises and government-linked companies.

Second, with regard to the consequences of contemporary reforms for citizens, there is potential for some favorable outcomes due the growing emphasis on service quality and customer satisfaction, which is one of the main objectives of the PS21 initiative. To a certain extent, public administration in Singapore has been restructured or reinvented in order to make it more client-centered by motivating and training street-level bureaucrats in courtesy and service mentality, by restructuring and improving service counters to deal with customers' needs and queries, by providing incentives to employees based on customer feedback, and so on (Jones, 1999). However, not all citizens can qualify as customers or clients as there are low-income families whose incomes have not improved (CPO, 2000: 7; 2001: 4), who cannot afford to purchase high-cost services, and who have not gained much from recent reforms and policy changes. For instance, in the health sector, there have been cutbacks on medical expenditures, especially after the implementation of the Medisave Scheme in the early 1980s (Lee, 2001). According to Khan (2001: 11), the public spending on health (as a percentage of GDP) appears to have a "downward trend," and the initiatives were taken by the government to privatize certain hospitals, which shifted the financial burden of health care to individuals, families, and employers.

Last, within the public service itself, the recent reforms in some other countries have raised concerns whether policies and reforms such as privatization, contracting out, and joint venture may create greater potential for bureaucratic corruption. In fact, in the aftermath of such reform initiatives, the incidence of corruption has worsened in many cases. However, in the case of Singapore, the anti-corruption measures and institutions have been so effective that it is ranked as one of the most corruption-free countries in the world. However, it is wise to be more vigilant as the reform processes are often replete with uncertainties. Another concern emerging from these current changes in governance based on organizational disaggregation (e.g. autonomous agencies), the use of multiple stakeholders (private, non-government, and foreign), and the expansion of budget autonomy, are potential barriers to the realization of public accountability due to the growing difficulty to coordinate, manage, and monitor these new structures and institutional arrangements. In this regard, the optimistic aspects of the Singapore case are its highly capable state to steer the situation and its relatively small public sector (due to a small population) that is more easily manageable.

However, there are certain real and potential challenges to the current mode of governance and public administration in Singapore. First, in the political sphere of governance, there is growing realization that the earlier rationale for the expansion of the state's role in the name of overcoming economic backwardness, building racial harmony, and ensuring national survival, is difficult to justify in the contemporary context (Lee, 2001). In addition, since most citizens are now highly educated, well informed, and politically aware, they may expect the state and government to be less interventionist and more consultative (Lam, 2000: 416-418). In line with this changing context, the former Prime Minister Goh Chok Tong began with the pledge of practicing a "consultative and participatory" leadership style, and set up the Feedback Unit to facilitate consultation with selected citizens regarding political disagreements on various policy matters (Lee, 2001). This newly emerging political context characterized by higher public demands and expectations has certain implications for rethinking state control over various sectors or domains of society.

Second, on the economic front, as Singapore faced serious economic recession in the mid-1980s, allegedly caused by over-regulation and high service charges, the state began to recognize the negative impacts of economic intervention and to identify alternative strategies with reduced control and regulation (Lam, 2000: 402-403, 416-418). The earlier economic success, based on a leading role played by the state and its public sector, came under pressure due to such economic downturn or recession during this period. There was also external pressure from the world economic powers to enhance openness to the global markets through measures such as liberalization and de-regulation, which often make the national economy vulnerable to the global business fluctuations (see Yeung, 2000b: 143). It is a challenge to reconcile between the established tradition of economic success based on an active interventionist role of the state on the one hand, and the adverse impact of such internal intervention as well as external pressure requiring the withdrawal of state control on the other.

Concluding Remarks and Prospects

In most countries, including Singapore, recent reforms in governance and public administration have been carried out based on two major rationales or objectives: to enhance public sector efficiency and quality and to increase customer choice and satisfaction. After carrying out such significant reforms for so long, unfortunately, there have not been any comprehensive and objective assessments of whether they have indeed improved the levels of efficiency, quality, and satisfaction. It is imperative to pursue comprehensive studies to evaluate all major dimensions of reforms in terms of their rationales, claims, and actual outcomes.

Even without such a study and assessment, it is becoming increasingly clear that the whole generation of contemporary reinvention or reform in public governance and administration has often been based on prejudiced or ideologically charged assumption of market superiority and state failure. In this regard, one major source for lessons to be learned was the Asian economic crisis of the late 1990s followed by severe declines in the rates on economic growth (Yeung, 2000b: 146), which should remind us how things may go wrong in this globalized world, how careless policies and reforms may produce adverse and unpredictable outcomes, how the economic disasters created by market forces may require policy reversal in favor of government intervention, and how the role of the state still remains critical. These lessons have become even more crucial in the current context of unprecedented economic recession worldwide, which is globally recognized as the most severe economic challenge since the Great Depression. In this regard, the tradition of Singapore's strong and capable state, interventionist governance, and efficient public administration cannot be easily dismissed.

References

Bellows, Thomas J. (1985). "Bureaucracy and Development in Singapore." *Asian Journal of Public Administration* 7 (1): 55-69.

Browning, Bob (2000). "Rethinking the Singapore Model." *News Weekly*, 19 September 2000. [http://www.sprint.net.au/~rwb/singapore.htm]

Budget Speech 1997 (1997). Singapore: Ministry of Finance. Available at: HYPERLINK "http://www.mof.gov.sg/budget_1997/ management.html" http://www.mof.gov.sg/budget_1997/management.html

Cheung, Wai-lam (2000). *Unemployment-Related Benefits Systems in Singapore*. June 2000. Hong Kong: Research and Library Services Division, Legislative Council Secretariat, Hong Kong.

Chua, B. H. (1997) *Political Legitimacy and Housing: Stakeholding in Singapore*, New York, Routledge.

Cima, Ronald J. and Donald R. DeGlopper (1989). "Government and

Politics." In Library of Congress (ed.), *A Country Study: Singapore.* Washington DC: Library of Congress. [http://lcweb2.loc.gov/frd/cs/sgtoc.html]

Clarke, J. & J. Newman (1997). *The Managerial State: Power, Politics and Ideology in the Remaking of Social Welfare*, London, Sage Publications.

CPO (Census of Population Office) (2000). *Economic Characteristics of Singapore Resident Population.* Singapore Census of Population, 2000. Advanced Data Release No.4. Singapore: Census of Population Office, Singapore Department of Statistics.

DBJ (Development Bank of Japan) (2001). *Public Service Sector in Singapore: PS21.* Tokyo: Development Bank of Japan.

DBJ (Development Bank of Japan) (2003). *Privatization and Contracting Out Trends in Singapore.* Singapore: Development Bank of Japan (Representative Office).

Department of Statistics (2008). *Yearbook of Statistics Singapore, 2008.* Singapore: Department of Statistics, Ministry of Trade & Industry.

Hamilton-Hart, Natasha (2000). "The Singapore State Revisited." *Pacific Review* 13 (2): 195–216.

Haque, M. Shamsul (2002a). "Globalization, New Political Economy, and Governance: A Third World Viewpoint." *Administrative Theory & Praxis* 24 (1): 103-124.

Haque, M. Shamsul (2002b). "Structures of New Public Management in Malaysia and Singapore: Alternative Views." *Journal of Comparative Asian Development* 1 (1): 71-86.

Haque, M. Shamsul (2004). "Governance and Bureaucracy in Singapore: Contemporary Reforms and Implications." *International Political Science Review* 25 (2): 227-240.

Jones, David Seth (1999). "Public Administration in Singapore: Continuity and Reform," in *Handbook of Comparative Public Administration in the Asia-Pacific Basin*, Hon Chan (ed.), New York: Marcel Dekker.

Jones, David Seth (2002). "Recent Reforms in Singapore's Administrative Elite: Responding to the Challenges of a Rapidly Changing Economy and Society." *Asian Journal of Political Science* 10

(2): 70-93.

Khan, Habibullah (2001). *Social Policy in Singapore: A Confucian Model?* Washington, D.C.: World Bank Institute.

Kong, Lily (2000). "Cultural Policy of Singapore: Negotiating Economic and Socio-Cultural Agendas." *Geoforum* 31: 409-24.

Lam, Newman M. K. (2000). "Government Intervention in the Economy: A Comparative Analysis of Singapore and Hong Kong." *Public Administration and Development* 20 (5): 397-421.

LaMoshi, Gary (2002). "Singapore's capitalism myth." *Asia Times*, November 7.

Lee, Eliza W. Y. (2001). "Public Sector Reform and the Changing State Form: Comparing Hong Kong and Singapore." Paper presented at the American Political Science Association 97th Annual Meeting, San Francisco, August 30~September 2.

Lim, Siong Guan (2005). "Leadership in the Public Service: Changing Role of Senior Public Officials in Governance." Paper presented at 6th Global Forum on Reinventing Government, Seoul, Republic of Korea, May 26.

Low, Linda (1998). *The Political Economy of a City-State: Government-Made Singapore*. Singapore: Oxford University Press.

Low, Linda (2000). *Reinventing the Singapore Developmental Corporate State*. Working Paper Series, No.2000-042, Department of Business Policy, National University of Singapore.

Low, Li Mei (2001a). *Emergence of "New Public Management" in Singapore: A Case Study of the Ministry of Manpower*. Unpublished Honours Thesis. Singapore: Department of Political Science, National University of Singapore.

Low, Linda (2001b). *Experience of Health Care Policy in Singapore*. Working Paper Series No.2001-013, Business School, National University of Singapore.

Low, Linda and Stephan Haggard (2000). *State, Politics and Business in Singapore*. Working Paper Series, No.2000-037, Department of Business Policy, National University of Singapore.

Painter, Martin (2004). "The Politics of Administrative Reform in East and Southeast Asia: From Gridlock to Continuous Self-Improvement?" Governance 17 (3): 361–386.

Phua, K. H. (1991). *Privatization and Restructuring of Health Services in Singapore*. IPS Occasional Paper No.5. Singapore: Times Academic Press.

PWC Consulting (2002). "Appendix D: Singapore Country Summary," in *Interim Report to the Task Force on the Review of Civil Service Pay Policy and System*, PWC Consulting (ed.), Hong Kong: PWC Consulting.Available at: [HYPERLINK "http:// www.jsscs.gov.hk/en/publications/pwc/appendix_d.htm" http://www.jsscs.gov.hk/en/publications/pwc/appendix_d.htm]

Quah, Jon S. T. (1996). "Wielding the Bureaucracy for Results: An Analysis of Singapore's Experience in Administrative Reform." *Asian Review of Public Administration* 8 (1): 1-12.

RBAP (Regional Bureau for Asia and the Pacific) (1999). Public Sector Management Reform in Asia and the Pacific: Selected Experiences from Seven Countries. Islamabad, Pakistan: RBAP, UNDP.

Shameen, Assif (2000). "What Singapore Has Done Right…" *Asiaweek*, March 24.

Tay, Janet (1999). "Public Service Reforms in Singapore." Available at: [HYPERLINK "http://mirror.undp.org/magnet/Docs/psreform/civil_service_reform_in_singapore.htm" http://mirror. undp.org/magnet/ Docs/psreform/civil_service_reform_in_singapore.htm]

Vasil, R. (2000). *Governing Singapore: A History of National Development and Democracy*. St. Leonards, Australia: Allen & Unwin.

Wirtz, Jochen and Cindy M.Y. Chung (2001). *Marketing in Singapore: Macro Trends and Their Implications for Marketing Management for 2002 and the Years Beyond*. Research Paper Series No.2001-033, National University of Singapore.

World Factbook: Singapore (2007). Washington, DC: Central Intelligence Agency. Available at: [HYPERLINK "https://www.cia.gov/cia/publications/factbook/print/sn.html" https://www.cia.gov/cia/publications/factbook/print/sn.html]

World Factbook: Singapore (2008). Washington, DC: Central Intelligence Agency. Available at: [HYPERLINK https://www.cia.gov/cia/publications/factbook/print/sn.html]

Yeung, H. Wai-chung (2000a). "Global Cities and Develop- mental States: Understanding Singapore's Global Reach." Paper presented at the Second GWC Lecture, 7 March, Loughborough University, U.K.

Yeung, H. Wai-chung (2000b). "State Intervention and Neoliberalism in the Globalizing World Economy: Lessons from Singapore's Regionalization Programme." *Pacific Review* 13 (1): 133-162.

Chapter 11 Viet Nam

Trinh Tien Dung

Introduction

Viet Nam ranks relatively highly (relative to GDP per capita) in terms of human development and poverty reduction. From 1985 to 2005 Viet Nam improved its HDI by nearly 25% (from 0.590 to 0.733), placing it closer to the medium HD category. However, it is still lagging behind the East Asian regional average. Interestingly, Viet Nam has made impressive achievements in poverty reduction. In fact, the country has already achieved Millennium Development Goal 1 (Eradicate extreme poverty and hunger), which was targeted for 2015. Building on this success, the country is making progress towards reducing the poverty rate further, from 32% in 2000 to 15~16% by 2010, as set in the Socio-Economic Development Plan for 2006~2010 (UNDP Viet Nam Website).

In terms of economic achievements, after reconstruction, which lasted until mid-1980s, economic development and reform was selected as a preference to political reform. Over time, this has proven to be a correct choice, as Viet Nam has been steadily and smoothly transforming its economy from being centrally planned to becoming a market-oriented one. The average GDP growth rate of more than 7% from 1994 to 2007 has ranked Viet

Nam among few countries in Asia having a high GDP growth, which has been maintained for many years during the last two decades. This has happened in a context where Viet Nam has had to be self-reliant, without the major external ideological, political, and financial support it had in previous years.

Regarding political development, Viet Nam started its political reform in the late 1990s, after the economic reform yielded major achievements to figuratively enlarge the cake before its division-a process that has been handled with extremely great care. This cautious approach has proven to be wise when compared to what happened in former socialist countries such as Russia, Romania, and Poland. Political stability is a crucial precondition for economic and social development. To that end, adopting a gradual political change process, built on the basis of a well known broad base consensus, has proven to be the right choice. In this sense, it might be interesting to look more closely at if and how effectively a single party system works.

Viet Nam's most recent political system can be characterized by selected features such as the dominating role of the Communist Party of Viet Nam (CPV), no power separation between executive, legislative, and judiciary branches, society structure changes, etc., which are briefly explained below. Before 1992, there co-existed two other much smaller political parties named the Democrat and the Social Party. They were dissolved, however, after the Communist Party reached an agreement with them as part of a more radical strategic preparation process for the adaptation of the 1992 Constitution by the National Assembly in April 1992, which was an attempt to face the major political changes in the world-namely the collapse of the former Soviet block in 1991. The 1992 Constitution is known by three fundamental features: (1) recognition of rule of law principles (the people and businesses can do whatever is not legally prohibited); (2) party organizations are to operate within the legal framework; and (3) at the same time, recognition of CPV's leadership role (Article 4). The party system exists in parallel with the government administrative system and it is entirely financed by the government's budget. This however requires improvement at times because some Party individuals attempt to overrule the rule of law principles in the name of the Party.[1)] To cope with this alarming situation, the Party has adopted a Judiciary Reform Strategy known as the Resolution of the Poliburo No. 49 in order to establish regional courts, thus reducing the dependence of judiciary institutions (court and prosecution agencies) on administrative interventions.

No power separation between executive, legislative, and judiciary branches is another important characteristic of the Vietnamese political system. Unlike many developed countries, Viet Nam exercises unified party leadership over all of these three areas. The Party appoints its senior cadres to act as heads of the executive government, the National Assembly, and of the Judiciary (court and prosecutions) although these positions are formally elected by the National Assembly.

Public Administration and Governance in Viet Nam

The government (the executive branch) is composed of the Prime Minister (PM), Vice Premiers, the Cabinet Minister and Ministers (and ministerial equivalents).[2)] As per tradition, the PM ought to be a member of the Politburo and usually represents the South.[3)] This position is in fact the third highest rank,[4)] just

1) Example: In Ca Mau province, during 2008, the Provincial Party Secretary abused his role by imposing the appointment of some civil servants into senior positions. This case was reported by the mass media and the Secretary has been removed from all position and duties.

2) The Government structure of the current(2007~2011) term is composed of 26 ministries and ministry like agencies

3) While State President(another member of the Politburo) usually presents the

below the Party General Secretary and the President and higher than the Speaker (President) of the National Assembly. Officially speaking, all government members are to be elected and dismissed by the National Assembly at the PM's proposal after a careful prior review and clearance is given by the Party; there is not more than one candidate for one post.

The law specifies non-confidence[5] voting of cabinet members and other posts elected by the National Assembly although, practically speaking, current legal provisions are difficult. However, in practice, as it is extremely hard to gather 20% of the deputies who consent to vote. As a matter of fact, all government members should be members of CPV's Central Executive Committee. In this regard, Viet Nam lags behind its ideological partner and neighbor-China, which has appointed some ministers who are not part of Communist Party Central Committee. The Government is organized and operates according to the principle of democratic centralism[6] combined with collective responsibility and the individual accountability of the Prime Minister and his Cabinet members. The important issues under its jurisdiction are collectively discussed and decided by a majority.

The most recent re-organization of the new Cabinet held after its election in mid-2007 marks remarkable changes in terms of

---

Centre, and General Secretary of the Party usually represents the North of the country. This pattern aims to ensure that three parts of the country are well represented in the most important political positions.

4) Under current circumstances, the actual power of the PM over heads of local governments is limited. Law provisions require that heads of respective local governments are elected by respective people's councils, whose leaders are powerful Party leaders of the same rank.

5) In Vietnamese, it is read as "confidence vote" to make it sounding more positive.

6) This is a well known principle of the former Soviet bloc. Namely: democracy in the Party is based on a principle that minority respects; majority decisions are collectively made while individuals should take care of their duties; lower levels follow the decisions made by upper levels etc.

size and mandate. Size-wise, there is a noticeable reduction from more than 40 central agencies to some 22.[7] Some ministries were merged into other principal ministries in an effort to turn them into multi-disciplinary and macro-management agencies. Due to the lack of analysis of the pros and cons, however, for such an important organizational measure, especially because of common weaknesses-limited operational capacities to ensure efficiency and effectiveness of state management function, which has been widely acknowledged-some experts[8] argue whether such a "physical merge" has really led to a good return.

Division and coordination of tasks between line ministries (horizontal coordination) remains a persistent problem and needs important improvements.[9] The Government has tried its best to cope with this problem, including through assigning respective deputy PMs in charge of a number of related sectors[10] and *via* discussions in government monthly meetings ending with a resolution, which is published in the Government portal. Root causes of the above situation include: poor incentive framework, both moral and material; poor competencies of civil servants to carry out newly assigned duties, which are much more difficult than the previous ones, thus requiring re-training (policy drafting, setting of quality standards for public service delivery, monitoring, etc.), as well as the reluctance of a majority of civil

---

7) 22 ministries and the like and 8 agencies reporting to the Government.

8) Example: Head of PAR Secretariat, Ministry of Agriculture and Rural Development, Viet Nam.

9) Example: inflation is hardly to deal with due to constrained collaboration between MOF-Ministry of Finance, State Bank of Viet Nam and MPI. Thus, there has been some proposal (Harvard Group, 2008) to merge these three agencies into a single policy advisory body for the government. This might be one option for government consideration in the near future although it has not only pros but also cons.

10) The standing Deputy PM is responsible for macro economic issues; one of the remaining four deputy PMs is assigned to political reforms; another one is in charge of economic development; the next is assigned to social development, etc.

servants to delegate power to other entities and decentralize to local levels. Any improvement solutions should address these causes.

There are three sub-national levels in Viet Nam, namely provincial, district, and commune.

Currently there are 63 provinces after Ha Tay was merged into Hanoi on 1st August of 2008. This number includes 5 cities, namely Hanoi and Hai Phong in the North, Da Nang and Ho Chi Minh City in the center, and Can Tho in the South. In legal terms, so-called "local governments" consist of executive (People's Committee) and people's elected body (People's Councils); members of the former are elected by the latter. In reality, power rests with the Committee leaving the Council's formal entities acting more or less as a rubber stamp. To overcome this shortcoming, there have been important efforts including reform initiatives discussed below. However, more radical institutional and legal reform measures are required to cope with this situation. Leaders of people's councils are usually Party senior officials at the respective local level. This creates difficulties in vertical coordination, thus limiting the effectiveness of administrative instructions issued by the central government. At times there have been cases of poor implementation of policies and decisions taken by the central government at local levels.[11]

Districts and communes are considered extremely weak in terms of responding to the needs of the local people and of locality development goals and are subject of important reforms.[12] In real

11) During 2001~2005, 32 out of 64 provinces provided extra legal investment incentives trying to attract foreign investors. This was considered as a serious violation or rule breaking, in Viet Nam being well known as "fence breaking." As a result, the more favorable conditions, which were additionally created by the local governments not only did not result in increasing foreign investment in provincial territory as expected, but also increased their financial burden (UNDP, 2007).

12) The National Assembly decided in late 2008 to pilot abolishing people's elected

terms, it would be very hard to talk about decentralization in today's Viet Nam. Perhaps de-concentration is a more realistic goal because effective decentralization would require a fairly good amount of clarity concerning tasks between national and sub-national levels. Today, one can observe self-confronting extremes caused by the poorly coordinated division of tasks, one being too many undesired interventions of the line ministries into the work of local governments; on the contrary, many local governments illegally "break fence" in important areas such as attracting foreign direct investment (FDI) by easily granting big areas of land to foreigners for golf courses at the expenses of agricultural production, thus threatening the food supplies and stability of rural people, many of whom are poor.

Local governments play a crucial role seen from fiscal glances. They contributed nearly 73% in revenue collection and spent as much as nearly 68% in 2007. In terms of fiscal self-financing (budget revenue minus expenditure), the majority (49 out of 63) of the local governments are dependent on subsidies granted by the central government.

Civil service is a new term in Viet Nam although similar values like the "four Ps" (pride, passion, pace, and professionalism) (UK Government web-site, 2009) have also been promoted for many years in the country, first by the former President Ho Chi Minh who focused more on nurturing moral values such as honesty, objectivity, integrity, impartiality, and not yet on professional skills. There exists no law or regulation that provides comprehensive provisions regulating civil service as a whole, other than the newly passed law on cadres and public officials, which will enter into effect on July 1, 2010.

Similarly, the term "civil servant" has not been regularly used in official documents. Instead, the term "cadre" or "managers"

---

bodies at district and ward levels.

is frequently used. This mainly inherits from the centrally planned regime, which lasted for many years until 2006, when a draft bill on civil servants started. The bill aims at introducing key changes narrowed down just to the personnel (and does not cover the whole civil service area as generally expected). Before the above law was passed, the personnel working in administrative agencies were either managers (in management positions) or civil servants-i.e. ordinary staff, which includes those who are working in public institutions providing administrative services as well as those professionals, technicians such as teachers, doctors, writers, etc. providing public services (usually named as "public employees"). The personnel can shift vertically or horizontally within state institutions (government, legislative and judiciary ones) and mass organizations (e.g. youth, trade and women, etc.). This has been possible since merit-based performance has not been paid due attention. There is a growing general consensus that the current predominating career-based system is the major cause of poor performance. This shortcoming is partly translated into the new law on civil servants, where a similar shift is expected. Performance of important shares of civil servants is alarming, having just up to 40% of the personnel performing satisfactorily, 40% extremely poor–far below expectations, and 30% whose performance is basically acceptable but needs important improvements, although it is not always clear which assessment criteria have been used. A low and non-competitive salary is just a part of the problem. demotivating working environment and unclear perspectives with career development, coupled with poor working facilities, make civil servants unhappy, thus causing an increasing number of staff to move out of public institutions. An official government report says that in the recent few years there has been some 16,000 of public officials who have left public offices, many of them at a very senior level (department director, deputy director etc.). Specialist estimates suggest an even higher figure. In absolute terms, this is not a big figure as compared to the whole number of civil servants, but it is a significantly new phenomenon as per the traditionally high respect given for public employees.

The law attempts to reduce the extent of so called "life-long" civil servants as the case to date; instead it calls for a merit-based recruitment, promotion, appointment, and performance review. The bill is clear on a big "divorcement" of about 2 million so-called public professionals, be it teachers, doctors, artists, writers, etc. While this is a sound direction and should have been taken earlier, socially speaking, this causes some major concern to those who would be no longer considered as government workers. This is not only a financial fear but also a psychological discouragement as, per traditional values, being government workers means a lot more for many Vietnamese than just monetary compensation.

People and observers argue that the personnel working for the Party and its associated political-social organizations such as Women's Union, Youth Union, Trade Union, Veterans' Union, Farmer's Association, etc. should be regulated separately, under another legal document for the reason that the civil servants law should deal only with those who actually work in the civil service area. This well justified call was not accepted due to currently prevailing political circumstances. It remains unclear if another tricky issue, whether managers have a real power in the promotion of their staff or if they would still have to rely on external interventions,[13] would be resolved through the law.

Among key issues of public sector management in Viet Nam, SOE and public financial management deserve some closer consideration. State Owned Enterprises (SOE) management has

---

13) This also implies a so called dual "appointment." In practice, it means that senior positions from vice ministers and above need to be cleared by the Party first.

been and remains a big headache in public sector in Viet Nam. For good reasons, SOEs have been granted more support from the government than they deserve in terms of land allocation, credit, loans, etc. The SOE "equitization" process started in the early 1990s and gained some initial results turning down a big number of loss-making and less productive SOEs. Already equitized SOEs are the easy and less lucrative ones. Yet, there remains a highly centralized, bureaucratic, and time-consuming process of evaluation. Public resources continue to be allocated to SOEs that are long lasting monopolies such as EVN (Electricity of Viet Nam), Vinashin (Viet Nam Ship industry Corporation), TKV (Coal and Minerals of Viet Nam), state commercial banks, etc. Deputies to the National Assembly have recently raised a question of an urgent need to issue a law to monitor SOEs financial management, as they believe that SOEs are the main cause of high inflation in the country. In its recent budget proposal to the National Assembly for 2009, the government kept requesting the National Assembly to allocate even more resources (up to 7% as compared to 2008's estimation) (IntellAsia, 2008) to support SOEs, state groups, and corporations.

Public finance is also the subject of lively debate in recent years for its low efficiency, effectiveness, and especially for its poor impact on development outcomes, although Viet Nam ranks very highly as compared with other countries in terms of mobilizing a big share of GDP into the state budget (on average 22~23%), ranking higher than some developed countries such as Thailand, the Philippines, Malaysia, Japan, etc. (UNDP, 2008). Formally speaking, the budgetary process is a relatively participatory and transparent process in budget estimates. Annually, before Mid-may, the Prime Minister issues a circular guide for socio-economic planning including budget revenues and expenditure estimates. The process should be conducted from the bottom up. This means at every level, executive government proposes development targets and prepares budget estimates accordingly. The local level is to review and approve them before their submission to the upper level. In reality, due to many constraints, the process actually involves mainly executive staff and, at a much lesser extent, representatives of oversight and representative bodies. In many cases, the people's council does not see the estimates before they are submitted to the upper level. The current budgetary process allows mainly routine and physical checks while there is almost no chance to pay attention to ensure policy outcomes of public financial resources. The people's representatives have debated a possibility of expanding the financial calendar (budgetary process). The proposed revision of the 2002 State Budget Law, which is expected to be tabled for Legislature's review and approval in 2009, anticipates this significant change.

The other major shortcoming of the current management system of public resources is its input rather than output/result-orientation. Moreover, budget revenues and expenditures are managed on an annual basis rather than on medium-terms as commonly practiced in many developed countries. A significant reform was achieved in late 2005 when the National Assembly passed a law regulating that Viet Nam's State Audit is to become an independent body established by and reporting to the Legislature (instead of the executive government). This significant change has helped considerably improve accountability and transparency in using public financial resources, as big amounts of public money are being illegally and/or improperly used by spending units including the poverty reduction program known as Program 135. However, much is still desired for the State Audit of Viet Nam (SAV) to become a professional agency with internationally accepted standards (e.g. INTOSAI). The SAV's work in recent years is still based on financial and compliance audits; little has been done to apply performance audits and comment on fiscal policies and relating regulations.

Systems and practices by which Viet Nam's public institutions are directed and managed have experienced visible improvements. It can be said that performance of public institutions and officials have been considerably enhanced over the last ten years, although it is still far below the expectations of the public, not to mention how far performance ranks under internationally acceptable standards. The public usually expects the public institutions and their officials to maintain high standards of stewardship, probity, transparency, and accountability. Effective and meaningful corporate governance is therefore a critical component to ensure the above public expectations.

Formally speaking, there has been a system and mechanism in place, whose mandate is supposed to ensure an ethical and accountable performance of public officials *vis-à-vis* citizens. For one, there is a law on supervisory activities by the National Assembly. Among others, this requires a regular and/or thematic oversight over performance of the executives elected by the National Assembly. If more than 20% of Members calls for a non-confidence vote that it should be conducted. Recently there has been a well received question and answer session, usually arranged before the National Assembly's session ends. Ministers and the like are confronted by many hard questions raised by the members. A mechanism has been proposed to monitor the follow-up on the Minister's promises. A revised law on legal normative documents (Law on Laws) has been also been passed, requiring a RIA – regulatory impact assessment–for every draft legal document. It also requires that draft documents have to be published for people's information and comments within 60 days before they are published for use. This would improve the responsiveness of legal documents to people's needs. Every public office is supposed to arrange a space and time schedule for senior management to receive and listen to citizen complaints and denunciation as per the provisions stipulated in the law on same topic. Offices are supposed to have a so called "people's investigation board" to monitor and report misconduct or wrong doings by public officials, provincial anti-corruption boards established to deal with briberies. A draft bill stipulating provisions to deal with compensation for damages caused by misconduct and/or illegal actions of public officials will be passed by the NA in 2009. The Father Land Front member's organizations (this includes civil society organizations) are also entitled to supervise executive agencies' work. Recently, live interactions have increased between top government leaders (Prime/deputy Prime Minister, Ministers and the like, provincial heads, etc.) and investors and businessmen to discuss hot issues (customs, taxation, land clearance for industry construction, etc.).

Significant improvements are, however, required to make the public sector more efficient, effective and responsive to the people. This includes enhancements on all fronts including accountability, transparency, reliability, etc. and in all stages from policy/decision-making through to their realization. Decision-making at present is still very top down, input-oriented, poorly consultative, not user-friendly, and poorly client-oriented. In real terms, people and civil society forces have very little say in the policy and decision-making process. Usually policy and decision-making is not based on evidence and in consultation with the people, especially those who are subject of the policies and regulations. There exists very little attention to setting up and maintaining a good monitoring and evaluation system and database to track progress. Thus, there should be no surprise if their implementation is poor.

Major Issues and Public Sector Reforms in Recent Years

What to attribute to Viet Nam's impressive achievements made in the most recent two decades in socio-economic development and poverty reduction? Has there been a good public administration that has resulted in the above mentioned outcome? Briefly, it is hardly to attribute the above achievements to the PAR (Public Administration Reform), simply because in formal terms PAR only started in the mid-1990s as part of a more complex and longer political reform process following the successful economic reform that was cautiously selected to be conducted first. In a nutshell, despite some initial accomplishments, basically at the input level, PAR has yet to achieve its expected results. Very modest results have been made in four key areas of the PAR Master Programme (2001~2010)–PAR MP, namely institutional, organizational, human resource development and public finance. PAR efficiency and effectiveness has been very low and there is little evidence proving that PAR is making a clear impact on socio-economic development. PAR has not been able to make the breakthroughs as expected by the business community, investors, and especially by the people because of its cumbersome and complicated procedures, resulting in increasing transaction costs.[14] PAR has been initiated and enforced mainly from the top. A stronger bottom up push would be required to make PAR more effective in responding to people's needs. Recently, there have been some considerations of PAR process in Viet Nam including: (1) the continued support for the comprehensive PAR MP, (2) the choice between service reforms and performance management as priorities, and (3) the compromise of consolidating on-going reform with the development of new actions (Jairo Acuna, 2008).

---

14) Speech of the Prime Minister of Viet Nam made at the Q&A session of the National Assembly, November 15, 2008. Web site: na.gov.vn

It would be more useful to choose the last option even though it is more challenging. In a sense, the Party Resolution adopted in its fifth plenary session of July 2007 contains some elements supporting this choice.

Despite the increasing efforts of the current cabinet to assign duties and accountability to heads of agencies, clarity of duties and accountability at every level and in every position remains blurry. Collective responsibility that partly inherits from the previous central planning working style might be one of the key reasons leading to this shortcoming. Poor accountability of civil servants causes a lot of complaints by citizens. Low accountability associated with the poor ethics of cadres is among the key things that cause people's frustration. In fact, under current institutional and legal frameworks, it is difficult to legally attribute malfunction and wrongdoing to any individual. Improving administrative procedures including through an on-going focus effort known as "Project 30"[15] may help improve accountability and responsiveness towards clients. However, more fundamental measures are also required, including some selected legal and institutional reforms towards actual independence of courts, strengthened independent oversight by the National Assembly and People's Councils, improving access to information by the people to enable their real supervision, etc. People have also started talking about constitutional protection, given increasing and obvious violations against the Constitution by executives, but little is happening to stop it. On the other hand, accountability problems are hardly to be virtually removed without encouraging performance-based motivation, competitive salary and good working facilities. In this sense, the new civil servants' law promises a good impulse.

Important initiatives have been taken in recent years by the

15) This project was decided by the Prime Minister under his decision numbered 30 in 2007 and is supported by USAID.

Government to improve transparency, efficiency, effectiveness, and participation of the people and accountability towards them. Most tangible outputs have been observed mainly in regulation work. The new issuance of the Ordinance on grassroots democracy in 2007 requests all communes to disclose the plans and budget allocation to the public. Reports (UNDP, 2008) say that 100% of communes disclosed their socio-economic development planning and budgeting information to the public. By mid 2008, 100% of communes established People's Inspection Committees for overseeing the implementation of the public/ community investment projects. The challenge is that people are sometimes reluctant to show such information and usually few of them review the documents simply because they question their reliability. Commune people's councils, who are supposed to represent the commune people, are facing severe difficulties due to constrained capacities in terms of knowledge and competencies, thus preventing them from virtual oversight over the executives.

Transparency at the national level has been also importantly improved. The Prime Minister's Instruction issued on June 11, 2007 and the amended law on required public consultation and people's participation in law making processes and stipulates that all draft laws, ordinances, resolutions, and decrees have to be posted for public comments on the Government's and the main drafting/issuing organization's official websites for at least 60 days and the drafting agencies have the obligation to consolidate and take into consideration all comments received. The State Budget Law (2002) also requires that budget estimates are to be submitted to National Assembly deputies at least ten days for their advance review to enable a more informative debate. In reality, however, they usually receive them shortly before the session, in some cases just few hours in advance and under a "top secret" stamp. Moreover, the way the budget data is presented is also worrisome as it is presented in big bulks and extremely difficult for the deputies to understand, since three fourths of them are part-timers and non-finance experts. The question and answer session of the National Assembly, enabled in the recent decade for a more transparent and accountable government, also needs a lot of improvements.

Transparency is also constrained due to inappropriate arrangements of all social surveys seeking virtual feedback from the people, as they are purely conducted by government institutions rather than independent institutions. Thus, the reliability of the obtained data (e.g. unemployment, amount of yearly job creation, households/people living under the poverty line, number and quality of public services delivery, etc.) is questionable.

Lack of transparency is one of key factors causing low efficiency and effectiveness of education, which is essential for Viet Nam's successful competition on the regional and international markets. Experts like Vu Quang Viet[16) argue that Viet Nam's current serious problems in education do not come from insufficient funding as education officials keep complaining, rather poor management (non-transparency and wasting of resources) is to blame. Mr. Vu argues that spending on education in Viet Nam accounts for 8.3% of GDP, which is even higher than that of USA (7.2%), Japan (4.7%), South Korea (7.1%), and the average level of OECD countries (6.1). Also, the self payment share of Vietnamese students, which is 40% of total education spending, is very high when compared to that of other developed countries (USA–26%; France–7%; Japan–26%; OECD–20%).

People's access to information as stipulated in the Constitution is constrained, not only for ordinary citizens, but also for academicians, professionals, press, and even for officials of

16) Vu Quang Viet, ex UN senior statistical specialist, New York. Article printed on VietnamNet on July 14, 2007.

the other units of same agency. There are several reasons leading to this situation: (1) the absence of a law specifying constitutional rights to information by the people; (2) the limited availability and quality of information, (3) the information being perceived as power; (4) the inappropriate behavior and lack of awareness towards information sharing, and (5) the insufficient societal pressure to produce quality outputs other than just to present the information. The law on access to information, to be tabled for the National Assembly's review during 2009, presents a big promise in this regard. The draft law on memorandum (to seek people's opinions) being pursued by the Viet Nam Lawyer's Association is another good signal.

Public Administration Education and Research

The Department of Training and Re-training under MOHA is in charge of drafting and monitoring of policies and guidelines for civil service training. The National Academy of Public Administration (NAPA), an agency which belonged to MOHA for many years until late 2007 before it was merged into the National Political Academy named after the President Ho Chi Minh, is responsible for short-term training of senior managers at central and provincial levels. NAPA has the following training programs: under-bachelor, bachelor, post-graduate, civil servant training, and specialized training; the latter two at the request of administrative agencies at the national and sub-national levels. The administration bachelor training programme runs in two forms, full-time (formal) and in-service training; its postgraduate certificate-based (Master and Ph. D.) training programs are only the in-service type. The bachelor education consists of 44 disciplines through 203 learning units, of which 32 are optional and lasts for 4 school years. The above said time does not include the 4-week national defense training. Apart from general education (consisting of 77 learning units), core professional education is made up of (1) the State and Law (6 disciplines/26 learning units), (2) state administration (6/22), (3) document presentation and administration technology, (4) state economics management, (5) state management of social and other issues, and finally, (6) internship or thesis work before completion (NAPA web-site).

In addition, each ministry and province has its own management/political/administrative training school . although resource persons usually come from central agencies, mainly in an *ad hoc* manner. Under the training framework identified by MOHA and the political training program, they are responsible for administering and servicing agency/provincial-wide training on national and general issues and on the professional/specialized areas of their relevance. The training program also includes basic training for newly recruited civil servants and pre-promotion training. There are management-training institutions in all central ministries/agencies and political/administrative schools in 63 provinces/cities. In big cities there are also training centers at its district level.

In short it can be said that currently education and training in the area of public administration is facing severe constraints and shortcomings as it is non-responsive to the country's needs, is repetitive, and not cost-or time-effective, thus it is considered as lagging far behind education and training for the public in general.

There are two main institutes engaged in public administration research, including the Institute of Administration Science Research (belonging to NAPA) and Institute of State Organization Science (associated to MOHA). Mandate of the former is mainly to back up NAPA's training work and develop administration science, while the latter focuses its activities mainly on supporting MOHA's work. A common feature of these institutions is their poor contribution to policy analysis which both NAPA and MOHA need badly. Similarly to other public sectors, the research work in this domain is seen by the society as very inefficient, ineffective, and makes very little impact on policy, law-making, and implementation. It is not certain how MOHA and NAPA would solve these chronic issues, which are not unique to this area only. The fact that the Institute of State Organizations Science (ISOS) has been appointed to act as a focal point for the drafting of the law on civil servants is a good move towards linking research institutions to policy making and debate. It is good to see how this shift will contribute to quality improvements.17)

Challenges and Newly Demanding Tasks

Integration provides Viet Nam with great opportunities but also places the country before newly arising challenges. This mainly relates to Viet Nam's obligations as a WTO member since late 2006. More specifically, national competitiveness remains extremely low (ranked 68 out of 131 countries in 2008) (UNDP Website) and, coupled with the newly emerging global financial crisis, protectionism in the markets where Viet Nam exports majority of its products such as Western Europe, USA, ASEAN, etc. could increase. In turn, national competitive capacity greatly depends on business environment. Raising competitiveness would require good public governance, namely an effective, efficient, responsive, and ethical public administration. In addition, raising competitiveness becomes even more difficult as Viet Nam is facing another challenge－climate change and its impact on the country, which is included in the group of five

17) Many line ministries have established a so called "Strategy and Policy Institute" to support policy drafting and decision making process. The results have been mixed and rather limited; below the expectations.

top countries being mostly affected by climate change. These external factors will place the country into a more difficult situation coupled at the same time with internal challenges as a result of Viet Nam's becoming a middle-level income country-rapidly increasing demand for democracy from within the country caused by, among others, continuously widening socio-economic disparities. This calls for a more effective and efficient social security, decentralization of power and responsibilities to sub-national levels, and outsourcing of public services to the private sector.

To successfully cope with the above newly emerging challenges, the pubic sector of Viet Nam would need more radical reform efforts to result in an effective, efficient, and ethical provision of administrative and public services to the people, investors and businesses, and to timely and proactively respond to newly arising needs, moving this country toward democratic and sustainable socio-economic development.

Viet Nam possesses invaluable human resources. Unfortunately, this huge potential has been poorly utilized for many years. Human resource development is the key to raising Viet Nam's competitiveness and productivity and maintaining it at high level. Some experts (Nguyen Trung, 2008) argue that industrialization and modernization may not be what Viet Nam needs, rather education to result in a more competent and qualified contingent of people, so this should be considered Viet Nam's most important strategy to move forward to a middle income level country. The dominance of politicians and too few technocrats in top levels of the country, in the Party, and in the legislative, executive, and judiciary institutions strongly support this urgent call. The fact that the Party got a high consensus among its Central Party's Committee and thus could issue a resolution on intellectuals for the first time of this kind, reaffirms this alarming situation. Education is a key means to result in vibrant and highly qualified trainees, not just on a formal basis, but also through continuous self-learning. In this regard, public governance and especially PAR play a crucial role in many aspects, including enabling, organizational, and individual levels.[18)]

Civil servants, as elaborated in the civil service sub-section above, who currently face fundamental weaknesses, such as incompetence and poor integrity, inadequate job descriptions and poor performance assessments, require both short and long-term solutions to address these problems. A key reason leading to this alarming situation is that the whole cycle of recruitment, promotion, dismissal, reward and discipline, etc. is not based on competency-merit criteria and lacks standard ethical requirements. The new provisions contained in the most recently endorsed law[19)] on civil servants promise some big moves forward, but still leave Viet Nam rather far behind internationally accepted requirements.

Raising honesty and integrity among civil servants is not completely new in Viet Nam. Recently the Party has re-launched a campaign of learning these core values following the outstanding example of Ho Chi Minh. For understandable reasons, the exercise has not been gaining the expected results simply because moral values need to go hand in hand with material ones.

Evidence-based policy and law-making is not new even in Viet Nam. Formally speaking, in the past the law-making process also required surveys and studies to be carried out in order to analyze the real (for existing laws) or expected impact (for new laws) of legal documents before drafting a new legal document or

---

18) UNDP Practice Note on capacity development may 2008. UNDP web site New York.

19) For example: The law stipulates a competitive recruitment; makes a preference to talented people; pays a lot of attention to raise integrity level by providing 4 articles detailing what civil servants and managers must not do.

revising existing ones.[20] Current debates in the country also stress the importance of enhancing policy analysis in the policy and law-making process toward intended policy outcomes, rather than the current practice of paying attention to technical and even procedural aspects. In this regard, the regulatory impact assessment (RIA) can be very useful. These requirements would hardly happen without an effective and lively monitoring and evaluation (M&E) system and associated indicators, supported by a good and functioning database to track the progress in public governance and PAR. This is a big challenge as almost nothing exists today except for some piecemeal information and data, which becomes quickly outdated. International donors[21] stand ready to support Viet Nam in its efforts in developing a functioning M&E system, indicators, and database.

Better informed and evidence-based policy, law, and even regulation-making requires substantial changes in the present way of organizing research and analytical works, including the following: (1) separate institutions in charge of data collection and processing from policy/law making bodies to make them independent, primarily in financing, human resource development, and corporate governance; (2) stronger advocacy for a higher quality of preparatory works for policy and law-making the high quality requirements would create room to engage qualified non-state institutions and would surely increase the quality of policies and laws; and (3) building a governance database and a system for measuring and assessing governance progress, which does not exist in real terms today.

Today's society is an information society. Information has

20) Practice/implementation review(in Vietnamese "Tổng kết thực tiễn") before new policies and laws are developed is well known in Viet Nam. This important work has however ended up as a formality with poor quality.

21) UNDP has been working with MOHA to develop a new project to be implemented in early 2009; one of key expected results is the M&E system, indicators and database.

become an integral part of the production force. "*Inforstructure*" (UNESCO Website) has been developed along side with conventional "infrastructure" with the aim to develop information standards and management tools, etc. to enable effective information sharing and communication. In Viet Nam, rights to be informed are stipulated in the Constitution as part of human rights. The challenge is how to realize them. The revision of the present Press Law, which is essential for access to information in the context of increasing power of the press in everyday life, is underway for approval in the last legislative session of 2009. The revision needs to consider newly emerging features, such as information technology, telecommunication, and the internet,[22] that enable private communication channels (i.e. blogs) as provided for in the Constitution.

Conclusion

Public governance in general, and public administration in particular, is a means to ensure sustainable and inclusive socio-economic development. To date, public governance and public administration have appeared to be far less effective and efficient than expected by the government and the people. It is therefore very hard to attribute Viet Nam's relatively big and impressive achievements to the modest performance of the public sector in recent years.

To fulfill the above expectations and in order to effectively cope with the rapidly changing internal and external environment and emerging challenges including low national competitiveness, rapidly widening social gaps, climate changes and their impact on the national development process, etc., Viet Nam needs to

22) At present, there are 813 press publications, 67 Radio TV stations, 10 E presses, 130 web sites and nearly 15,000 registered journalists. None of the above is under private ownership(Website of Ministry of Information and Communication).

prioritize reform initiatives to improve key elements of good governance systems, namely transparency, accountability, people's participation, and the rule of law. These values could be gradually accomplished by addressing some selected fundamental building blocks including human resource development in general and raising competency, honesty, and integrity among civil servants, improving access to information, building an effective and better informed and evidence-based policy and law-making system including a functioning M&E system and indicators, building a good governance database, and measuring and assessing systems. To date, these issues have been paid insufficient attention, thus they lag much behind the expected levels and will require timely and bolder attention from now on. In all the above tasks, PAR would play a crucial role. That is also the reason why the Party has recently paid increasing attention to this important reform program–it is an important vehicle to achieve success in Viet Nam.

References

Acuña-Alfaro, Jairo (2008). *UNDP Policy Brief: Public Administration Reform and Anti-Corruption*. Hanoi: UNDP Viet Nam.

Balme, Stephanie and Sidel, Mark (2006). *Vietnam's New Order: International Perspectives on the State and Reform in Vietnam*. London: Palgrave Macmillan.

Jefferies, Ian (2006). *Vietnam: A Guide to Economic and Political Developments*. London: Routledge.

Karnow, Stanley (1997). *Vietnam: a History*. New York: Penguin.

Porter, Gareth (1993). *Vietnam: The Politics of Bureaucratic Socialism*. Ithaca, NY: Cornell University Press.

Sardesai, D. R. (2005). *Vietnam: Past and Present*, 4th ed. Boulder, CO: Westview Press.

UNDP Viet Nam (2007). *The Top 200: Industry Strategies for Viet Nam's Larger Firms*. Hanoi: UNDP Viet Nam.

UNDP Viet Nam (2007). *Provincial Extralegal Investment Incentive in the Context of Decentralization in Viet Nam.* Hanoi: UNDP Viet Nam.

UNDP Viet Nam (2008). *Mid-term (2006~2010) Review of SED Plan.* Hanoi: UNDP Viet Nam.

UNDP Viet Nam (2008). *Public Financial Management: Research Project on Governance and State Management* (by Clay G. Wescott, Nguyen Huu Hieu, and Vu Quynh Huong). Hanoi: UNDP Viet Nam.

Womack, Brantly (2006). *China and Vietnam: The Politics of Asymmetry.* Cambridge, UK: Cambridge University Press.

Appendix

Websites of some public institutions relating to public administration and related organizations

Ministry of Planning & Investment	http://www.mpi.gov.vn
Ministry of Finance	http://www.mof.gov.vn
Ministry of Justice	http://www.moj.gov.vn
Ministry of Home Affairs	http://www.moha.gov.vn
Ministry of Foreign Affairs	http://www.mofa.gov.vn
Communist Party of Viet Nam	http://www.cpv.org.vn
National Assembly	http://www.na.gov.vn
Ministry of Industry	http://www.industry.gov.vn
Ministry of Science & Technology	http://www.most.gov.vn
Ho Chi Minh National Academy of Politics and Administration	http://www.npa.gov.vn
Viet Nam Academy of Social Sciences	http://www.vass.gov.vn
Institute of State & Law	See http://www.vass.gov.vn

Chapter 12 Republic of Korea

Sang-Il Han and Pan Suk Kim

Introduction

In August 2008, the Korean people celebrated the sixtieth anniversary of their government. Since the initial inauguration of the government in 1948, the Republic of Korea has achieved remarkable economic development and political democratization, bringing it into the world's spotlight. The Korean economy has grown into the fourth largest in Asia and thirteenth largest in the world and is considered one of the most successful economies in the world, growing faster than any other major economy in the twentieth century. In addition to such economic success, the Korean democracy that followed about 40 years of authoritarianism has progressed steadily to the point that regular free elections are now conducted, the military is fully under civilian control without any possibility of potential military intervention, and the strong voices of civil society organizations are expressed freely and publicly.

Since Korean public administration has been pivotal in both the country's economic and political success, this chapter will introduce the nation's historical development over the most recent six decades as well as its current status, in order to identify the prospects and challenges for the future. To establish a common foundation for this discussion, it is necessary to present the major historical and developmental steps of Korean public administration. The authors share the widely held assumption that Korean public administration experienced a three-stage developmental process: state-building, developmental state, and the democratization and globalization period.

Historical Development of Korean Politics and Public Administration

The historical development of Korean politics and public administration encompasses four phases: (1) state-building (Tilly, 1975) to design a constitutional framework and institutional arrangement; (2) developmental state (Woo-Cummings, 1999) to industrialize and urbanize society for economic prosperity; (3) democratization, which involves enhancing civil and political society simultaneously in order to articulate better the citizens' voices and enhance interaction with other countries across national borders; and (4) advancement toward more advanced levels. Throughout these phases, the Korean government has made contributions to advancement in many ways.

State-building (1948~1960)

Since Korea's liberation from Japanese colonial rule (1910~1945), Korea was dominated by authoritarian regimes for nearly 50 years. The first presidency of Rhee Syng-man (1948~1960) sought to strengthen control of the government through autocratic leadership, creating government ministries to maintain public safety and perform the very basic functions of the state. Thus, the first government of Korea consisted of 18 subunits: 11 ministries, four offices, and three boards. After the Korean War (1950~1953), the government reframed its structure in 1955, establishing the Ministries of Interior, Foreign Affairs, National Defense, Finance, Justice, Education, Commerce, and Transportation. Most of the ministries were responsible for public order and general administration. The total number of ministries was just under 20. During this period, slight changes emerged in the composition of the ministries.

[Table 12–1] Number of Korean Ministries during the State-Building Period

Year	Board	Department	Office	Bureau	Administration	Commission	Total
1948	0	11	4	0	0	3	18
1949	0	12	5	0	1	3	21
1950	0	12	5	0	1	3	21
1951	0	12	5	0	1	3	21
1952	0	12	5	0	1	3	21
1953	0	12	5	0	1	3	21
1954	0	12	5	0	1	3	21
1955	0	12	0	2	3	3	20
1956	0	12	0	2	3	1	18
1957	0	12	0	2	3	1	18
1958	0	12	0	2	3	1	18
1959	0	12	0	2	3	1	18
1960	1	12	1	0	3	3	20

Source: Ministry of Government Administration and Home Affairs (2004~2007).

In the late 1950s, Rhee pushed through a constitutional amendment that made the presidency a directly-elected position and exempted him from the eight-year term limit, suppressing several congressmen who were expected to vote against it. His repressive reign brought in political turmoil and strong protests by students that spread throughout the country in 1960. After the student revolution, Rhee resigned and the presidency was handed over to a transitional administration. A new parliamentary election was held on July 29, 1960, and the Second Republic was established. In this election, the Democratic Party, opponents of the former Republic, easily gained power. The National Assembly revised the Constitution, decreeing that the Second Republic take the form of a parliamentary cabinet system with a Prime Minister (Chang Myun) and with the President (Yun Bo-Seon) playing only a nominal role. This was the first and only instance in which South Korea turned to a cabinet system instead of a presidential system.

Developmental State (1961~1979)

Although the Second Republic was established, political turmoil and student unrest continued due to political clashes among inner groups of the new ruling party and mismanagement of corruption of the former government. Unhappy with the cleanup measures undertaken by the government, some military personnel assured themselves that the current disoriented state would give way to communism and consequently chose to take matters into their own hands. A military coup d'état (5 · 16 *coup d'état*) led by Major General Park Chung-Hee in 1961 terminated the Second Republic. The military leaders promised to return the government to a democratic system as soon as possible, but they governed Korea for 19 years.

The military's newly established 13 ministries and offices included the Board of Economic Planning and the Ministry of Construction, which coordinated economic policy and built social overhead capitals. Supporting and implementation functions like the Cabinet Office, Prosecutor's Office, Ministry of Government Legislation, Ministry of Labor, and Public Procurement Service were also founded during this military regime.

On December 2, 1962, a referendum was held to return power to a presidential system; it purportedly passed with a 78% majority. Park and the other military leaders pledged not to come forward as candidates in the next elections. However, Park ultimately ran for president, narrowly winning the election of 1963. Park made economic development a top priority, claiming a program for "emerging from extreme poverty and reducing immediate human sufferings" as soon as he was inaugurated. The Park government firmly promoted a "growth-first developmental policy" and formulated economy-friendly government organizations and expenditures.

The figure below shows the growth of government organization and public employment from 1962 to 1987. In particular, the number of ministries increased to 40 during the Third Republic (1962~1978). With the Board of Economic Planning and Board of Reunification, the two-board system was completed and continued for 30 years. The boards coordinate economic policies and relations with North Korea among the different ministries. Most of the new ministries, including the Ministry of Science and Technology, National Tax Service, Korea Customs Service, Military Manpower Administration, and so forth focused on implementing economic policy.

As the Constitution of 1963 prevented a president from looking for a third consecutive term, Park amended the Constitution to allow the current president to run for third term in 1971. In 1972, he dissolved the National Assembly and suspended the Constitution. In December 1972, the Restoration (*Yusin*) Constitution was approved in a highly manipulated plebiscite. The new Constitution transferred the election of the president to an electoral college, the so-called "National Conference for Unification." The presidential term was increased to six years, with no limits on reelection. The Yusin administration created several new ministries in 1979, including the Ministry of Energy and Resources, bringing the number of ministries to 42, one of the largest on record. Since the developmental state led by non-civilian military government placed great emphasis on industrialization and economic development, new organizations were necessary to bolster national economy and to administer export-oriented industry.

[Figure 12–1] Ministries and Public Employment during the Developmental State Period

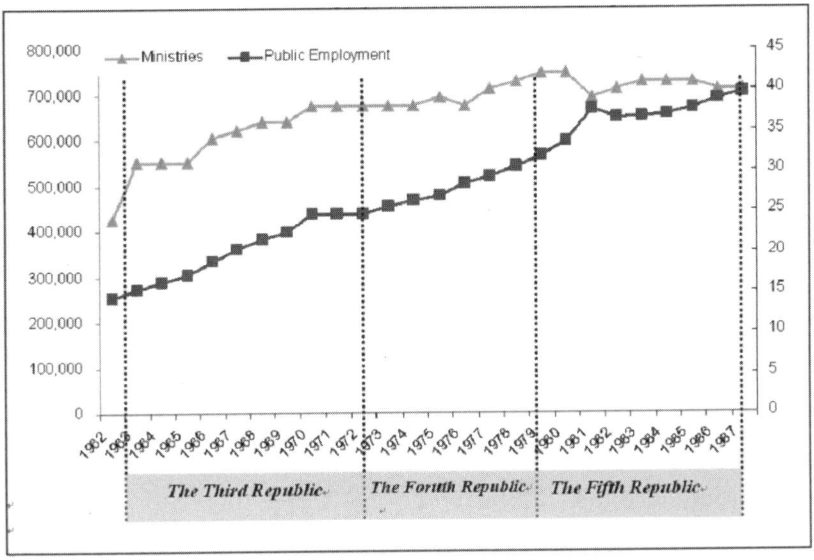

Source: Ministry of Government Administration and Home Affairs (2004~2007).

In October 1979, Park was assassinated by one of his allies and an interim government was organized under an interim President (Choi Kyu-hah, 1979~1980). However, Major General Chun Doo-Hwan emerged in the December 12, 1979, coup d'état and declared martial law (Katsiaficas and Na, 2006). To make up for the significant deficit of political legitimacy, the Chun Doo-Hwan administration (1980~1988) made extensive efforts at social and economic reform and brought in rhetoric like social justice, welfare state, and small government. The two ministries were privatized and merged into the administration. During the developmental state period, the number of government ministries and public employees was increased significantly, mostly in an effort to promote economic development. Indeed, the newly created government ministries focused on economic policy.

Democratization (1980~2007)

Public outrage over the authoritarian regime and the *Gwangju* Uprising (Katsiaficas and Na, 2006) consolidated nationwide support for democracy, paving the road for the first democratic elections in 1987. The Chun Doo-Hwan authoritarian regime was forced to make important political concessions to the opposition as a result of massive street demonstrations in the June Democratization Movement of 1987. The transition to democracy was carried out through the presidential election of December 1987 and the National Assembly election of April 1988. Roh Tae-Woo (1988~1993), President Chun's protégé, was elected to the presidency by a slim margin, winning only 36% of the popular vote due to the failure to unite the presidential candidate with opposition groups. Moreover, the three opposition parties comprised a majority in the National Assembly, which fundamentally limited the new regime's political capacity. Equally important was the expansion of political space in which the hitherto suppressed distributional interests could be spelled out.

In 1991, three existing political parties (an amalgamation of the then-ruling party and two opposition parties) had merged and a new big party was born under the name of the Democratic and Liberal Party as a way to extend the governing of the then-ruling party. The Democratic and Liberal Party nominated Kim Young-Sam, a long-time opposition party leader, as presidential candidate and he was elected in the fourteenth presidential election of December 1992, which opened a new era of civilian government. There was high expectation for the Kim Young-Sam administration (1993~1998) to move from a stage of "transition to democracy" (that of the Sixth Republic) to one of "consolidation of democracy." Under the banner of "constructing a new Korea," the Kim Young-Sam government carried out a series of sweeping reforms, contributing to the further consolidation of the Korean democracy.

Kim Young-Sam's reform politics followed the typical "reform from the top" process, which relied heavily upon the political leader's charisma. As one scholar noted, the *modus operandi* entailed "mobilizing the aspirations of the people and public opinion against vested interests" and demonstrated "a strong nationalist character." Yet, despite these early reform efforts, the Kim Young-Sam administration was ineffectual when it came to solving fundamental problems such as the deeply entrenched collusion between government and business, the resulting corruption within the power structure, and a political party structure that had grafted a personality cult with regionalism.

During this period, the Kim Young-Sam administration searched for government reform and cutback management. In the earlier period of this government, five ministries were abolished but public employment was not reduced, resulting in a transition to a "large ministry system" rather than cutback management. In this sense, the government's reforms were considered political rhetoric. Many scholars argue that the administrative reforms simply became the instrument of politics.

Moreover, the Kim Young-Sam government's globalization policy, which was implemented without sufficient preparation and with an inadequate understanding of its merits and shortcomings, precipitated the arrival of the 1997~1998 financial crisis. The government's efforts to advance the principles of a market economy within a distorted economic structure with limited competitiveness and overgrown conglomerates, as inherited from the previous authoritarian developmental regime,

[Figure 12-2] Ministries and Public Employment during the Democratization Period

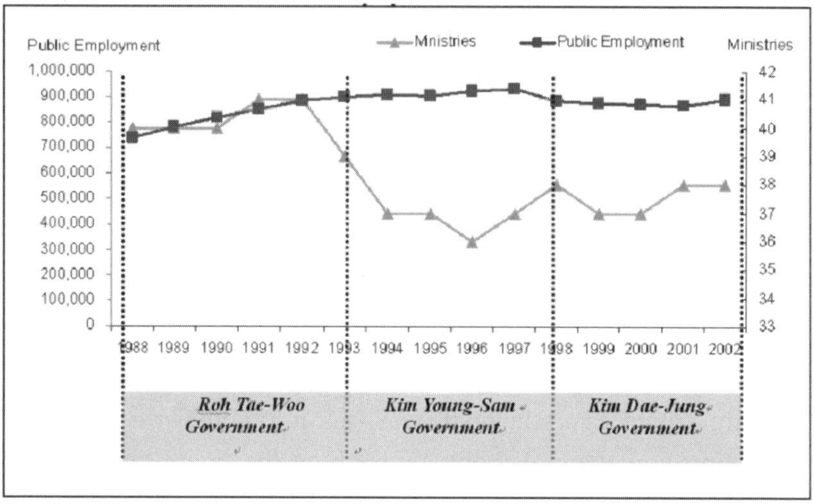

Source: Ministry of Government Administration and Home Affairs (2004~2007).

were doomed to fail.

With the election in December 1997 of Kim Dae-Jung (1998~2003), the candidate of the National Congress for New Politics (NCNP), the Korean democracy entered a new era. For the first time in Korean history, a peaceful transfer of power to the

[Table 12-2] Increasing Rates of Government Ministries

Government	Increasing Rates	Government	Increasing Rates
The First Republic	0%	The Fifth Republic	0%
The Second Republic and Military Government	72%	The Sixth Republic	2%
The Third Republic	23%	Kim Young-Sam	5%
The Fourth Republic	29%	Kim Dae-Jung	0%

Source: Ahn et al. (2007: 178).

Note: Increasing rate is a percentage of the number of Ministries at the end of the governments compared with the starting point.

opposition party took place. Moreover, the election of a president from southwestern Korea (i.e. the Cholla Provinces in Korea) meant that Korean democracy was given a chance to overcome regionalism and promote regional harmony.

Table 12-2 shows the increasing rates of the government ministries since the First Republic. The Second Republic and the military government recorded the highest rates. The military government after the Second Republic initiated significant growth of the government while the Third and Fourth Republics continued to establish the ministries and offices to handle the industrialization and modernization of the state. After the developmental state period, industrialization and urbanization slowed down and neoliberalism reinforced cutbacks in the management of public organizations. The governments started to merge and/or abolish the ministries.

In December 2002, the sixteenth South Korean presidential election took place, with Roh Moo-Hyun (2003~2008) of the Millennium Democratic Party, a relatively new politician, surprisingly defeating the well known ruling party candidate (i.e., Lee Hoi-Chang of the Grand National Party) by more than half a million votes. With such a surprising victory, Roh could continue the reign of the liberal party, promoting the controversial Sunshine Policy toward North Korea, enhancing corporate transparency, and reforming education and tax systems. Pursuant to the government's progressive orientation, new public management principles and practices in the public service were brought into public management reform. The Roh government actively encompassed mission-driven, decentralized, and incentive-based reform packages designed to enhance the performance management system, develop a senior civil service system, and instituted a top-down budgeting system. At the time, the composition of the government budget changed significantly because the government placed a top priority on

[Figure 12-3] Composition of the Government Budget (%)

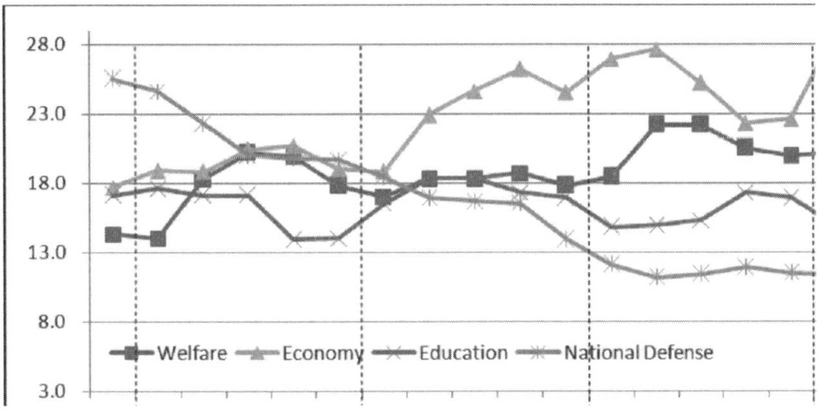

Source: Presidential Commission on Policy Planning (2007: 202).

social welfare policy. Thus, social welfare spending became the largest portion of central government expenditure (see Figure 12-3). Despite such changes, the number of government organizations did not change under the Roh government.

Advancement (2008~Present)

A conservative party, the Grand National Party, took over the Korean presidency in 2008, while the ten years of progressive regimes (Kim Dae-Jung and Roh Moo-Hyun administrations) were over by the 2007 presidential election. President Lee Myung-Bak was inaugurated on February 25, 2008, and announced his policy goal to move toward advancement through cooperation between the state and society, promotion of qualitative growth (establishment of a virtuous cycle between growth and welfare) rather than quantitative growth, establishment of the rule of law and respect for the Constitution, and fostering human resources in line with the values of pluralism, individuality, and creativity.

As soon as Lee took over the presidency, he restructured the central government and merged a number of ministries so that the number of ministries was reduced to 15. Furthermore, he announced continuous public sector reform, including public enterprise reform and deregulation. However, he faced a number of challenges such as the anti-American beef agreement protests in April 2008 (Jurenas and Manyin, 2008), so that Lee's administration reshuffled several ministers and top advisors. Since the current economic crisis has spread all over the world, both the Korean government and business sectors now face serious challenges. No one knows how long this crisis will continue, so public sector reforms are not currently moving forward as planned.

Current Status of Public Administration and Public Governance

The Central Government

The President, who heads the executive branch, is elected directly by the people and serves for one five-year term. The President can declare a state of emergency or martial law, subject to the National Assembly's subsequent approval, but does not have the authority to dissolve the National Assembly. This protection measure reflects the experience of authoritarian regimes in the past. One of the unique features of Korea's central government is its Prime Minister, appointed by the president and approved by the National Assembly. The Prime Minister has the power to recommend the appointment or dismissal of cabinet ministers. The current government comprises 15 ministries and two ministry-level agencies (the Ministry of Government Legislation, and the Ministry of Patriots and Veterans Affairs).

Among several ministries, the Ministry of Public Administration and Security (MOPAS) is in charge of government's organizational management, personnel management, local autonomy and local finance, electronic government, emergency and disaster management, government ethics, and labor relations. In March 2008, the Ministry of Public Administration and Security (MOPAS) was established by integrating the Ministry of Government and Home Affairs (MOGAHA), the Civil Service Commission (CSC), the National Emergency Planning Commission (NEPC), and the electronic government (informatization strategy) functions of the Ministry of Information and Communication (NIC). The Korean government had a Civil Service Commission (1999~2008) but it now is part of the MOPAS.

[Figure 12-4] Organizational Chart of the Korean Executive Branch

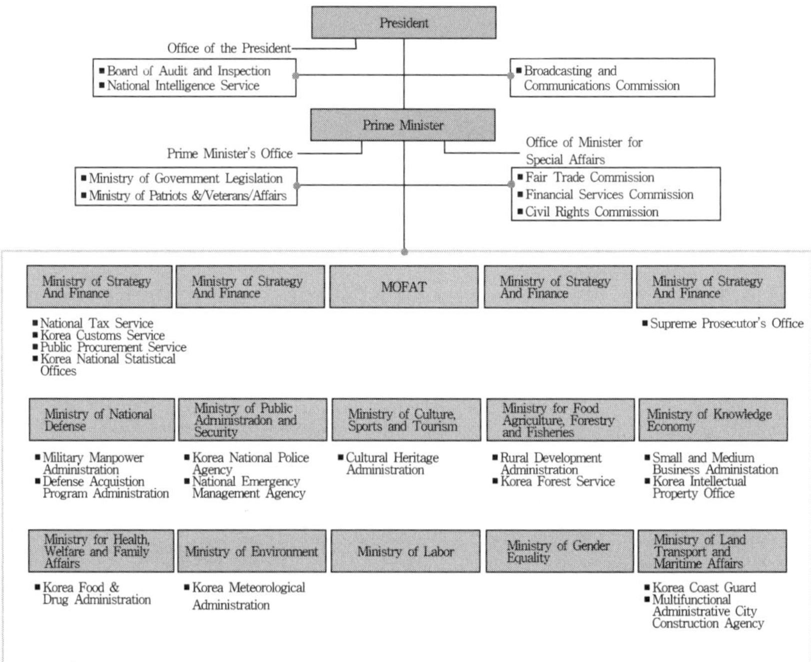

The Local Governments

Beginning with the First Republic, local autonomy was established as a constitutional principle of South Korea. In 1949, local autonomy was introduced by President Rhee Syng-man (1948~1960) as the Local Autonomy Act (LAA), which was promulgated under the framework of the unitary system. Korea has a unitary system, while the United States and many Western countries have a federal system. Every local government under the unitary system is regulated by a single-law system and the LAA became the basis for executive local autonomous power.

However, local autonomy was overturned by the military coup in 1961. The local council was abolished by the military dictatorship and all heads of local authorities were appointed by the central government until 1990. In 1988, the restriction against full scale implementation of local autonomy was removed by the amendment of the Local Autonomy Act so that follow-up measures such the re-creation of local councils was permitted. Accordingly, local autonomy was reestablished in 1991 with elections for local council members started as part of a move towards democracy in Korea. In addition, chief executives (governors, mayors, and county chief executives) of each local government were elected directly by local residents in 1995. Since then, local elections take place every four years. Now,

[Table 12-3] Major Historic Changes of Local Autonomy in Modern Korea

Year	Major Changes
1948	Local autonomy was guaranteed as a basic tenet of the democracy under the Republic's first Constitution in 1948
1949	The Local Autonomy Act (LAA) was enacted for the introduction of local autonomy
1961	After May 16, 1961 (Park's military revolution), a full scale implementation of local autonomy was postponed
1988	Removing this restriction led to a later amendment of the Local Autonomy Act that permitted the recreation of local councils in 1991
1991	Reestablished local councils (provincial level local councils were reconstituted)
1995	Chief Executives (governors and mayors) and Local Council Members were elected in all localities. Since then, local elections take place every 4 years

each local authority (province, metropolitan city, city, county, and autonomous district) has a local council, and the head of each local authority is elected by the residents every four years. Moving into the 1990s, the local autonomy system started to be reinvigorated after a long suspension, and an institutional framework for local autonomy is now fully in place.

Civil Service

The civil service in Korea is divided into national and local civil services. Civil servants are managed by their respective governmental bodies and are regulated by the national or local statutes accordingly. The National Civil Service Act was passed in 1949, while the Local Civil Service Act was promulgated in 1963. Since then, these laws have been amended several times to meet new demands and challenges. There have been some fluctuations of the total workforce size in government over time, but in 2008 the total numer of government employees, including national and local government employees, was close to one million. The number of national government employees is approximately 600,000, including public school teachers and police, while the number of local government employees is approximately 350,000. Civil servants in Korea do not include employees of any public corporations (state-owned or state-invested enterprises) or soldiers. The size of the civil service increased steadily from the 1950s to the late 1990s. After the Asian financial crisis in the late 1990s, the government's workforce was downsized somewhat, but the size of the workforce has grown slightly in recent years.

There are many occupational groups along with different occupational series, while there are nine grades vertically in the general service or equivalent pay system: Grade 9 (basic entry level) is the lowest and Grade 1 (assistant minister level) is the highest in the career civil service. Political appointees such as ministers and deputy ministers are above Grade 1. In general, members of the Senior Civil Service are those who are in Grades 1~3. The new senior civil service covers all positions at the bureau director level or higher in the central government ministries and agencies that require management and leadership abilities. It covers a total of nearly 1,500 positions, including career, special, excepted, contract, and Foreign Service positions.

Career civil servants make up the bulk of the civil service and promotions are determined according to a combination of seniority, training, and performance appraisal. At present, performance appraisal is the most important factor in promotion. In performance appraisal, three different approaches are used: (1) a performance agreement system for those in Grade 4 (director level) or higher, (2) a performance appraisal system for those in Grade 5 or lower, and (3) 360-degree feedback as a supplementary evaluation for all levels of employees. Individual-level performance assessment is executed by the personnel authority of each agency.

After a long delay in legalization of public unions, the Act for the Establishment and Operation of the Civil Servant's Labor Union was promulgated in the National Assembly on December 31, 2004, and it became effective on January 27, 2006. Since January 2006, the establishment and operation of a labor union in government is permitted for those in Grade 6 or lower levels (some employees–who deal with personnel, budget, security, accounting, and secret service–are not permitted to join the labor union).

Public Governance

The South Korean government used to be an administrative state, but lately it has been slimming down substantially. That is the current direction of South Korea, whether it is appropriate or not. The role of traditionally powerful agencies (i.e. military and national intelligence service, etc.) is also diminishing, declining, or being repositioned from the public setting. At the same time, there is an increasing role of the private sector as well as an increasing role of citizens and civil society, plus an increasing role for the judiciary and the legislative bodies. Whereas in the past, particularly in the 1970s, the legislative bodies were basically a rubber stamp for executive policy, they are now quite a provocative and an important part of policy making. Thus, there is evidence of such governance change in South Korea as shown in Table 12-4.

The most influential organizations and their relative positions of influence and trust in Korean society have been studied by the East Asia Institute (EAI) since 2005. A national opinion survey was conducted by the EAI every year since 2005, based on a random sample. The EAI identified the most influential and trustworthy organizations and came up with about 25 leading organizations, including major companies, governmental agencies, political parties, courts and prosecutors, labor unions, and civil society. After that, the EAI asked how much each respondent sees the degree of influence and trust of each organization in Korean society (EAI, 2005, 2008).

The EAI's report showed that the most influential and trustworthy organizations in 2008 were Hyundai Automobile, Samsung, and SK Company, followed by LG and the Constitutional Court. No government agency was included in the top four categories of the most influential and trustworthy organizations in Korean society. Typically, in the 1970s~90s, people thought the Office of the President was the most powerful and influential organization. However, as shown in Table 12-4, the Office of the President is not high anymore. Now, the most influential or trustworthy organizations are in the private sector: Hyundai, Samsung, SK and LG, followed by the courts (the

[Table 12-4] Most Influential and Trustworthy Organizations in Korea

Rank	Influence in 2008	Influence in 2005	Trust in 2008	Trust in 2005
1	Samsung	Samsung	Hyundai Automobile	Samsung
2	Hyundai Automobile	Hyundai Automobile	SK	Hyundai Automobile
3	SK	Constitutional Court	LG	SK
4	LG	SK	Samsung	Constitutional Court
5	Constitutional Court	Supreme Court	Constitutional Court	LG
6	Prosecutors	LG	Supreme Court	Supreme Court
7	Supreme Court	Prosecutors	Board of Audit	Police
8	National Tax Service	Police	National Tax Service	People's Solidarity for Participatory Democracy (PSPD)
9	Office of the President	Federation of Korean Industries	Police	Prosecutors Lawyers for a Democratic Society (Min byun)
10	Police	National Tax Service	Federation of Korean Industries	

Source: East Asia Institute (2005, 2008).

Constitutional Court and the Supreme Court) and a few law enforcement agencies. Interestingly, the Constitutional Court received great attention in Korea's national politics. Another interesting development is the rise of civil society. For example, the People's Solidarity for Participatory Democracy (PSPD) was ranked as one of the top ten trustworthy organizations in 2005 and it was ranked eleventh among the most trustworthy organizations in 2008. This is quite an interesting phenomenon and it is fair to say that national governance is changing in South Korea (Kim, 2007).

Public Sector Reform

Since the early 1990s, every president established an organization in charge of government reform and utilized it as a major vehicle to promote organizational change and development in the public sector. The Kim Young-Sam administration (1993~1998) established the Administrative Innovation Committee (promoted organizational restructuring, management reform, improvement of service delivery, deregulation, and anti-corruption). The Kim Dae-Jung administration (1998~2003) organized the Administrative Reform Committee and later renamed it the Presidential Committee for Promoting Government Reform (initiated organizational restructuring, management reform, deregulation, anti-corruption, public enterprise reform, and building e-government). The Roh Moo-Hyun administration (2003~2008) established the Presidential Committee on Government Innovation and Decentralization, which made several roadmaps for public sector reform. The Lee Myung-Bak administration (2008~present) established the Presidential Council on National Competitiveness (initiated deregulation, public sector reform, etc.). There are numerous issues to discuss, but two particular issues are elaborated as follows: neoliberal domination of administrative restructuring and lack of consistency.

The Korean government has implemented many structural reforms at the central level. In spite of the reforms, the government still is criticized in some aspects. By and large, recent reforms in the Korean public sector have followed New

Public Management (NPM), which applies a set of market-oriented principles and practices in public services that aim to reduce government size, privatize state-owned enterprises, devolve government authority, and create an incentive-based system. The main objective of the neoliberal measures is to break up the monopolistic nature of the production of public goods by increasing the number of producers, which may improve efficiency and competitiveness. This approach seeks to transplant business-oriented concepts to the public organizations. As a consequence, public managers have become more attentive to performance, more result-oriented, and more familiar with cost-effectiveness.

However, Korean public sector reform has been based on ideas of small government and business orientation, thereby failing to enhance social equity and public welfare. It falls into the misleading idea of regarding the public sector as a market by overemphasizing the business management aspect to increase efficiency. Business or market-oriented concepts cannot be accepted completely in the public sector, because the circumstances–and, more importantly, the core public values–are different. Public management also has a politico-administrative dimension, which means that bureaucrats at all levels are involved deeply in formulating and implementing various public policies. In recent years, however, the Korean government primarily has pursued efficiency, productivity, and profit, rather than democracy, accountability, and equity.

Over the years, the Korean government claimed that the role of the government is to help market mechanisms function appropriately, not to intervene directly in the distribution of resources, aiming at small but efficient government. As such, the main role of government would guarantee rules by which the market could function smoothly. Contrary to the market-oriented approach, however, administrative reforms of the

Korean government were based mainly on development-centered administration, with economic technocrats and ministries in charge of the economy as key actors focused on regulations controlling the private sector. Such practice actually is against the ideas of small government and private sector initiative. For example, the Kim Dae-Jung administration upgraded the Minister of Finance and Economy (MOFE) to the Deputy Prime Ministerial level and the Lee Myung-Bak administration merged two ministries, the Ministry of Finance and Economy (MOFE) and the Ministry of Planning and Budgeting (MPB), into the Ministry of Strategy and Finance (MOSF). It is clear that the administrative reforms strengthened and centralized the authority of ministries in charge of the economy and followed the government-driven approach, though government officials said that they attempted to pursue the ideas of neoliberal reform. As a result, it is fair to say that the reforms were implemented in a top-down manner and lost consistency.

Public Administration Education and Research

Public Administration Education

Modern public administration education began in Korea right after independence from Japanese colonial rule (1910~1945). Many public administration programs have been offered in tertiary institutions since the 1950s. During the Park Chung-Hee administration (1963~1979), particularly, public administration programs grew quickly, along with the growth of the public sector and the developmental state. As of 2008, 112 Korean universities offer public administration programs at the undergraduate level. These programs include many courses on public management and public policy. A variety of courses are offered in each school, including such core courses as public personnel management, public financial management, organization theory and behavior, public policy (agenda setting, formation, implementation, and evaluation), local and urban administration, and many others, including new courses designed to meet current demands and future needs. Successful students are recruited by the central and local governments through Civil Service examinations; others are hired by state-owned enterprises, quasi-government organizations, non-governmental organizations, and private enterprises.

For incumbent public officials, the Central Officials Training Institute (COTI), founded in 1949, provides general and specialized training for central government employees. COTI offers 64 programs to educate several thousand public officials, including senior civil servants. The programs include change management training, grade-based general training, specialized training, and international training. Recently, COTI initiated various innovations in terms of training methods, training materials, and its facilities in pursuing outcome-centered training and development programs based on actual situations and experiential learning, as well as nurturing government officials' national agenda execution capabilities to fulfill national advancement and new development systems. In doing so, COTI regained the confidence of public officials and general citizens.

There is another national training institute for local government employees: the Local Government Officials Development Institute (LOGODI). The Local Administration Training Institute was established in 1965 and its name and functions have been changed. In addition, each provincial level government has its own training institute.

Public Administration Research

The two major research communities of Korean public administration are the Korean Association for Public Administration (KAPA) and the Korean Association for Policy

Studies (KAPS). KAPA, established in 1956, is the largest research community in the field of public administration. Its membership includes individual and institutional members, practitioners, scholars and graduate students. KAPA's 2008 membership comprises 1,662 scholars, practitioners, students, and institutions. It has become a central venue for members' interactions. KAPA functions include annual quarterly academic conferences and an annual international conference. KAPA also publishes *the Korean Review of Public Administration* (in Korean) and *International Review of Public Administration* (in English). It has seven regional chapters and sections focusing on specific subjects.

Meanwhile, the Korean Association for Policy Studies (KAPS), established in 1992, organizes quarterly conferences and publishes the Korean Journal of Policy Studies (in Korean). In addition, there are several other professional organizations, such as the Korean Association for Local Government Studies (KALGS), the Korean Society for Public Personnel Administration (KoSPPA), the Korean Association for Organizational Studies (KAOS), the Korean Political Science Association (KAPS), and many others.

Moreover, there are two major government-sponsored research organizations: the Korean Institute for Public Administration (KIPA) and the Korean Research Institute for Local Administration (KRILA). KIPA, established in 1991, is a government-sponsored organization devoted to independent research on public policy and administration. It has six research centers and three project units that provide high quality research, policy recommendations, and analysis on the full range of public policy issues.

KRILA was established in 1984, supported and financed by local governments to conduct research and promote policy development for the development of local autonomy, as well as to support local governments.

Challenges and Prospects for the Future

Korea experienced a rocky road to its present state: rapid economic growth but a lack of social welfare systems. As the Korean national economy faces difficulties, the so-called "growth-first policy" is no longer welcomed in Korea. In other words, government has no choice but to pursue two goals simultaneously: economic growth and distribution. Consequently, the Korean government is required to catch up to the pace of the global economy and expand a social safety net in Korea.

In order to meet these kinds of complicated challenges stemming from rapid developments in globalization and diversification in international arenas, more proactive and responsive approaches are required in government. Today's open trading world has had a significant influence on Korean public administration. For example, it is necessary to pursue strategic management of key markets and resolve issues on trade restrictions through bilateral/multilateral channels or the international organizations' dispute settlement procedure, nurturing new growth engines and reviving the domestic economy.

Although some socioeconomic indicators represent that Korea is reaching to a level close to that of advanced nations, there are still many weakness and challenges. For example, the existing current social safety net is not sufficient to cover all the populations or tackle the aging population, low fertility, and long-term unemployment problems. Furthermore, the Korean government is attempting to reform the National Pension System, the National Health Insurance system, and the delivery system of community services, but all these issues are highly complicated and it is not easy to find quick solutions. At the same time, the voices of citizens and civil society are growing substantially; government must work with multiple stakeholders toward democratic governance. Pursuing democratic governance is the right thing to do, but, at the same time, the cost of public governance is increasing significantly. In recent years, public officials have faced various daunting challenges that are more complex than ever before. Therefore, public officials need to develop better competencies and capacities for more collaborative public management in order to handle diverse demands and complicated challenges in an age of governance and globalizations.

Conclusions

Developing countries have more constraints in enhancing public trust than advanced countries. In general, the good governance agenda is far too ambitious in developing countries and needs to be more realistic in considering relative importance, sequences, and feasibility (Grindle, 2004). Accordingly, prescriptive policy options for enhancing public trust in developing countries need to be different from advanced countries because developing countries have different capacities than advanced ones. For example, authoritarianism, lack of responsibility among public officials, lack of evaluation, and lack of participation are major constraints in promoting public accountability in developing countries, in addition to relatively lower economic well-being.

A reasonable way to decide what and how to reform is to first analyze various public affairs independently and then, based on sound theory established in home-grown public administration research, select reform goals and methods carefully. However, one common problem in developing countries is a tendency to try to imitate foreign experiences that have many differences from those of developing countries without fully independent assessment of the reality.

If a country simply follows the experiences of the advanced countries and mechanically imitates their systems without indigenizing efforts, it is likely to make mistakes or fail. Some reasons for such problems might include lack of understanding of sociopolitical dynamics between developing countries and advanced countries, and failure to recognize that every country has a different background (tradition, history, culture, religion, etc.) and a different path (nation building, industrialization, democratization, modernization, and institutionalization).

The best practices might be transferable to another society, but not always. Those who lead public sector reform should not neglect differences between developing and developed worlds; neither should they ignore the unique characteristics of a home country. Historically, there has been a long debate on the role of flunkies or toadies in many developing countries. When countries select reform measures, it is necessary to review or realistically analyze the nature of the issue and best possible solutions in a home country. In other words, it would be better to consider differences in environmental factors and carry out pragmatic reforms based on an indigenized study of reality.

Korea has tried to imitate or utilize many things from the experience of advanced countries and has actually made substantial progress in doing so. However, such a way is no longer effective. Korea now must find its own creative ways. That is the biggest challenge Korea faces today.

References

Ahn, B. Y., Chung, M. K., and Han, S. I. (2007). *Korean Public Sector.* Seoul: Bakyoungsa (in Korean).

Cho, Y. H. (2006). "Korean public administration and indigenous theory building," *International Review of Public Administration* 10 (2): 1-5.

Cummings, B. (1997). *Korea's Place in the Sun: A Modern History.* New York: W. W. Norton.

Grindle, M. (2004). "Good Enough Governance: Poverty Reduction and Reform in Developing Countries," *Governance: An International Journal of Policy, Administration and Institutions* 17 (4): 525-548.

Haggard, S, and Moon, C. (1993). "The state, politics, and economic development in postwar South Korea." In Hagen Koo, *State and Society in Contemporary Korea.* Ithaca: Cornell University Press.

Jun, J. S. (2006). "Rethinking the theoretical perspective: Beyond the quest for indigenous theory of Korean public administration," *International Review of Public Administration* 10 (2): 6-15.

Jun, J. S. and Campodonico, L. (1998). "Globalization and Democratic Governance: A Contradiction," *Administrative Theories and Praxis* 20 (4): 478-490.

Jurenas, Remy and Mark E. Manyin (2008). "U.S.-South Korea Beef Dispute: Negotiations and Status," *CRS Report for Congress* (Order Code RL34528). Washington, DC: UN Congressional Research Service (CRS).

Katsiaficas, Georgy and Na, Kahn-chae (eds.) (2006). *South Korean Democracy: Legacy of the Gwangju Uprising.* London: Routledge.

Kaufmann, Daniel, Kraay, Aart, and Mastruzzi, Massimo (2008). "Governance Matters VII: Aggregate and Individual Governance Indicators, 1996-2007." *World Bank Policy Research Working Paper,* No. 4654. Washington, DC: World Bank.

Kim, Pan Suk (2008). "A Daunting Task in Asia: the move for transparency and accountability in the Asian public sector," *Public Management Review* 10 (4): 527-537.

Kim, Pan Suk (2007). "Emerging Challenges to the Public Capacity in the Era of Evolving Public Administration: Toward Collaborative Public Management," *Asian Journal of Political Science* 15 (3): 282-302.

Kim, Pan Suk (2004). "Management Innovation of Quasi-Governmental Agencies in Korea," *International Review of Administrative Sciences* 69 (4): 535-552.

Kim, Pan Suk (2003). "Strengthening the Pay-Performance Link in Government: A Case Stud of Korea," *Public Personnel Management* 41 (4): 447-463.

Kim, Pan Suk (2000). "Administrative Reform in the Korean Central Government," *Public Performance and Management Review* 24 (2): 145-160.

Lee, C. (2004). "A critical review of the administrative reforms in the Korean central government: A case study of the Kim Dae-Jung administration," *International Review of Public Administration* 9 (2): 113-120.

[Korea] Ministry of Government Administration and Home Affairs. Various years (2004~2007). *Government Administration and Home Affairs Statistics Yearbook*. Seoul: Ministry of Government Administration and Home Affairs.

Pollitt, Christopher and Bouckaert, Geert (2004). *Public Management Reform*, 2nd ed. London: Oxford University Press.

[Korea] Presidential Commission on Policy Planning (2007). *Report on the Roh Moo-Hyun Administration*. Seoul: Presidential Commission on Policy Planning.

Rozman, Gilbert, In-Taek Hyun, and Shin-wha Lee (eds.) (2008). *South Korean Strategic Thought toward Asia*. London: Palgrove Macmillan.

Tilly, C. (ed.) (1975). *The Formation of National States in Western Europe*, Princeton, NJ: Princeton University Press

Woo-Cumming, M. (ed.) (1999). *The Developmental State*. Ithaca, NY: Cornell University Press.

Major websites related to public affairs and public administration in Korea

Office of the President: http://www.cwd.go.kr

Office of the Prime Minister (OPM): http://www.opm.go.kr

Ministry of Public Administration and Security (MOPAS): http://www.

mopas.go.kr
Central Officials Training Institute (COTI): http://www.coti.go.kr
Korea National Statistical Office (NSO): http://www.nso.go.kr
Local Government Officials Development Institute (LOGODI): http://www.logodi.go.kr
Government-for-Citizen (G4C) Portal: http://www.egov.go.kr
Korean Institute of Public Administration (KIPA): http://www.kipa.re.kr
Korea Research Institute for Local Administration (KRILA): http://www.krila.re.kr
Korean Association of Public Administration (KAPA): http://kapa21.or.kr
Koran Association for Policy Studies (KAPS): http://www.kaps.or.kr
Korean Political Science Association (KPSA): http://www.kpsa.or.kr

Index

N

S

T

U

V

W

List of Contributors
(Listed by the alphabetical order of the author's last name)

Suresh Balakrishnan is Chief Technical Advisor with the United Nations Development Programme (UNDP) for the Governance and Public Administration Reform (Support for Better Service Delivery Programme) in Laos. He previously served as executive director of the Public Affairs Centre, a nonprofit think tank based in Bangalore, India, that is devoted to improving governance by strengthening civil society in its interface with the state. He has more than two decades of experience with monitoring and evaluating in the governance and development sectors, which spans training, research, and consulting. He has worked closely with national, provincial, and city governments and nongovernmental organizations in Asia and Africa to strengthen service delivery.

Alain Benicy is a former executive officer of the Canadian Federal Public Service. His career evolved around planning and managing reforms in central agencies and in ministries. He was part of the first UNDP mission fielded after the 1993 national elections to recommend a course for reforming the Cambodian Public Administration. Since then, he has worked with Cambodian officials to build and strengthen State institutions with a particular focus on the Civil Service. He is an experienced practitioner of change management. The text reflects his understanding of the Administrative Reform underway as directed and managed by the Council for Administrative Reform under the leadership of Samdech Prime Minister in Cambodia.

Alex B. Brillantes, Jr. has a Ph. D. and MA from the University of Hawaii, and an MPA and AB from the University of the Philippines. He is currently Dean and Professor at the National College of Public Administration and Governance (NCPAG), University of the Philippines (UP), Secretary-General of the Association of Schools of Public Administration of the Philippines (ASPAP), and Deputy Secretary General of the Eastern Regional Organization for Public Administration (EROPA). He served as Executive Director of the Local Government Academy (LGA) of the Department of Interior and Local Government (DILG). He was visiting Professor at Kobe University, in Kobe, Japan; Visiting Fellow at Queensland University of Technology in Brisbane, Australia and Guest Professor at Meiji University in Tokyo, Japan. He has written three books and has published numerous papers on local government, development administration and civil society in local and international journals.

Trinh Tien Dung obtained a Ph. D. degree in the Czech Republic (in 1978) specializing on development economics and immediately started working for the government of Viet Nam until 1991. Afterwards he moved to the Swedish Embassy and worked there as a development officer for 4 years before joining UNDP Viet Nam in January 1995, where he continues working today. He is now UNDP Viet Nam's most experienced national officer in Viet Nam's governance and public sector reform issues. He has been Assistant Country Director (since 2003) and currently UNDP Viet Nam's Head of Governance Cluster.

Maricel T. Fernandez is a currently a University Researcher at the University of the Philippines National College of Public Administration. She was a former instructor of Saint Paul University Philippines (SPUP) where she obtained her Bachelor of Science in Public Administration (BSPA) and completed her academic units in Masters in Business Administration (MBA). She is an expert in module writing and has been writing and updating courses for Integrated Modular Curriculum Delivery System of SPUP. She has written teaching modules on governance and development, enhancing fiscal sustainability, and decentralization and local governance, among others. She has carried out research work on decentralization governance, and agricultural extension services.

Sang-Il Han is Assistant Professor of Public Administration in the College of Government and Business at Yonsei University. He graduated from University of Southern California with a Ph. D. degree in public administration. His research interests cover public management, public organization theory, and public philosophy. He is the author of several books and a number of articles on learning organization and community participation. He teaches organization theory, and public management, and global public administration.

M. Shamsul Haque is Professor at the Department of Political Science, National University of Singapore. He is interested in diverse research and teaching areas based on a multi-disciplinary approach, including development theory, public governance, comparative administration, public sector reform, ethics and accountability, policy and politics, environmental politics, globalization and the state, and other contemporary issues. He has published books and numerous international refereed journal articles on these topics or issues. He is currently the Editor of *Asian Journal of Political Science* and sits on the editorial boards of several academic journals. He is also currently involved in research on issues such as crisis in public administration, governance in Southeast Asia, sustainable development, Non-government Organization, public service reinvention in developing nations, and so on.

Brian Hunt is a full-time faculty member and Assistant Professor at the College of Management Mahidol University, Bangkok where he held the post of Director of Research from 2000~2004. He is a graduate of the universities of East Anglia (UEA), Reading (UR), and Bath (UB), and has conducted research projects at City University Business School and at Imperial College, London. He holds a Ph.D. from the University of Technology Sydney (UTS), and his thesis investigated culture and management in the Thai public administration. He has published widely in the areas of business and management. His most recent book (co-edited with Toni Ivergard), *Handbook of Control Room Design and Ergonomics: A Perspective for the Future*, was published in 2008 by CRC Publishers (New York).

Toni Ivergard is Director of Innovation and Entrepreneurship, Master of Management at Rangsit University, Bangkok. Previously, he headed a Master of Management program for the Thai public sector in a cooperative partnership between the Office of Civil Service Commission (OCSC) and Mahidol University. He has a Docentship from the Royal Institute of Technology, Stockholm and holds a Master and a PhD from Loughborough University, UK. During his career he has been a Director of Scandinavian Airline System (SAS) University, Regional Labour Director and Deputy Director General of the

Swedish Labour Market Administration. He has been an advisor to Royal Thai Government and many other Governments. Toni has more than 220 publications including many books in different fields such as human sciences, people-technology, leadership, and public administration.

David Seth Jones is Associate Professor in the Faculty of Business, Economics and Policy Studies. Previously he held various academic posts in Singapore and elsewhere. These included Associate Professor, Department of Political Science, National University of Singapore, Adjunct Professor, School of Economics, Singapore Management University, Local Director in Singapore, Masters in Public Administration Programme, Australian National University. His research interests cover public sector reform, public service management, public budgeting, government procurement, land administration, and agrarian reform. He has published numerous articles in these fields in international journals and in edited collections, as well as a book on land reform in Ireland. He has also undertaken extensive consultancy work in recent years, and conducted professional training programs in Southeast Asia.

Pan Suk Kim is Professor of Public Administration and the Director of the Institute of Regional Studies and Development in the College of Government and Business at Yonsei University in Korea. He earned his doctoral degree in public administration from the American University. His areas of research interests are public sector reform, human resource management, public governance innovation, international development, and organizational change. He is currently a member of the UN Committee of Experts on Public Administration (UN/CEPA) and the IIAS Executive Committee, and the IASIA Board of Management. He is Vice President of the International Research Society for Public Management (IRSPM) and Co-Chairperson of the ASPA Action Team on International Outreach. He is Deputy Editor of the *International Review of Administrative Sciences* and sits on the editorial board of several international journals. In 2009, he received the International Public Administrating Award from the American Society for Public Administration (ASPA).

Tin Hla Kyi is Professor and Head (Retd.), Director (Retd.) of the Master of Public Administration Programme, Department of Applied Economics, Yangon Institute of Economics in Yangon, Myanmar. She holds a B.A. Hons (Economics) degree from the Yangon Institute of Economics and an M.Ec. degree from the University of New England in Armidale, NSW, Australia. Her field of specialization is Development Economics, but her interest is focused more on socio-economic issues of the poor. She has carried out research work on socio-economic issues of HIV/AIDS (Cost of HIV/AIDS to households; KAP study on HIV/AIDS; HIV/AIDS and Transport and Migrant Workers) for UNDP, UNICEF, ADB and on road safety (Road Accident Cost in Myanmar) for ASEAN.

Hong-Hai Lim is currently Associate Professor in the Department of Political Science at Universiti Sains Malaysia. He earned his master degree from University of Michigan at Ann Arbor and his doctoral degree from University of Malaya. He teaches Introduction to Public Administration, Development Administration, Complex Organizations, Public Sector Management, Administrative Ethics, and Malaysian Politics and Government. He was invited as Erasmus Mundus Scholar at Trondheim University (Norway) and Linkoping University (Sweden) during the autumn semester of 2007 and lectured on public administrative ethics in the Erasmus Mundus Masters Programme in Applied Ethics jointly run by Trondheim, Linkoping and Utrecht (Netherlands).

Ismail Mohamad is currently Deputy for State Minister of Administrative Reform in the Field of Management System and Procedures in the Republic of Indonesia, and is heading the National Working Team for Bureaucacy Reform in Indonesia State Apparatus. He earned his DBA degree from School of Business and Management at the United States International University, San Diego, California in 1986. He was the Deputy for Policy Management and Public Service Studies, at the National Institute of Public Administration (LAN) of the Republic of Indonesia when his paper was written. Much of his latest work is concerned with the implementation of bureaucracy reform in Indonesia, and research in the field of public policy, public accountability, strategic management, and public service management.

Khammoune Viphongxay is Vice Chairperson of the Public Administration and Civil Service Authority (PACSA), in the Prime Minister's Office, Lao PDR. He earned his MPA degree from University of Canberra and Doctorate of Law from Joseph Attila University of Science in Hungary. He is a career civil servant, specializing in public administration. His recent areas of work include decentralization reforms, development of civil society and creation of local councils. He is on the faculty of the National Academy of Politics and Public Administration. He is a member of several key committees including State Committee for Organizational Improvement. He is also the Project Director for UNDP's Governance and Civil Service Reform Project, as well as the Civil Society Project.